APPROACHES TO EDUCATIONAL AND SOCIAL INCLUSION

In this insightful text, the editors reflect on contributions from scholars representing Bangladesh, Greece, India, Israel, New Zealand, Switzerland, UK and USA, by showing how the majority of educational and social institutions in both developed and developing countries have failed to overcome the many barriers to an effective integrated system of education, suggesting ways as to how these barriers might be challenged.

By looking closely at the overt and covert injuries of educational and social exclusion, a variety of approaches to overcoming the consequences of those challenges is proposed, drawing together strands of social theory, research data and conceptualisations for social action.

Gajendra K. Verma is Emeritus Professor of Education at the University of Manchester, UK.

Devorah Kalekin-Fishman is Senior Researcher at the University of Haifa, Israel.

APPROACHES TO EDUCATIONAL AND SOCIAL INCLUSION

International perspectives on theory, policy and key challenges

Edited by Gajendra K. Verma and Devorah Kalekin-Fishman

LONDON AND NEW YORK

First published 2017
by Routledge
2 Park Square, Milton Park, Abingdon, Oxon OX14 4RN

and by Routledge
711 Third Avenue, New York, NY 10017

Routledge is an imprint of the Taylor & Francis Group, an informa business

© 2017 selection and editorial matter, Gajendra K Verma and Devorah Kalekin-Fishman; individual chapters, the contributors.

The right of the editors to be identified as the authors of the editorial material, and of the authors for their individual chapters, has been asserted in accordance with sections 77 and 78 of the Copyright, Designs and Patents Act 1988.

All rights reserved. No part of this book may be reprinted or reproduced or utilised in any form or by any electronic, mechanical, or other means, now known or hereafter invented, including photocopying and recording, or in any information storage or retrieval system, without permission in writing from the publishers.

Trademark notice: Product or corporate names may be trademarks or registered trademarks, and are used only for identification and explanation without intent to infringe.

British Library Cataloguing in Publication Data
A catalogue record for this book is available from the British Library

Library of Congress Cataloging in Publication Data
Names: Verma, Gajendra K., editor. | Kalekin-Fishman, Devorah, editor.
Title: Approaches to educational and social inclusion : international perspectives on theory, policy and key challenges / edited by Gajendra K. Verma and Devorah Kalekin Fishman.
Description: Abingdon, Oxon : New York, NY ; Routledge
is an imprint of the Taylor & Francis Group, an Informa Business, [2017] | Includes bibliographical references.
Identifiers: LCCN 2016025022 | ISBN 9781138672635 (hbk) | ISBN 9781138672642 (pbk.) | ISBN 9781315562414 (ebk)
Subjects: LCSH: School integration--Cross-cultural studies. | Social integration--Cross-cultural studies. | Multicultural education--Cross-cultural studies.
Classification: LCC LC214 .A77 2017 | DDC 379.2/63--dc23
LC record available at https://lccn.loc.gov/2016025022

ISBN: 978-1-138-67263-5 (hbk)
ISBN: 978-1-138-67264-2 (pbk)
ISBN: 978-1-315-56241-4 (ebk)

Typeset in Bembo
by Taylor & Francis Books

CONTENTS

List of illustrations vii
Editors and contributors ix
Acknowledgements xv

Introduction and overview 1
Gajendra K. Verma

PART I
Theoretical and conceptual issues 7

1 Education and social integration for all: Challenges and responses 9
  Gajendra K. Verma

2 Furthering social inclusion through citizenship education: Cultivating civic action in early childhood education 22
  Devorah Kalekin-Fishman

3 Pedagogies and partnerships for educating the whole child 38
  Carl A. Grant and Elisabeth Zwier

4 Broadstreaming through creative learning: An approach towards educational inclusion 53
  Vijoy Prakash

PART II
Perspectives on policy and practice — 77

5 Inclusive education and societal development: An Indian perspective — 79
   Ran Bijay N. Sinha and Rupa Lakshmi

6 The field of education in New Zealand: Inclusion/exclusion in schooling — 89
   Charles Crothers

7 European Union policies for lifelong learning: A 'portal' to social inclusion? — 105
   Eugenia A. Panitsidou

8 Educational policies and teachers' professional development: Disability issues — 119
   Panagiotis Giavrimis, Stella Giossi and Adamantios Papastamatis

9 Gender parity: Inclusion in Bangladesh education — 131
   Samir Ranjan Nath

PART III
Challenges and possible responses to inclusive education — 145

10 Challenges for education and inclusiveness in India — 147
    Mohd Akhtar Siddiqui

11 Bilingual immigrant students and inclusive learning: Issues and challenges — 157
    Eleni Griva

12 Dyslexia: A learning disability in the Indian context — 171
    Mona Tabassum and Manju Kumari

13 Inclusive learning: The challenge of special needs — 183
    Royston Flude

14 Reaching the unreached: Traverse of alternative and innovative schools — 194
    K. Gireesan

Afterword — 207
Devorah Kalekin-Fishman

Index — 213

ILLUSTRATIONS

Figures

4.1	Three phases of learning	67
4.2	Processive phase of creative learning	67
11.1	Pre-writing processes	161
11.2	While-writing cognitive strategies	162
11.3	While-writing compensation strategies	162
11.4	While-writing meta-cognitive strategies	163
11.5	Writing difficulties	164

Tables

4.1	Comparison of mainstreaming and broadstreaming	56
7.1	Profile of the majority of participants in the sample	110
7.2	Primary profile of respondents	111
7.3	Overall cluster profile	112
9.1	Increase in the number of institutions, students and teachers in Bangladesh, 1970–2014	132
9.2	Percentage of female students at various levels of education in Bangladesh, 1970–2014	136
9.3	Percentage of female teachers at various levels of education in Bangladesh, 1970–2014	137
9.4	Gender difference in education and literacy rates (7+ years) in Bangladesh, 1974–2013	138

9.5 Percentage of female candidates in secondary and higher secondary school certificate examinations in Bangladesh, 1990–2014   139
11.1 Differences between poor and good writers in cognitive, compensation and meta-cognitive strategies in Greek   164
12.1 Prevalence of children with learning disabilities   177

EDITORS AND CONTRIBUTORS

Editors

Gajendra K. Verma, Ph.D., is Emeritus Professor of Education at the University of Manchester, UK, a title conferred on him for life in recognition of his international standing and for his services to the university. Whilst Professor of Education at the University of Manchester, he succeeded in 1994 to the Sarah Fielden Chair of Education, which he held for several years. He was appointed the first Dean of the Research and Graduate School of the Faculty of Education for four years in 1991, which was extended to 1998. In March 2010 he was awarded the most prestigious University of Manchester Medal of Honour for his many contributions to the university and to educational thinking worldwide over a period of 30 years. He has been, and remains, an active researcher. During his career he has directed over 20 national and internationally funded educational research projects. He was also British Coordinator of four international projects funded by the European Union, spanning nine nations: United Kingdom, India, Germany, France, Portugal, Israel, Greece, Finland and Estonia. He was a member of an influential Royal Commission, the Swann Committee, on 'Education for All' (1980–1985). He has published widely on educational issues. He has published over 100 papers in international journals, contributed numerous book chapters and written several book reviews for professional publications. As author, editor or co-editor he has published some thirty books, among them: *International Perspectives on Educational Diversity and Inclusion* (2007, Routledge, Ed. with C. Bagley and M.M. Jha), *The Ethnic Crucible* (1994, The Falmer Press, with Paul Zec and G. Skinner), *Challenges for Inclusion* (2008, Sense Publishers, Ed. with C. Bagley) and *Researching Education: Perspectives and Techniques* (1999, The Falmer/Routledge Press, with K. Mallick). He has served on the editorial board of six international journals and has been a regular reviewer for various journals and research councils.

Devorah Kalekin-Fishman (Dr. Rer. Soc., University of Konstanz, Germany; Dr. Rer. Soc. honoris causa, University of Eastern Finland – formerly University of Joensuu) is Senior Researcher at the University of Haifa, Israel. In the Faculty of Education, she was founding head of the Department of Educational Sciences, headed the pedagogical staff of the Department of Teaching and Teacher Education and coordinated workshops dedicated to furthering Arab-Jewish co-existence. She is the founding editor of the *International Sociology Review of Books* and associate editor of Sociopedia@isa. Among her publications are over 75 articles in refereed journals, many book chapters and several books, among them *Ideology, Policy, and Practice: A Study of Education for Immigrants and Minorities in Israel Today* (2004, Kluwer Academic Publishers), *The New International Handbook of Sociology: Conflict, Cooperation, and Competition* (2009, Ed. with A. Denis, Sage), *Everyday Life in Asia: Social Perspectives on the Senses* (2010, Ed. with K.E.Y. Low, Ashgate) and *The Shape of Sociology Today: Tradition and Renewal* (2012, Ed. with A. Denis, Sage).

Contributors

Charles Crothers completed his Ph.D. in Sociology at Victoria University of Wellington (VUW), New Zealand, after earlier study at the University of Waikato. He joined Auckland University of Technology as professor in 2001 after five years as Head of Sociology at the University of Natal, Durban, South Africa. Prior to that he worked at the Universities of Auckland and VUW and in the Town and Country Planning Division of the Ministry of Works and Development. His current areas of research include Social Theory, Methods of Applied Social Research and policy processes, the history and current situation of Sociology, and Settler Societies (especially in New Zealand and South Africa). He co-edits *New Zealand Sociology* and has also edited a theme on the 'History and Development of Sociology' for the UNESCO On-Line Encyclopaedia.

Royston Flude, Ph.D., is a dyslexic multidiscipline polymath, educated at the University of Manchester, UK. He is an active Rotarian and Governor of the British Association for Counselling and Psychotherapy. He has completed a review of Primary Education for the UK National Audit Office that provides insights into improved education systems which are self-sustaining and is currently working on the development of SMART Learning Centres. He is a leading thinker in both social and economic inclusion and is a global Thought Leader for change. As President of CSPOC, a not-for-profit United Nations-accredited NGO based in Switzerland, he is focused on the development of Self-sustaining People, Organisations and Communities through the primary inputs of Health, Education and Enterprise to deliver trans-generation outputs in Wealth, Citizenship and the Environment. He has published several papers in this field.

Panagiotis Giavrimis studied at Kapodistrian University of Athens, Greece, where he completed a B.A., a Diploma in Special Education, an M.A. and Ph.D.

in Education. He also has an M.A. in Sociology and Local Development from the Department of Sociology, University of the Aegean, Greece. He was elected Lecturer in the Department of Sociology at the University of the Aegean in 2009. Prior to that he worked as a teacher and school counsellor in primary public schools for 22 years. He currently teaches 'Sociology of Education', 'Didactic of Sociology' and 'Educational Policy' at undergraduate level and theory of organisations to postgraduates. He has published seven books and several articles in Greek and international journals. His scientific interests focus on sociology of education, educational inequalities, multiculturalism and heterogeneity of students.

Stella Giossi is an adjunct Lecturer in the Department of Educational and Social Policy and the Department of Accounting and Finance at the University of Macedonia, Thessaloniki, Greece. She has carried out a postdoctoral research on innovation and e-entrepreneurship. She holds a Ph.D. in Continuing Education, an M.B.A. and degrees in Business Administration and Pedagogy. She has worked for many years as manager in the financial departments of a Greek bank. Consequently, she is a freelance consultant and certified quality auditor as well as a specialised adult educator. She has served as associate editor, reviewer and member of the editorial board of international journals. She has published several papers in international journals, conference proceedings and chapters in books and is author of *Entrepreneurship 2.0 and its Didactics* and *Teaching Economics and Business Administration*.

K. Gireesan, Ph.D., is Faculty Head, School of Governance and Public Policy at the Rajiv Gandhi National Institute of Youth Development, Sriperumbudur, Tamil Nadu, India. He obtained a Post Graduate degree and a Doctoral degree in Public Administration from Panjab University, Chandigarh, India. He has undertaken a number of studies for the Ministry of Human Resource Development, Government of India. As a National Evaluator, he conducts monitoring, evaluation and impact assessment studies for the Ministry of Rural Development and Ministry of Panchayat Raj, Government of India, across the country. He is an examiner/Member of Doctoral Committee in various educational institutions. He has published/edited six books and research reports. In addition, he has published several research papers/articles in refereed journals. He is a life member of Indian Political Science Association, Indian Adult Education Association and Kerala Association for Non-Formal Education and Development.

Carl A. Grant, Ph.D., is Hoefs-Bascom Professor in the Department of Curriculum at the University of Wisconsin–Madison, USA. He has authored or edited more than 50 books and has written more than 100 journal publications. His recent book publications include: *The Moment: Barack Obama, Jeremiah Wright and the Firestorm at Trinity United Church of Christ* (2013 with Shelby Grant, Rowman & Littlefield), *Intersectionality & Urban Education: Identities, Policies, Spaces and Power* (2014, Ed. with E. Zwier, Information Press), *The Selected Works of Carl A. Grant*

(2014, Routledge) and *Black Intellectual Thought in Education* (in press, with Keffrelyn and Anthony Brown, Routledge).

Eleni Griva, Ph.D., is an Associate Professor of Applied Linguistics in the Faculty of Education at the University of Western Macedonia, Greece. She is also the coordinator of the postgraduate module 'Testing and Assessment in Language Learning' in the School of Humanities of the Hellenic Open University (HOU). Her research interests include: Methodology of teaching a second/foreign language, language learning strategies, bilingualism/multilingualism, Foundations of Bilingual/Multicultural Education, Methods and Materials in Bilingual/SL Education, and assessment in language learning. She has participated in a number of research projects and is a member of various international scientific committees and Associate Editor of five international academic journals. She has published four books (in Greek) related to teaching a second/foreign language and bilingualism, as well as more than 140 papers, in international and national refereed journals, collected editions and conference proceedings. She has also participated in more than 140 international and national conferences.

Manju Kumari graduated in Psychology from Bihar University, Muzaffarpur, India, where she also completed her Ph.D. in 2002. She joined Marwari College, LNM University, Darbhanga, in 1975. After serving in various teaching capacities there, she joined RN College, Hajipur, Bihar University where she is an Associate Professor of Psychology. She has published a number of papers in international and national journals. She was Indian associate on a study project 'Cross-cultural study of family life and adolescent stress' in 1999. In 2005, she was invited to provide an Indian Perspective on 'e-learning' and 'dual citizenship' projects, in the Faculty of Education, University of Manchester, UK.

Rupa Lakshmi is currently working as Associate Professor, Department of Psychology, RN College, Hajipur, Bihar University, Muzaffarpur, India. She did her M.A. and Ph.D. at Patna University, India. She has published more than 15 research articles in national reputable journals. She is a life member of the Association of Social Engineering, Research and Training (ASSERT), Patna and also a life member of the Association for Promotion of Creative Learning (APCL), Patna. She is the consulting editor of the journal, *Perspectives in Psychological Researches*. Her current interests are psychology of personality and social capital.

Samir Ranjan Nath, Ph.D., is Head of Educational Research at BRAC University, Bangladesh. He has postgraduate degrees in Statistics from Jahangirnagar University and in Educational Research Methodology from the University of Oxford, UK. He is a major researcher for Education Watch, a civil society research initiative in education. He also provides consultancy services to UNICEF, UNESCO, Plan Bangladesh, Save the Children and Directorate of Primary Education, Dhaka. His research interests include early intervention, pupils' assessment, inequity and marginalisation, and supplementary private tuition. He has contributed to journal articles, book chapters and books, both nationally and internationally.

Eugenia A. Panitsidou, Ph.D., is Assistant Professor at the College of Education, Department of Foundations of Education at the United Arab Emirates University (UAEU), Al Ain. Her research interests pertain to education policy and leadership. She has authored a large number of publications in international journals and books, with numerous citations to her published work. She sits on numerous Reviewers' and Editorial Boards internationally.

Adamantios J. Papastamatis, Ph.D., is Associate Professor of Teaching Methodology in Continuous Education at the Department of Educational and Social Policy at the University of Macedonia, Thessaloniki, Greece. He has a long administrative and academic career in education and training. He has organised and participated in scientific committees at many international and Greek conferences. Additionally, he has participated in several research projects. He has been an invited speaker at several universities in Greece and abroad. He has a number of national and international publications including books, journal articles and conference proceedings.

Vijoy Prakash, M.Sc. M.Phil., is a senior bureaucrat with the Government of India, and has built a reputation for bringing social and economic metamorphosis among people from excluded communities, through breakthrough work across prestigious positions such as human resource development, agriculture, planning, rural development and social welfare. His work centres around promoting 'creativism' – a society based on creativity as a core value for all human transactions and he is known for developing an innovative system of holistic education known as 'Creative Learning', which has become the basis for an innovative school that he supports for children from underprivileged communities. His methods have also proved useful in enhancing the learning abilities of children with special needs. He has written several thought leadership books for the development of concentration, memory, imagination, visualisation and emotional management. Working in one of the most impoverished regions in the world, he also champions the cause of food diversification and tolerance.

Mohammad Akhtar Siddiqui obtained a Ph.D. in Education and has been engaged in teaching, research and educational administration for more than three and a half decades. He is a Professor of Education at the Institute of Advanced Studies of Education, Jamia Millia Islamia Central University, New Delhi, India. Until recently, he was Chairperson of the National Council for Teacher Education (NCTE), a national regulator and apex body for teacher education under the Ministry of Human Resource Development, Government of India. As its head, he presented before the national Curriculum Framework for Teacher Education 2009 and was acknowledged for initiating many systemic reforms in teacher preparation and qualifications. He has completed many research projects including one multi-country Asia Link Project on development of inter-cultural understanding funded by the European Union. He writes on teacher education, educational policy and administration, comparative education and education of the disadvantaged, particularly of the Muslim minority in India.

Ran Bijay Narayan Sinha is Professor and Head of the Department of Psychology at B.S. College, Danapur, Patna, India. He gained an M.A. at Bihar University, India and completed his Ph.D. at Patna University. He has been a General Fellow of the Indian Council of Social Science Research (ICSSR), New Delhi, India, life member of the Association of Social Engineering, Research and Training (ASSERT), Patna, and a participant at the Advanced Research Training Seminar (ARTS), Singapore. He has published over 50 research articles in refereed national and international journals. He attended and presented a research paper at the 13th World Association for Dynamic Psychiatry (WADP) in Munich, Germany and 15th International Congress of Applied Psychology (ICAP), Singapore. He is the Managing Editor of *Social Engineer* and consulting editor of *Perspectives in Psychological Researches*. He is author of the book *Culture and Development* and his current interests are social capital and inclusive development.

Mona Tabassum received her B.A. and M.A. in Psychology from LN Mithila University, Darbhanga, India. She obtained her P.G. Diploma in Clinical Psychology and Ph.D. from Patna University, India. In 2003, she joined the P.G. Department of Psychology at Bihar University, India as an Assistant Professor. Since 2005, she has worked at R.N. College, Bihar University where she became an Associate Professor in 2012. Her current research interests include health psychology with focus on studies of depression among adolescents, and she has published ten papers in reputed national journals. She is a life member of Indian Science Congress, Indian Academy of Applied Psychology and Bihar Psychological Association.

Elisabeth Zwier is the Curriculum Development Coordinator at Zamorano University, Honduras. Formerly, she was an adjunct professor of education, consultant, and elementary teacher. She holds a Bachelor's degree in Elementary Education from Goshen College, Indiana, USA, and a Master's degree in Curriculum and Instruction from the University of Wisconsin–Madison, USA. She is currently a Ph.D. candidate in Curriculum and Instruction at the same institution. She has co-authored several articles and chapters on intersectionality and education. Her research interests include: education policy, comparative and international education, civil society, parent involvement, teacher education and curriculum design.

ACKNOWLEDGEMENTS

We are grateful to friends and colleagues who gave their support in making the 2011 Conference a success.

Preparation of a manuscript, particularly an edited one, is a daunting task. The editors are thankful to Louise Jones, for organising the material, liaising with all the contributors and for updating, revising and amending where necessary. She has been extremely helpful to us in bringing the project to the final stage of its submission. Thanks also to the University of Haifa, Israel, for their part support towards the cost of the production of the material.

We also wish to thank all the contributors for their positive response to suggestions for amendments/deletions/additions to their chapter as required.

G. K. V.
D. K.-F.

INTRODUCTION AND OVERVIEW

Gajendra K. Verma

This book grew out of an International Conference on 'Educational and Social Inclusion' held in Patna, Bihar, India, in November, 2011. The broad rationale of the Conference was to provide a platform for educational and social thinkers and practitioners from different parts of the world to come together and share/debate/ examine their thoughts, understanding and experience as to how we can tackle the evils of educational and social exclusion of children and young people which exists in most developed and developing societies in some form or another.

Given the context, the Conference specifically focused on two major challenges facing democratic countries in particular: firstly, that certain sections of society's citizens are not able to participate in educational and social spheres, and secondly, that marginalised children and young people include those who are forced to exist on the outer fringes of society and as a result do not have access to education. Roma and Traveller children in Europe, street children in large urban cities in Latin America, Dalit and untouchable children in India, children and young people in war refugee camps, particularly in Africa, are just a few examples.

Educational and social inclusion has become an international movement in the twenty-first century. The Conference covered themes for presentation, discussion and debate which are relevant for the new social movement in a fast-changing technological world: learning difficulties, health education, gender issues, teacher education, home-school partnership, curriculum, disability, equality and quality in determining the possibility of inclusiveness. During it there was an opportunity for educational researchers, practitioners, social reformers and policymakers to present their views and compare experiences in developing and promoting strategies to prevent children from being marginalised on the basis of race, gender, culture, caste or disability. All children including physically challenged ones have the right to have their educational, social and psychological needs met by society. Education is the birthright of all.

The chapters in this volume have raised pertinent issues and questions with some possible solutions, which have implications for modern societies as they seek to come to terms with an increased understanding of the 'exclusion' and 'inclusion' dichotomy. These are:

- What theory, principles and needs underlie the aims and objectives of social and educational inclusion?
- What are the main obstacles that prevent children and young people, particularly those from marginalised groups, from enjoying inclusivity in terms of education, as well as in employment and welfare?
- What are the key challenges that face teachers, social reformers, parents and all those involved in the educational integration and inclusion of such children?
- How does society respond to such challenges and are there any promising solutions?
- How can educational systems and policy makers in democratic societies foster the will to reverse the hopelessness of disadvantaged groups and facilitate inclusiveness as a celebration of diversity?

Broadly, the three parts in this volume offer some answers and give signposts to possible solutions.

Authors from Bangladesh, Greece, India, Israel, New Zealand, Switzerland, the United Kingdom and the United States show in their respective chapters how the majority of educational and social institutions in both developed and developing countries have failed to overcome the many barriers to an effective system of integrated education. They also suggest models, strategies and ways as to how it may be possible to challenge and even dismantle these barriers.

The volume also closely examines the overt and covert damage to individuals' self-esteem and identity as a result of social and educational exclusion while proposing a variety of interventions and strategies (educational, social and political) to overcome the consequences of exclusion and marginalisation.

Part I opens with four contributions, each suggesting a different way of analysing issues of social and educational integration of disadvantaged and vulnerable groups. Verma examines the concept of inequality, discrimination, prejudice, racism, stereotyping and other forms of exclusion in educational and social settings which are likely to affect individuals' life chances. He focuses on the concept of equal opportunities and the varying perspectives of the stakeholders involved, including the teacher whose role is central for positively meeting diverse needs. Underlying Verma's analytical reflection is a critical question as to what initiatives are needed to create a society in which all individuals and groups have an equal chance to succeed in life.

Given the fact that education is a powerful socialising agent, Kalekin-Fishman focuses primarily on education as a force for 'social inclusion'. She believes that the promotion of 'social inclusion' of diverse groups (culturally, economically and cognitively) in educational institutions from early childhood onwards will ensure their inclusion in adult society. The experience of social participation in the educational setting will ensure, if successful, that when reaching maturity, participants will not tolerate exclusion from decision-making in any social and political institutions. In this model the author has outlined a plan of action for cultivating inclusive civic action in early childhood education through to formal schooling.

Complementing this chapter, Grant and Zwier highlight the importance of school partnerships, with families and community members, for the development of culturally responsive approaches to teaching the whole child as preparation for life in a democratic society. They assert that only parents, teachers and community members as a whole relate to children with the respect they deserve as complete human beings. Having critically examined various pedagogies and partnership models in practice, the authors conclude that education for full development of the human personality requires pedagogies and partnerships that involve all educational actors in a collective way – teachers, parents, students and community members.

Prakash goes more deeply into an approach to teaching for inclusion. He has proposed 'broadstreaming' as the natural process of learning in contrast to the stressful policy of mainstreaming. According to him, one such model is Creative Learning, which has been applied to find a new approach to identifying learning difficulties. A framework for diagnosis of the strengths and weaknesses of an individual child and methods of planning for remedial action has been suggested. The author believes that 'broadstreaming' can make a difference in children's self-assessment of their cognitive powers, and thus would enable them to avoid the experience of 'meaninglessness'.

In Part II, contributors from Bangladesh, Greece, India and New Zealand present perspectives on educational and social policies and practices designed to further social inclusion. Although these are described in specific contexts, they draw conclusions that are applicable to states throughout the world. These contributors point to problems, some of which are being dealt with by programmes within the system, and some requiring new initiatives by the government concerned. Education in India for 200 million children aged 6 to 14 (population of 1.2 billion people with 18 different major languages, many religious faiths and about a third of the world's poor) presents gigantic challenges for the system to respond to. Given the complexity and diversity in terms of caste, class, religion, language, and social-economic status, Sinha and Lakshmi point to the challenge of such diversity which presents barriers to educational and social inclusion. The authors also suggest that because of the conflicts between various segments of society on the basis of caste, religion, language, social class, sometimes there is a tendency to withdraw, to exclude themselves, which leads to alienation from educational and social institutions.

Crothers relies on historical evidence to explain the nature of educational and social issues and some possible solutions in New Zealand. He describes the interplay of inclusion and exclusion in the education system there by examining key policy decisions, research findings and also inclusivity and its problems in practice. It is clear from his analysis that changes in educational policy have been cosmetic. Whilst there would seem to be some social mobility between generations, educational policy has preserved the status quo in minority discrimination. The minority group has responded by tending to isolate themselves from the privileged dominant white group. In short, the impact of education policy has been shaped by biases of gender and class, reinforced by teachers' belief in static cultural values, which leads to social isolation on the part of the minority.

Surveying European Union (EU) programmes of Lifelong Learning, Panitsidou describes the outcome, including the problems encountered by such programmes when implemented in Greece. She has shown through a comprehensive research study that opportunities for mature adults to acquire new skills, or upgrade their existing ones, promote social inclusion of disadvantaged groups who were in a hopeless situation before they acquired these new skills. The author concludes that such initiatives encouraged by the EU highlight the necessity for implementing programmes that will equip adults with key competencies for coping with the challenges of living in the twenty-first century.

Giavrimis, Giossi and Papastamatis offer an approach to deal with disability issues in the Greek educational context, which involves teachers as well as the whole school staff as part of the process. According to these authors, Greek teachers need to be educated to increase their understanding about students' difficulties in the learning environment. Professional development of teachers would seem to be a crucial element in helping students escape from social and educational alienation and isolation.

Nath, whilst examining the issues within the context of Bangladesh (only within 45 years of its anniversary of independence) also relies primarily on historical evidence with regard to educational issues. Women-friendly policies, affirmative action and targeted developmental goals are identified and some progress has been made. In spite of various ecological and political catastrophes, Bangladesh has enhanced the accessibility of education for girls and women's participation at various levels. The author admits that in spite of the policy formulation and efforts by the government as well as non-governmental organisations, there are policy gaps. A number of plausible solutions are proposed to counteract the challenges facing Bangladesh.

In Part III, Siddiqui, whilst discussing challenges for the education sector and inclusiveness in a diverse population like India, shows how India is emerging as a global economic power. The author argues that the pace of development has increased in the last two decades because of the Education Policy of 1986 which resolved to substantially improve access to education at all levels. It also helped to make education more relevant and inclusive in its reach. Some would argue that there is still a big divide between rural and urban education, between haves and have-nots. The author admits that there are several challenges to be addressed for access to quality education for all which would enable young people in India to meet the demands of a fast-changing, competitive technological world.

Griva discusses some of the challenges within the context of Greek education which is faced by the system in teaching bilingual immigrant students. The author provides evidence to suggest that Greek teachers often express anxiety and uncertainty in teaching bilingual immigrant students perhaps because of their preconceived ideas. Teachers fail to understand that for immigrant students coming to school with their home language and being required to adapt to a new language of the host country, contributes to their inability to grasp the lesson and to their consequent alienation from school and society. The author points out that teachers' biases and stereotypes also hinder the process of immigrant students' inclusion in educational and social institutions. She suggests that courses in teacher education should aim to promote bilingual students' cognitive and linguistic development, to encourage training in meta-cognitive and social skills. She describes holistic learning and participation in all aspects of school life for all students. Collaboration between school and family is also essential to achieving education for all these children.

The problem of dyslexia is another issue which faces teachers and schools in most countries. It is estimated that 13 to 14 percent of school children in India have a learning disability. Tabassum and Kumari suggest that dyslexia is the most common learning disability in India and it is an important barrier to integrating these children in mainstream schools. It is widely accepted that very little is known about the etiology of dyslexia. Furthermore, it is more difficult to conduct any systematic piece of research into dyslexia in India because of the multilingual and multicultural nature of society. This makes it a difficult task to identify and understand the problem in the initial stages. The lack of appropriate tools in various languages is another issue which is one of the major challenges for the Indian education system. The sources of dyslexia may be neurological and/or genetic but it affects the ability to read, the ability to discriminate voices, and often the ability to write. These weaknesses require early diagnosis and intensive treatment, particularly in the digital age. Some psychologists believe that dyslexia is not a disease but a lifelong issue which needs to be dealt with by well-planned education, and support from teachers, parents, and family. Parents and teachers can be trained to understand the symptoms initially, which will strengthen the self-confidence of these children and help them to lead productive and successful lives as members of an inclusive community.

Showing a similar approach, Flude asserts that the digital age provides resources and opportunities for the educational and social inclusion of children who manifest a wide range of learning disabilities. Discussing the challenges presented by children with special needs of different kinds, the author suggests that inclusivity must be part of a lifelong learning strategy, which should be open to all potential learners without labelling their disability. This requires an approach involving the whole school in focusing on the efficacy of integration, tools of self-management and e-learning for solving problems of all children with special needs. Like other writers in this volume, he strongly believes that parents, grandparents and the community should be involved in this network to facilitate societal change.

Following a similar line of plausible solutions for inclusive education, Gireesan shows how, as a result of policy legislation since the 1990s, novel pedagogies and model strategies have evolved in India to ensure the participation of children from underprivileged and marginalised groups. Based on a well-planned research study, conducted in one of the Indian states where 'Alternative and Innovative Education' was developed, he discusses how to 'reach the unreached'. The rationale behind the strategy was to address the issue of non-enrolment and higher dropout rates in remote areas and to provide primary education for all. The findings showed that critical thinking, problem-solving, self-confidence, self-esteem, interpersonal relations, cooperative learning and empathy were more evident in learners. The rise of experimental schools, according to the author, is an important move to enable 'Universalising Primary Education' among the underprivileged and marginalised sections of Indian society. This is also seen as an important step in the context of Right to Education (RTE).

As can be seen from the foregoing analysis by these scholars from different countries, education is a critical element together with social, economic and political inclusivity, all of which need to be advanced thoughtfully and systematically. This volume seeks to capture the complexity and breadth of educational and social inclusion. It also touches on political, social, cultural and educational development and the meaning of 'equality' and the 'rights of citizens'. There is also a common view among the contributors that discrimination, stereotypes, biased assumptions, prejudice and dismissive disparagement cannot be sustained in this newly globalised, open and dynamic world society. The views and critical analysis in this volume are based on research evidence, authors' many years of experience in their respective field, and close observations as part of the institution in question. It is hoped that the material presented here will contribute to the current debates and discussions taking place in most developed and developing countries and will help us to increase our understanding of the processes involved. Clearly, there is no turning back from globalisation and its promise of growing diversity among populations in different territories. This requires policymakers and practitioners to think imaginatively and act positively. Education as a socialising agent must further a pluralistic dimension, an education for all, quality education for all.

PART I
Theoretical and conceptual issues

1
EDUCATION AND SOCIAL INTEGRATION FOR ALL

Challenges and responses

Gajendra K. Verma

Introduction

The issues arising from educational and social inclusion seem to have powerful backing throughout the world. At its World Conference on Education in 1994, UNESCO acknowledged the losses incurred by social and educational exclusion and argued that schools should accommodate all children regardless of physical, intellectual, social, linguistic or other issues. Thus, the United Nations (UN) insisted on the inclusion of disabled and gifted, street and working children, children from remote or nomadic populations, children from linguistic, ethnic or cultural minorities and children from other disadvantaged groups and from all areas of the world (UNESCO, 1994a).

At the Salamanca Forum on education for children with special needs, UNESCO called for inclusive principles to operate in education. The Salamanca Statement recognised the fact that no matter how well-trained and dedicated the teachers, there are serious consequences in segregated schooling for those students with grave learning difficulties (UNESCO, 1994b).

Again, a recent UNESCO seminar on open and distance learning (UNESCO, 2002) emphasised to its delegates that they would 'have an important role in achieving the great vision which motivates UNESCO's work, the vision of a world in which everyone gets an education', the vision of Education for All (D'Antonio, 2003).

The UN declarations of 1994 were updated in 2016, at the ninth World Assembly of the Disabled People's International,[1] by the Prime Minister of India, Narendra Modi, who sent the message that India is taking measures to ensure that the demographic dividend of people with special needs is adequately tapped for nation-building. He emphasised that the cost of exclusion of people with disabilities from the workplace is estimated by the World Bank to be around 37% of the country's GDP (Press Trust of India, 11 April, 2016). The message also pointed out that as the world advances, people with disabilities must be included in accomplishing the Sustainable Development Goals by 2030, particularly the eradication of extreme poverty. The Prime Minister translated the philosophy of 'Vasudhaiva Kutumbakam' (the world is one family) and stressed that India believes in the principles of inclusion and integration (Press Trust of India, 11 April, 2016).

The implication of UN discussions, as of the declarations of the Indian government, is that the planned and committed inclusion of all disadvantaged and vulnerable children is both a moral obligation and a way of fulfilling the needs and aspirations of children from these groups. All children including emotionally and physically challenged ones have the right to have their educational, social, personal and physical needs met by the state which is responsible for acknowledging explicitly that the country's future and its development depends on its children growing up to be creative citizens. Yet, in many democratic and 'civilised' states, these needs are still not met. More than twenty years have passed since the uncompromising statements were formulated by UNESCO and well over a decade since the seminar on distance learning. But the vision embodied in those declarations has not yet been fulfilled. Consequently, various disadvantaged and vulnerable groups fall into the category of an underclass. Among them, none, not even immigrants and their descendants, have the right to choose between the privileges of inclusion and integration and those of separatism and diasporism (Bagley, 1986; Verma, 2007).

In the following we look at *what is really happening* with the aspiration to Education for All, at *the outcomes*, and at *what should be done*.

Despite the committed declarations of UNESCO, a glance through international literature discloses that there are many bases for exclusion from social, educational, religious and political arenas. Among the excluded are the poor, the disabled, the minorities who speak a language different from the majority tongue, groups that follow foreign traditions and customs, carry out unfamiliar religious practices and have adopted an unusual lifestyle, as well as groups with ascriptions of caste, class, and gender. In Western Europe, for example, apart from cognitively and physically challenged groups, the excluded are usually immigrants and their children, religious minorities, linguistic minorities, such as Roma and Traveller people as well as African Caribbean, descendants of slaves who were forced to assimilate. In schools there are often bitter clashes between teachers' values (derived from their mind-sets) and the expectations of children from the deprived groups.

Roma have experienced centuries of stigma and are still Europe's most downtrodden minority (Bagley, 2007). The Roma people's greatest concentration is in the population of Romania and they suffer extreme educational and social disadvantage. Roma families try to escape from Romania from time to time under new EU (European Union) rules on migration. Often they are deported by the governments concerned; even democratic states ignore the EU rules on free migration in regard to them (Bagley, 2008).

Indian society, like many others, has failed to realise fully the value (at both individual and societal levels) associated with optimising the development of all children (Siddiqui, 2007). It is estimated that in India there is a terrible waste of human resources, with perhaps the highest number of out-of-school children in the world, most of whom are working or are street children at the mercy of an exploitative adult world (Siddiqui, 2007). Quite often access to education is restricted because individuals and communities belong to a certain caste, social class, or to a family with low social status. In fact, Dalits and Untouchables, at the lowest rung of the caste system, are among the most marginalised groups in India and their education presents significant challenges. They are derogatorily known as the tribal people, and in schools their children are usually cited as physically and cognitively challenged. As a result, they are often expelled from school and become urban street children and child labourers.

It is clear that in an increasingly globalised world, diversity is rapidly becoming the norm rather than the exception. Over the last three or four decades most European countries have experienced an increased diversity of their population as a result of international migration. Still, the risk that immigrants suffer from multiple disadvantages has not disappeared and, indeed, has been commented upon by researchers (Pitkänen, Kalekin-Fishman and Verma, 2002). There have always been economic, religious, linguistic, class, caste and physical disability differences in state populations. Immigrants and their descendants have always felt that there has been little or no recognition of their religions, lifestyles, traditions and languages. What differs now is the extent to which individual societies acknowledge this reality. Developing countries demand a different approach when analysing the issues associated with the educational and social exclusion of certain sections of society. For example, such countries have a high proportion of children who may rarely attend school or even drop out after a year or two, often because they suffer from economic and social disadvantages. There have been only hesitant attempts on the part of the EU (European Union) to develop policies of inclusion by ensuring equity at educational, social and personal levels.

As briefly pointed out in the earlier section, differences, *per se*, are not the 'problem'; the meanings we attribute to such differences turn into 'issues'. Deprivation does not stem only from the indifference of policy-makers, 'top down'. Examples of 'bottom-up' signals of indifference to minority needs and mandatory assimilation are many. Typical is an example of a head teacher talking to linguistic minority pupils in his school, telling them: 'Do not communicate in your language within your group in the playground because my English-speaking boys feel offended.' Such statements are not uncommon and obviously have an undesirable impact on the socialisation process of the individual through family structures and schooling.

The situation of vulnerable populations is exacerbated because of the rapid social, political, technological and economic changes taking place in the world today. But the reality is that we live in an increasingly interdependent and globalised world in which we interact with varying cultural, social, religious and political individuals or groups not only within our borders, but often beyond national boundaries. Consequently, globalisation confronts individuals, groups and nations with new learning challenges, sometimes extremely sensitive in nature, that policy-makers and educational planners find daunting (Calloids, 2003; Verma, 2007).

At this point it would seem pertinent briefly to mention the concept of self-exclusion which seems to operate in some discriminated groups. The cultural and social self-exclusion by certain groups can be seen as a conscious or unconscious withdrawal from the cultural field of the dominant group in society. This may mean reluctance or even refusal to adopt norms and values of the mainstream. Self-exclusion can also be explained by the desire to avoid assimilation. This form of self-exclusion can be reinforced by a negative attitude of the mainstream group towards religious, cultural, linguistic and ethnic minority groups. This self-exclusion can also be motivated by personal choice, cultural choice or a sense of alienation. Self-exclusion can be reinforced by a negative attitude of the majority group towards minority groups, political refugees and migrant workers. This is seen when the majority group expresses disregard or disrespect for others' beliefs and cultural or religious symbols. Two salient examples are that of the disrespect for Muslim women wearing a scarf or Sikhs wearing a turban. Whatever may be the underlying reason for self-exclusion, it can reinforce the marginalisation of that individual or group.

In sum: among the critical issues of paramount importance being debated over the last two decades are those surrounding educational/social equality, social justice, the mainstreaming of 'disadvantaged', 'underprivileged' and 'vulnerable' groups. There is sufficient evidence in the literature to suggest that differences in socio-economic status, tensions between ethnic/religious groups, discrimination of scheduled castes/tribes by the upper caste in India (just a few examples) have been the product of religious, ethnic or cultural minority groups finding themselves subject to discrimination, prejudice, segregation and exclusion resulting in their inability to access education, employment and welfare services. Thus, certain characteristics of diversity, such as colour, caste, language, socio-economic status and physical and emotional challenges can label individuals as potential educational winners or losers (Grant, 1995). Such marginalised minority groups find their life chances impaired by gross inequalities in the system as a whole (Grant, 1995; Verma, 1999).

There is no consensus amongst nations about the approaches to be adopted for educational and social inclusion of such groups. Experience shows, however, that the factors underpinning any form of exclusion have a powerful bearing on shaping the historical, cultural, economic and social context. Furthermore, in most countries, the common experience of groups excluded from educational opportunities and experiences is that they face discrimination, prejudice, racism, and educational and social exclusion of varying forms in their adult lives. The discriminated groups suffer from multiple disadvantages, and there are indications that underachievement in schools and a high rate of school dropout are connected with lack of skills, poor health, inferior employment or chronic unemployment in adulthood. Therefore, educational inclusion is proposed as a long-term solution.

Indeed, in most democratic countries, the concept of 'social and educational inclusion and integration' of disadvantaged groups has become an accepted slogan.

Although it is agreed that the educational system is a powerful instrument for promoting social inclusion or exclusion, the ways forward for this intellectual movement are often far from clear. Let us admit that most democratic societies have failed to develop practices that advance the fundamental right of each individual to education, health and welfare so as to benefit the growth and development of the nation as a whole. Thus, education has an important part to play in the development of individuals – intellectually, affectively, physically, socially and morally – and through those individuals, in the development of the wider society. Many educational planners continue to pose the question: what initiatives are needed to create a society in which the life chances of all individuals and groups will be equal?

Sebba and Ainscow (1996) have defined the concept of educational inclusion as follows:

> Inclusion describes the process by which a school attempts to respond to all pupils and individuals by reconsidering its curricular organisation and provision. Through this process the school builds its capacity to accept all pupils from the local community who wish to attend and in doing so reduces the need to exclude pupils.

Broadly, there would seem to be different perspectives when analysing the issues associated with social and educational inclusion. Jha (2007) neatly puts them into two distinct categories – first, those emerging from developed countries, and second, those prevailing in the developing world. Inclusion within the educational context involves the right of an individual or the group to be accepted within the institution of their choice. Inclusion also involves the right of an individual or group to retain a well-defined identity whether based on religion, language or culture. Inclusive societies and governments are expected to promote a system in which all their citizens can fully participate and share its educational, social and welfare provisions irrespective of their social origin, economic status, gender, ethnicity, disability whether physical or emotional. Inclusion must cover, among other fields – education, employment, health, social security and the domain of politics. Policies for educational and social inclusion ought to aim at promoting the values of equality, justice, democratic rights and respect for individual identity.

Education systems are society's crucibles, so the issue of fair education for all children and young people sharply focuses priorities relating to inclusion. The questions posed by a consensus in favour of 'inclusion' and 'integration', and the policies formulated differ from one state to another. Many developed and developing countries advocate or legislate inclusive education for all, regardless of social class, caste, 'race', ethnicity, religion, gender and gender orientation, language, cognitive and emotional status, and physical abilities and challenges. However, it is well known that many societies are strong on rhetoric, but weak on action.

It is also a fact that all governments use their educational system to inculcate certain attitudes and beliefs as part of their political objectives (sometimes hidden objectives) including some degree of inclusiveness. Most societies have traditionally regarded formal schooling as the major institution for the transmission of society's core values, even when the values and aspirations of different social and cultural groups are in conflict with those of the so-called mainstream society and even its core values. Whenever there are overt or covert disagreements over these values and beliefs, there are tensions within educational institutions ranging from teacher education institutions to school at all levels.

Inclusion: Some challenges

There are, however, many places where sincere efforts are being made to further educational and social inclusion through education. The concept of inclusion has now moved away from simplistic notions, implying the integration of children with emotional and physical disabilities and special educational needs (Warnock Report, 1978). Now inclusion refers to the enrolment and successful participation of all groups of children in mainstream education, which requires changes in pedagogies, organisational structure, policy-making and cultural understandings within education systems and the wider society (Tomlinson, 1996). In the 1990s the consensus emerged amongst educational practitioners and policy-makers that the whole school approach is needed if inclusive education is to be successful (Smith and Tomlinson, 1989). Inclusive education is now an international movement, far beyond the boundary of special education.

Efforts are being made by the Indian government to redress the situation by introducing quota systems in education, in public sector employment and welfare schemes. There is strong pressure from some political parties in India to reserve places for a quota of deprived groups in schools and in employment in the private sector. Progress has been painfully slow because of strong traditions, customs and cultural norms controlled by the dominant group. The mainstream, however, resists on the grounds that this kind of policy will discriminate against those more qualified.

Another crucial aspect of the teaching process is the 'hidden curriculum'. Formal attitudinal changes are likely to come from the prescribed curriculum process which may teach knowledge, facts and competencies but the hidden curriculum has a powerful part to play in fixing values. This curriculum is realised when educationists are unaware that attitudes and beliefs demonstrate opposition to completing the process of personal adaptation, interpersonal interaction, and sensitivity to diversity of different kinds.

There is also an even more important aspect in the educational process, namely teachers. When reflecting on our education, many of us would, I suspect, tend to recall first and foremost those who taught us, rather than necessarily the curriculum we studied. This reminds us of the centrality of teaching and teachers in the educational process. If an inclusive education is to be offered to young people, then the training of the teaching force is of paramount importance. One is tempted to say that a curriculum is only as good as those delivering it. Thus delivery of effective and inclusive education in a diverse classroom is heavily dependent on the quality and training of the teaching force (Verma, Zec and Skinner, 2012).

Programmes of teacher education must address the stereotypes, which are barriers to effective teaching and planning for the adoption of inclusive education policies. Indeed, any planned changes such as the social and educational inclusion of disadvantaged and minority groups requires the involvement of many stakeholders including politicians, policy-makers, educational institutions including teachers, head teachers and teacher trainers, and not least parents of 'challenged' children, and their community leaders. There must be dialogue, exchange of information, research and synthesis of research, the allocation of fresh resources as well as new modes of teacher training through school inspection. We must begin with understanding the meaning of being a 'special' pupil (and surely, all children and youth fall into this category, each in particular ways), and conduct institutional analyses of the parameters for change. These changes may be complex and difficult to achieve, and require new cognitive and affective mind-sets in policy-makers and teachers alike. Indeed, nothing less than a change in how society regards children and young people is required. We need also, in achieving these goals, to incorporate new electronic technologies and modes of communication in this exciting programme of change.

New technology provides opportunities for creating an inclusive society. However, like all other things with a potential for providing education and social integration for all, these new developments hold within themselves the potential for misuse if educators are not equipped with the skills, knowledge and understanding in dealing with the issues of inequality and underlying factors responsible for it in society. The barriers that exist between the 'excluded' groups and the mainstream will not disappear in the short term. However, education can begin to dismantle the barriers which exist in our minds. As noted, education should adopt a holistic approach to dealing with inequality. That means that the system of addressing educational and social inequalities should be integral to the structure of the institution as a whole. It is time to move these issues from the periphery to become central to teacher education. It is also important for all of us to understand more about the discrepancies of prejudice, discrimination, stereotypes and inequality at both individual and group levels (Verma, 1993). It is now widely accepted that education and knowledge are the main instruments for change, innovation and growth in society.

Changing mind-sets

The means and methods by which educational structures and curricula work are indications of the governing mind-sets perpetuated in education. A 'mind-set' incorporates preconceptions that may be derived from popular prejudice and stereotypes about certain sections of society. They may rely on civilisational, national and societal contexts. Within the background of overflowing knowledge and information transmission through modern technology, citizens are exposed to repeated opportunities to revise conceptions and misconceptions about people, as about objects and events. Misconceptions are often reinforced by laypersons' constructions of 'reality', constructions that are not necessarily powered by recognition of shared evidence. 'Mind-set' also refers to a collection of collectively held beliefs, preferences, actions, faiths which ought to be analysed within the historical, cultural, social and political contexts. The formation of such mind-sets takes place during socialisation through family structure and later are reinforced through schooling. Mind-sets are often reinforced through self-confirming interactions, in which the dominant group structure the cognitive and emotional worlds of the least powerful groups of society. The stereotypes which prevent healthy educational inclusion are often reinforced by a biased and ill-informed media. In Britain this has led, for example, to a form of institutionalised Islamophobia. In India, prejudice and stereotype against Dalit, Maha Dalit groups is similarly self-confirming.

All mind-sets are, of course, related to 'group thinking'. This implies that the groups to which people belong control the values, beliefs, actions and behaviours of those who subscribe to the group thinking acceptably. When we talk about changing mind-sets we imply that those beliefs and values are not in line with the norms of society, and with current trends in thought. Mind-sets can be developed by acquiring knowledge within the educational context. Education has been seen as the most powerful strategy to bring about changes in mind-sets. This involves new ways of recognising the form and content of knowledge, redefinition of worthwhile knowledge, updating knowledge relevant to the times, inculcating new sets of values, new concepts and new language usage. Admittedly, in this process there is likely to be conflict with certain beliefs, old customs, traditions and values.

'Changing mind-sets' through the process of teacher education has become the focus of much European research (Caena, 2014; Huber and Mompoint-Gaillard, 2011). To challenge existing 'mind-sets', innovative approaches are required, approaches that empower pupil learning through peer-group learning approaches. Expecting that pupils' mind-sets are based on collectively held beliefs, attitudes, choices and behaviour that may defeat their capacity for learning, it is important to ascertain that learners from deprived groups acquire what Dweck (2006) calls a 'growth' mind-set, one that will enable them to deal with learning challenges because they believe in their ability to grow. Her research shows that responding to people, events and learning materials with a fixed mind-set, with an understanding that one's capacities are inborn, will be self-defeating and likely to reproduce the vulnerabilities of the (excluded) groups of origin. Given a flexible growth mind-set, a good education can play an important role in challenging stereotypes, prejudice, discrimination and ethnocentric perspectives of both individuals and groups. Education can at least begin to identify and dismantle the fences which exist in our minds.

Access to 'Education for All' is of course important to all forms of educational outcomes including health and employment. Without access, the chances of attaining social and economic equality are insignificant (Rizvi et al., 2007). However, the researchers also acknowledge that mere access is not enough to realise the full potential of education. It is clear that equality of opportunity and equality of outcome are incompatible. The processes between equality of opportunity (input) and the outcome (output) are critical in maximising the potential of individuals. In others, these intervening variables include the curriculum, the teacher, the testing/ examination, the hidden curriculum experience of the individual in society at large, all have a strong bearing on the outcome at the end of compulsory schooling.

Inclusiveness or integration must be viewed in terms of a series of conscious steps taken by various institutions. The aim should be to ensure equality of educational provision, tailored to the individual's needs, in order to achieve the maximum outcomes in terms of achievement and the life fulfilment of which the individual is capable. The aim, above all, should be to achieve the 'normalisation' of outcome for every student. Principles of inclusion and integration also imply that all children and youth should be equipped with the necessary skills, attitudes and understanding of their society to make them self-reliant and self-actualising, as equal participants in a democratic society. Educators, professionals, social activists, politicians and decision-makers have key roles to play in this process. The strategies to be adopted in order to achieve these realistic goals are, however, contested, and imply bold incursions into contested political and social arenas.

Equal Opportunities, Protection of Rights and Full Participation was passed in India in 1995. The Act allowed a 3% quota for differently-abled people in Government services. Following this special drive, just over 1% of the vacancies were filled as against the stipulated three. This resulted in filling 10,000 posts only between May 2015 and April 2016 (*The Indian Express*, 3 May, 2016). It was also announced that reservation of 1% will be made for people with blindness or low-vision, hearing impairment and locomotor disability or cerebral palsy in posts identified for each disability (*The Indian Express*, 3 May, 2016). Thus it can be seen that efforts are being made to provide employment of differently-abled people in public and private sectors.

For given educational inclusion, we must turn as well to the arena of social inclusion. In many societies there are barriers to participation in social, religious and cultural activities on the basis of social origin, gender, caste, religion, traditions, customs or ethnicity. When it is a question of inclusion and/or exclusion, we can draw a clear-cut distinction on the level of gender. Acute examples of cultural and social differences in the status of women have been noted in connection with the conservative principles of religions. Women are sometimes cornered between familial traditions, customs and beliefs and the requirements of life in a modern and technological society. This is true of young women born and educated in the twenty-first century, and desirous of preserving their bonds with family and community.

Recently religious prejudice on the basis of gender countered a small group of women social activists who tried to enter Haji Ali Dargah in Mumbai, India; their attempt was foiled (*Times of India*, 28 April, 2016). The Haji Ali Dargah is a very old and famous shrine. This is a 'classic' example of how women are not accorded equality to pray in religious places such as temples, mosques and shrines.

But here, too, there is promise of change. Recently, for the first time in its history, the 1,000-year-old Juma Masjid in India, situated at Kerala's Thazhathangady, has thrown open its doors to Muslim women. The mosque is famous for its rich architecture and wood carvings. This is one of the heritage zones of Kerala (Press Trust of India, 25 April, 2016). Until now, women were allowed to enter the mosque on specified dates, but only to see the famous architecture and not for 'any celebrations or for offering prayers', President of the mosque committee told the Press Trust of India (25 April, 2016). It is obvious that this is the first step towards equality of women in religious places.

Another very recent event provides positive signposts for gender equality. A 400-year-old tradition was broken by a small group of women activists (TNN and Agencies, 11 April, 2016). For centuries women were not allowed to enter the inner sanctum of the Shani Shingnapur temple. Bowing to the Bombay High Court order, the temple announced that both men and women could enter the inner sanctum to offer their prayers. The Highest Court of Justice in India, the Supreme Court, asked the Management Committee of the temple, 'Can you deny a woman her right to climb Mount Everest?' It further added in its judgement that customs cannot override constitutional values.

Now this movement of 'Inclusion for All', even in regard to religion, irrespective of gender, social origin and economic disadvantage, has started, as the above recent events show. It is hoped that this movement will spread and benefit all deprived groups.

Conclusions

It is clear that the world is rapidly coming to terms with the underlying issues of the exclusion of certain sections of the population and its impact on society's health and development. Some educators might argue, perhaps naïvely, that education alone should not be held responsible for the exclusion of disadvantaged and/or discriminated groups in society. Since this is beyond its direct control, particularly in the case of certain socio-economic, and traditional/cultural and rural–urban divides in society. Nevertheless, it is unalterably true that education can play an important role in leading the battle against exclusion, prejudice and discrimination (Verma, 1993). Of course, the first step has to be strong legislation followed by a firm commitment by policy-makers and educational planners. Political commitment is critical for the success of the movement.

As we have seen, developed, as well as developing, countries have used formal education as the primary medium for promoting (social and educational) inclusion. Yet, there is no denying the fact that to date educational policies and practices have failed to attain the objectives of inclusion for all. One of the main reasons would seem to be that they have failed to adopt a holistic approach by taking into account the cultural, socio-economic backgrounds and social deprivation of children and young people, and this has consequently hampered their success in the educational system (Verma, 1989). The lack of effectiveness of educational institutions in integrating disadvantaged and excluded groups and enhancing their educational opportunities to realise their full potential is still a major issue in most countries.

Admittedly, adopting the whole school approach to the inclusion of all children is not an easy task, since it involves meeting the educational and personal needs of all children and of their teachers as well.

In spite of the challenges posed, some educators retain optimism about the future. As Verma (1997) has expressed with some conviction:

> Education in the twenty-first century can become an essential contributor to integration, to a culture of peace and understanding. Through this we can assure respect for diversity, whether diversity of behaviour, or diversity of philosophical or religious belief.

In principle, most commentators agree that 'social and educational inclusion for all' is a noble goal: in practice, there is not only a lack of agreement on how to reach these goals, but also a failure to take the needed steps to reach them. This is true of North America, Britain, Greece, Eastern Europe, India, Bangladesh and Nepal (Bagley and Verma, 2008). There is still no example to which we can point in which successful inclusive education has been achieved in a holistic way. In practice, the majority of social institutions in developed and developing countries have failed to overcome the many barriers to an effective system of integrated education. Young people who are most in need of an effective educational system are often deprived of access to equality and equal rights to an educational system which addresses their individual needs. Thus the goals of inclusive education for the many millions of the world's children and youth have yet to be realised.

It is very useful and timely to reflect hard on the nature of educational and social inclusion and its broader implications for modern society. It is also critical that societies develop an over-arching framework which can support those differences rather than accentuate them. We need a framework that will enable all members to move freely and in harmony. However, that process will not occur overnight and there are likely to be many challenges to be faced before such a situation is reached. In the meantime, it is of crucial importance that all of us come to understand more about the dynamics of inclusion and society. In so doing, we can help to keep the issues to the forefront in the debate about the shape of our modern societies (Verma, 2002).

There are no easy answers to the issues surrounding educational and social inclusion for all citizens. But there is also no turning back from globalisation and the international movement which has begun its march for social and educational reforms. As noted here from different angles, combating prejudice and discrimination has been a central tenet of the international movement in the twenty-first century. Now this international movement has a platform, the *International Journal of Inclusive Education*, which is a stimulating initiative for those educators and policy-makers who are optimistic about the success of inclusiveness. This journal provides a forum for researchers, educational practitioners and policy-makers to share their ideas and research findings for the promotion of inclusive educational practices. Such initiatives are designed to prevent marginalisation on the basis of race, caste, ethnicity, gender, language, disability and any other forms of disadvantages. If we do not communicate or debate the issues, then we will allow distorted stereotypes to flourish unchallenged and divisiveness to increase. It is hoped that educators, policy-makers, educational planners and all those concerned with the health and development of the nation will join the forum. This social and educational revolution must embody the principles of equity, diversity, quality and democracy. These are fundamental to social justice and human dignity, the basic rights of All.

Note

1 It should be noted that Disabled People's International (DPI) has members from over 150 countries, and is supported by the United Nations.

Bibliography

Bagley, C. (1986). Multiculturalism, class and ideology: A European–Canadian comparison. In: S. Modgil, G. K. Verma, K. Mallick and C. Modgil (eds). *Multicultural Education: The Interminable Debate*. London: Falmer Press.

Bagley, C. (2007). Dalit children in India: Challenges for education and inclusiveness. In: G. K. Verma, C. Bagley and M. M. Jha (eds). *International Perspectives on Educational Diversity and Inclusion: Studies from America, Europe and India*. London: Routledge.

Bagley, C. (2008). The logic and morality of social and educational inclusion. In: C. Bagley and G. K. Verma (eds). *Challenges for Inclusion: Educational Social Studies from Britain and the Indian Subcontinent*. Rotterdam: Sense Publishers.

Bagley, C. and Verma, G. K. (eds). (2008). *Challenges for Inclusion*. Rotterdam: Sense.

Caena, F. (2014). *Initial Teacher Education in Europe: An Overview of Policy Issues*. Brussels: European Commission.

Calloids, F. (2003). The changing role of the state: New competencies for planners. *International Institute for Educational Planning Newsletter*, XXI(2), 1, 3–4.

D'Antonio, S. (2003). Open and distance learning: Technology is the answer but what was the question. *International Institute for Educational Planning Newsletter*, XXI(2), 14.

Dweck, C. (2006). *Mind-set: How You Can Fulfil Your Potential*. New York: Ballantine Books.

Grant, C. (1995). *Educating for Diversity: An Anthology of Multi-cultural Voices*. Boston: Allyn and Bacon (sponsored by the Association of Teacher Education).

Huber, J. and Mompoint-Gaillard, P. (eds). (2011). Teacher education for change: The theory behind the Council for Europe Pestalozzi programme. F-67075 Strasbourg Council of Europe Publishing. Available at: Cedexhttp://book.coe.int (retrieved 2 May, 2016).

Jha, M. M. (2007). Barriers to student access and success: Is inclusive education an answer? In: G. K. Verma, C. Bagley and M. M. Jha (eds). *International Perspectives on Educational Diversity and Inclusion*. Oxford: Routledge.

Pitkänen, P., Kalekin-Fishman, D. and Verma, G. K. (eds). (2002). *Immigration Settlement Policies and Current Challenges to Education*. London: Routledge/Falmer.

Press Trust of India. (11 April, 2016). Demographic dividend of special need people must be tapped: P.M. Modi. New Delhi: Press Trust of India.

Press Trust of India. (25 April, 2016). Entry of Muslim women in Juma Masjid. New Delhi: Press Trust of India.

Press Trust of India. (25 April, 2016). Thazhathangadi Mosque reeks with history. *The Hindu Daily*, 25 April, 2016.

Rizvi, F., Engel, L., Rutkowski, D. and Sparks, J. (2007). Equality and the politics of globalisation in education. In: G. K. Verma, C. Bagley and M. M. Jha (eds). *International Perspectives on Educational Diversity and Inclusion*. Oxford: Routledge.

Sebba, J. and Ainscow, M. (1996). International development in inclusive schooling: Mapping the issues. *Cambridge Journal of Education*, 26, 5–18.

Siddiqui, M. A. (2007). Inclusive education for working children and street children in India. In: G. K. Verma, C. Bagley and M. M. Jha (eds). *International Perspectives on Educational Diversity and Inclusion*. Oxford: Routledge.

Smith, D. J. and Tomlinson, S. (1989). *The School Effect: A Study of Multi-racial Comprehensives*. London: Policy Studies Institute.

The Indian Express. (2016). Equal Opportunities, Protection of Rights and Full Participation Act, 1995. New Delhi, 3 May, 2016.

Times of India. (28 April, 2016). Haji Ali for All. ANI @ ANI_news, April 2016.

TNN and Agencies. (2016). 400 years tradition broken: Shani Temple allows women to enter inner sanctum. *The Indian Express*, 11 April, 2016, Delhi, India.

Tomlinson, S. (1996). Conflicts and dilemmas for professionals in special education. In: C. Christensen and F. Rizvi (eds). *Disability and the Dilemmas of Education and Justice*. Buckingham: Open University Press.

UNESCO. (1994a). *The World Education Forum*. Paris: UNESCO.

UNESCO. (1994b). *The Salamanca Statement and Framework for Action on Special Needs Education*. Paris: UNESCO Special Education Programme.

UNESCO. (2002). *Open and Distance Learning: Trends, Policy and Strategy Considerations*. Paris: UNESCO.

Verma, G. K. (1989). Postscript – Cultural pluralism: Strategies for change. In: G. K. Verma (ed). *Education for All: A Landmark in Pluralism*. London: Falmer Press.

Verma, G. K. (1993). *Inequality and Teacher Education: An International Perspective*. London: The Falmer Press.

Verma, G. K. (1997). Inequality and intercultural education. In: D. Woodrow and G. K. Verma (eds). *Intercultural Education: Theories, Policies and Practice*. Aldershot: Ashgate.

Verma, G. K. (1999). Inequality and educational implications for the psychologist. *Education and Child Psychology*, 16, 6–16.

Verma, G. K. (2002). Migrants and social exclusion: A European perspective. In: *Integrated Approaches to Lifelong Learning*. Asian-Europe Institute, University of Malaysia.

Verma, G. K. (2007). Diversity and Multicultural Education. In: G. K. Verma, C. Bagley and M. M. Jha (eds). *International Perspectives on Educational Diversity and Inclusion*. Oxford: Routledge.

Verma, G. K., Zec, P. and Skinner, G. (2012). *The Ethnic Crucible: Harmony and Hostility in Multi-ethnic Schools*. Oxford: Falmer Press/Routledge.

Warnock, M. (1978). *Children and Young People with Special Educational Needs*. London: HMSO.

2

FURTHERING SOCIAL INCLUSION THROUGH CITIZENSHIP EDUCATION

Cultivating civic action in early childhood education

Devorah Kalekin-Fishman

Context

While mobilizing education as a force for 'social inclusion' is a task of the highest importance, placing emphasis only on learning materials limits its potential contribution to realizing the comprehensive goal. The aspiration to include people (of diverse cultures, diverse socio-economic strata and diverse cognitive aptitudes) in educational institutions and through education to ensure their inclusion in adult society, requires sustained efforts to further students' capacities for social participation throughout their schooling. If successful, such education can develop people who, when reaching maturity, will be equipped to reject exclusion from decision-making in social and political institutions. I wish to outline a plan for cultivating inclusive civic action in early childhood education and throughout formal schooling. I base this proposal on three arguments: (a) wide-ranging theoretical definitions of citizenship (state-individual relationships) cohere with theoretical definitions of civil society (non-governmental collectivities and organizations); (b) actions of state and non-state collectivities in democracies are effected through politics, i.e., deliberation and participatory decision-making; (c) up-to-date practices for advancing learning cohere with procedures that shape civic action in a robust democratic state.

Introduction

The year 2011 was the year of the Arab Spring. It began in March with the suicide of Mohamed Bouazizi, a Tunisian street vendor who set himself on fire after he was hounded and humiliated by police and bureaucrats, and signalled the onset of rebellious protests in all of Tunisia. Later protests broke out in Egypt, in Yemen and in Libya, and more meekly but significantly in Iran, Jordan, Saudi Arabia and perhaps most poignantly in Syria. The Arab Spring also spurred the events of the Israeli summer, two months of protest which began in Tel Aviv and spread to all the large Israeli cities as well as to villages, including those of Arab citizens of Israel. All the protests in the Middle East were distinguished by the fact that they were *inclusive* in the fullest sense of the word. They engaged people of all ages, different social strata, various ethnic backgrounds, religious affiliations and even different political convictions. Despite significant differences, all the groups were disgruntled by economic and social injustice as well as by the arbitrariness of national politics. Evidence that solidarity in the face of globalizing neo-liberal policies was not merely the whim of people in one region was seen when, in October 2011, people in forty states throughout the world demonstrated, identifying themselves with the tenor of the protests of the Middle East. Many sociologists hailed these inclusive demonstrations as the 'rise of civil society'. The denotation proved overly optimistic. At best, the 2011 'spring', 'summer' and 'autumn' highlighted a lacuna in education for social inclusion.

Events of the Israeli summer illustrate one type of civic confusion; those who participated in the protests, about 4% of the population, congregated in vociferous, albeit orderly displays. A goodly number set up tents on main thoroughfares and, in order to make their point, withstood the trials and discomforts of encampments. Among the long-time homeless for whom living in the street was not a novelty, becoming part of a population-wide protest seemed to be a source of hope. Media enthusiasm knew no bounds. 'Events of the protest' were highlighted daily on television; attention turned to the young people who rallied crowds everywhere with calls for egalitarianism and for revising unwarranted bureaucratic rules and regulations. A wide range of not necessarily compatible goals clustered under the slogan: 'The people want social justice!' Determination fired the imaginations of the students turned leaders, of workers, farmers and people with small businesses, as well as of pensioners, 'contract workers' and women with baby carriages calling for affordable child care and improvements in public education that would enable them to participate in the labour market. A sign of the impact of the protest was the fact that it attracted words of support from representatives of the wealthiest segments of the population and opportunistic politicians outdid one another in showing their identification with 'the people'.

Fearing further civil action, the ultra-right-wing government co-opted the action. They appointed a committee ostensibly to formulate guidelines for meeting the demands of the protesters. Among the immediate consequences of the Israeli summer was a communiqué to teachers by the Minister of Education who insisted that 'the protest' was in itself evidence of how successful the educational system is, and has been, in imparting principles and practices of active citizenship. This, of course, was patently untrue. In fact, the entire project of the months-long protest reaffirmed the sad truth that even in states which style themselves democracies, schools often fail to cultivate students' sensitivity to injustices or to equip them with the tools they need for translating alertness into meaningful initiatives. There are grounds for claiming that programmes of education for a working civil society should not lead to protests that are unfocused and prolix after years of apparent indifference. Were educators to involve children in collective decision-making throughout their school careers (from their earliest encounter with formal education), graduates would be capable of monitoring government and restraining their unreasonable acts rather than resorting to the random mechanisms of protest.

Background

Although education for citizenship is part of the curriculum in many countries, there is very little emphasis on attaining collective goals, that is, on decision-making which is the heart of citizenship (Parsons, 1960). Let us look at some different approaches.

In the UK, citizenship education became a core theme of schooling for the first time with the introduction of the National Curriculum in 1988. Its aims specified the need to impart knowledge about government, law and citizens' rights, as well as to foster critical inquiry and '[learn] to participate in community-based citizenship activities' (National Curriculum, 2016). Interpretation of these principles, however, remains relatively hazy. Since the mode of introducing citizenship into the school schedule remains the prerogative of each school, some have introduced regular lessons while others consider that citizenship can somehow be taught 'throughout the curriculum' (OFSTED, 2005; Smith and Verma, 2007). In a word, the meaning of citizenship education remains ambiguous.

In Germany, a post-fascist society struggling with its past, the very idea of teaching citizenship was feared for a long time after World War II lest it lead to a renewed descent into dictatorship. Civics was introduced hesitantly, therefore, as 'Staatsbürgerkunde' which dealt mainly with knowledge about formal procedures in a democratic regime. In the aftermath of the student uprisings in 1968, a curriculum for critical political education was elaborated, generalized and disseminated in institutions of youth work as well as in schools (cf. Schröter and Jäger, 2007; Sünker and Swiderek, 2010). But, as shown by the stubborn emergence of neo-fascist bands, its success has been only partial.

In China, citizenship education is a course of 'moral education' from elementary to secondary education. Planned by the government, this type of education is associated with the instrumental study of economics and the institutionalization of political ideology (Kan, 2010).

In Pakistan, citizenship education is the site of conflict between the religious establishment and the state. Attempts by the state to initiate programmes that promote democratic participation have repeatedly been foiled by the insistence of theocrats on uncritical devotion to traditional Islamic principles as the single determining criterion for good citizenship (Ahmad, 2004).

In India, citizenship education is widespread, but not obligatory. There are initiatives designed to make citizenship education a lively part of students' experiences (Nurturing Youth, 2009). Still, critics point out that as a school subject, civics often promotes the tedious learning of facts rather than fostering the development of mature well-rounded citizens who identify emotionally with the largest democracy in the world (Chhokar, 2006; Thapan, 2008).

In Israel, programmes in civics have been a mandatory part of the curriculum since the establishment of the state school system in 1953. Classes take place once or twice a week in both junior and senior high schools, and civics is among the required subjects for matriculation. In addition, secondary school students are required to carry out a project of service to the community, a project that is evaluated as part of the student's academic record (Kalekin-Fishman, 2004). Basically, the Israeli programme is modelled on US courses of study which highlight goals of imparting positive attitudes toward democracy, ensuring that children acquire knowledge of how the country is run, and equipping them with the skills necessary for choosing representatives to carry out collective goals. In Israel, as in the USA, there is much criticism of students' long range achievements in this area.

The differentiated failings of citizenship education in diverse states cannot be ignored. Embedded in local historical processes, formulated according to local establishment understandings, and articulated in content that is ideologically acceptable at a given time, outcomes of programmes of citizenship education often fall short of expectations. Interpretations of failure vary, however, between traditionalists who decry changes in conceptions of loyalty to the state and activists who complain of what they see as the nurturing of excessive compliance. Reference to theoretical and empirical literature can shed light on complex models of citizenship and on how education can contribute to their concrete realization.

What is citizenship?

Citizenship is a core status in democratic states which have various ways of defining it. According to Janoski (1998), citizenship regimes may be liberal (emphasizing individuals), communitarian (emphasizing collectivities), or social-democratic (with emphasis on integration). Pointing out that the term betokens 'a constitutionally based relationship between the individual and the state', Delanty (1997: 285) defines four dimensions of citizenship: *rights, duties, identity* and *participation*. In the literature, the emphasis on *rights* is most extensive. It derives from Marshall's (1949) perception of citizenship as a historically evolving accretion of civil, political and, in the post-World War II era, social rights, i.e., government delivery of education, health and welfare services. In Marshall's view, the realization of civil, political and social citizenship is the means to counter the competitive mechanisms of the market, and thus an important step toward ensuring equality.

Throughout the twentieth century, theorists elaborated on the generalized headings initiated by Marshall to highlight the right to practise one's religion and to enjoy a way of life in one's own way (Koopmans et al., 2005; Kalekin-Fishman and Pitkänen, 2007). Recent writings also insist on rights to a healthful environment (ecological citizenship) and rights to access electronic media (*e*-citizenship) (Dobson and Bell, 2006; Mossberger, Tolbert and McNeal, 2007; see also Selbourne, 1994). Arguing for the universality of rights, Soysal (1994) supports the idea that citizens' comprehensive claims on government should be read as personal attributes and since they move with persons across all state borders, they must be recognized and honoured in all states.

The Hobbesian emphasis on *duties* as the key to entitlements indicates demands that citizens must support the territoriality and internationally recognized sovereignty of their states (Benhabib, 2004) by obeying laws, paying taxes and serving in the armed forces, among others. By limiting naturalization and the inroads of people who do not share bonds presumed to be hallowed by tradition, states not only preserve the state as a sovereign unit but also acquire legitimation as 'nations' (Castles and Davidson, 2000; Janoski, 2010; Joppke, 2005). Citizens of such states, those with a presumption of a common history and shared traditions, enjoy the emotional reward of *belonging* as they acquire a 'national' *identity* (Etzioni, 1995, 1998; Yuval-Davis, 2010). In sum, formal legislation that institutionalizes duties and nationality as integral to citizenship enables the state to exact both compliance and loyalty. On their part, citizens who perform their duties have a basis for claims to entitlements and, with rights, they can hold the state responsible for fulfilling basic human needs. With their acceptance as belonging to a nation, it may be presumed that they also gain psychological security.

The fourth dimension noted by Delanty – *participation* of the active citizen – can refer minimally to voting and choosing representatives to run the state. But *participation* can also refer to involvement in the community and/or taking part in decision-making in different contexts (Mohanty and Tandon, 2006).

In relation to each of the dimensions cited by Delanty, there are at least two more important distinctions – between formal and substantive citizenship as granted by the state; and between passive and active citizenship as performed by the citizenry. States may make formal legal provisions to ensure rights and evade fulfilling the substance of citizenship. Citizens, on their part, may be active in carrying out their duties, as well as in realizing their rights; or they may evade action and accept a position of passivity and dull reactivity to government action (Turner, 2001).

In the view of most political philosophers, democratic states ensure substantive citizenship, and citizens have ample opportunities for participation (Holston, 1999; Li, 2002). Thus, 'vicarious' (passive) rather than 'practical' (active) participation has no place in states which truly seek to model democracy (Walzer, 1998: 293). Following Habermas (1998, 2006), Gutmann and Thompson describe citizenship as the foundation of just governance, and this can be encapsulated in a definition of deliberative democracy. In their perception,

> [Deliberative democracy] is a form of government in which free and equal citizens, and their representatives justify decisions in a process in which they give one another reasons that are mutually acceptable and generally accessible with the aim of reaching conclusions that are binding in the present on all citizens and open to challenge in the future.
>
> *(Gutmann and Thompson, 2004, Chapter 1)*

This description of substantive, active citizenship can apply to an understanding of citizenship behaviour at micro, meso and macro levels of civil society, the social formation that can be understood as preceding institutionalized politics (Bowles and Gintis, 1987; Sünker, 2009). It is understood, after all, that citizens have the right to participate in the sense of making demands on government, but they also have the right to expect reciprocity from peers (cf. Enjolras and Sivesind, 2009). A conceptualization of citizenship as interactional as well as active and participatory broadens its meaning to include the relatively unregulated relationships among members of collectives which are not institutionalized by government. This is the point at which citizenship education becomes key to the creation of civil society. It must be admitted, however, that the realization of participation as crucial to the bond of citizens to the state together with a lived experience of interaction and mutual responsibility as the core concern of individuals in their daily lives has the ring of an unrealistic, even a utopian ideal. Research has shown that in practice, there is a low level of active participation in the concerns of collective living even in democratic states, and that in everyday life mutual responsibility is a rarity. Citizens' participation in the polity is patently at a low ebb (Torney-Purta and Lopez, 2006), and theorists argue that civil society is weakened by the surrender to consumerism, an addiction to spectacle and commitment to virtual communication (Castells, 2000; Debord, 1967; Lefebvre, 2003). Yet, they are equally adamant in asserting that the very survival of humankind requires that people take on responsibility for participating and actively contributing to improving the conditions of living together (Castells, 2000). These are arguments for seeking effective citizenship education to ensure the viability of both civil society and a formal democratic state (Bowles and Gintis, 1987; Smith and Verma, 2007; Sünker, 2009).

There is reason to believe that citizenship, a status which, as Marshall insisted, was designed to be inclusive, can be the 'apparatus' for ensuring participation and collective involvement. For educators, it is clear that collaborating knowledgeably in a collective, participating as a citizen, requires preparation. Programmes of education which take account of what there is to do in order to educate students to be effective citizens of a deliberative democracy are, therefore, an important component of schooling (Smith and Verma, 2007).

Education for citizenship

In many ways, the field of education for citizenship is unique. Widely viewed as essential to the development of a responsible adult, it has no specific disciplinary underpinning, no distinct body of knowledge according to which it is possible to determine the form and content of a viable curriculum. Solutions to the question of what to include in a programme of citizenship education, in what stages of schooling and how to measure its success vary.

A highly detailed and extensively researched curriculum is the programme for 'Developing Citizenship Competencies from Kindergarten through Grade 12', which was elaborated by the Education Commission of the States (Torney-Purta and Lopez, 2006). Building on concepts of citizenship elicited in 24 countries, researchers headed teams that produced an operationalization of goals such as disseminating knowledge considered necessary for a citizen, fostering the dispositions needed to support the citizen in her role, amassing skills such as voting, obeying laws and following rules related to civic action. The programme assumes that every aspect of the teaching – learning process designed to impart knowledge, dispositions and skills can be measured. Thus benchmarks for accomplishments were established as a developmental process. Conclusions from the research have influenced curriculum programmes across many states in the USA, and in countries on other continents.

In their research, Torney-Purta and Lopez (2006) found that courses of study that stress introducing children to information about how things are run in political life and who the contemporary guiding figures are foster a conceptualization of citizenship as a passive status. Moreover, they invoke a stance of political neutrality among teachers who, perhaps unwittingly, are placed in the position of supporting the preservation of the familiar forms, the status quo. Emphasizing citizenship as an activity, on the other hand, appears to lay the basis for positive civic activity in adult life (Torney-Purta and Lopez, 2006). In some places, there have been efforts to encourage pupils to carry out civil acts, and these have usually taken the form of simulations of voting, or integration into activities related to needs that adults locate in the community (Hart, 2008). So even when the intention is to enable participation, the tendency is to introduce children to elements of citizenship that educate them to imitate adult activities as relatively passive followers.

Goals can also be defined according to models of citizenship orientations. In their survey of the literature, Westheimer and Kahne (2004, p. 240, Table 1) found that there are essentially three desirable types of citizens: the 'personally-responsible citizen, the participatory citizen and the justice-oriented citizen'. In their view, each type of citizen is moved by different core assumptions and can be recognized in the kinds of civic activities she undertakes. One conclusion could be that a curriculum educating students to become specific kinds of ideal typical citizens would have to be based on learning experiences differentiated according to individuals' inclinations. It is interesting to note, however, that although they characterise the 'participatory citizen' as a distinct type, their descriptions of two other types of civic behaviour actually indicate ways in which people are likely to participate in affairs of the collective. Thus, their analyses suggest educational experiences of a completely different kind from the benchmarked stages proposed by Torney-Purta and Lopez (see above).

Outcomes of citizenship education

The success of citizenship education has been assessed in a variety of ways; mostly by finding ways to measure students' attitudes, their orientations to citizenship and the methods teachers deploy in the classroom. In relation to every kind of programme, there are, of course, variations in delivery depending on available facilities as well as on teachers' inventiveness, and perhaps on biases. Litt (1963) found, for example, that with ostensibly the same curriculum, children in three neighbouring communities were directed by their teachers to different conceptions of what it meant to be an active citizen. While students from a working-class background were taught to be obedient and compliant in carrying out civic duties, students in a community of relatively high S-E-S were taught that citizens could influence government by deliberate action. While another early study (Langton and Jennings, 1968) found that civics classes made almost no contribution to the development of democratic citizenship, later research in selected classes challenged these findings (for example,

Hahn, 1998; Ichilov, 1998; Kennedy, 1997). Indeed, lessons in civics were shown to have a positive influence on 'democratic consciousness' in places such as Malaysia, Hong Kong, New Zealand, Argentina and Hungary. The findings of Keeter et al. (2002) show that young people who have been exposed to civic instruction avow that they pay more attention to government and about half find that they have a greater interest in politics. Studies show, however, that in countries marked by civil conflict, such as Northern Ireland and Israel, even minimal outcomes – small changes in consciousness – are far less frequent (Yates and Youniss, 1999).

In many key aspects of citizenship, the effects are ambiguous. Some recent research has shown that civic education is indeed likely to make a difference in students' attitudes toward citizenship as well as in their knowledge. There are, for example, impressive positive results of the IEA Civic Education Study in which 90,000 14-year-olds in 28 countries were tested on knowledge of civic content and skills in a survey that related to concepts of citizenship, attitudes toward governmental and civic institutions, and political actions (Torney-Purta, 2002). Still the positive effects are very modest. Torney-Purta and Lopez (2006) report on success as indicated by a self-reported interest in doing community work among 15% of the 15–25-year-olds they researched, and an interest in voting by 17%. Similarly, in a study carried out in post-apartheid South Africa, the largest effects of civic education were found in political knowledge. There were only weak effects in (self-reported) democratic values and skills.

In a review of research, Galston (2007) finds that civic knowledge acquired in schools can be said to lead to enhanced, though unspecified, 'civic engagement'. Studies of teaching methods have provided some clues as to the possible terms of such engagement. In checking the outcomes of one civics course, for example, Kahne, Chi and Middaugh (2006) used scales developed by Westheimer and Kahne (see above) and found that as a result of classroom use of role-play, exposure to role models and service-learning, there were small statistically significant gains in responsibility, participatory citizenship and orientation to justice, as well as in knowledge of social networks and in social trust. In a study that entered into details of classroom procedures, Billig (2000) discovered that service-learning based on well-structured tasks with clear goals, and on *tasks that meet actual needs* encouraged students' civic engagement. All told, moreover, positive results were found to be more evident when open discussion is encouraged in classrooms.

In summary, achievements noted in the literature are at best limited. Despite some indications of ways and means to improve learning, and scattered evidence of how didactic approaches may succeed in fostering civic skills, there is scant evidence of how to determine which goals are most viable.

Inclusive citizenship education

It is possible, however, to pinpoint key concerns related to enhancing inclusion through citizenship education.

1. In most programmes there is no clear specification about what model(s) of citizenship underlie(s) current school programmes and what their implications are for practices of citizenship. This is the result of taking a narrow view of what contributes to citizenship education.

As we have argued, the core concern of citizenship is participation in networks of relations and collective practices. This implies that education for citizenship is not limited to specially planned lessons and investigating outcomes of courses cannot provide reliable information. By definition, citizenship is the relationship between populations and their governments. Thus we can surmise that, in fact, citizenship education is conveyed in the structuration (Giddens, 1990) of hierarchical relations and of peer relations in all teaching situations and in situations that arise between lessons. Specific realizations of citizenship are, furthermore, evident in routine classroom procedures. Therefore, an estimate of the kind of citizenship that is taught and what practices are learned has to take into consideration a comprehensive picture of how human relations are handled in the classroom and even in the school, rather than limiting itself to a focus on a particular programme. No set of lesson plans, however detailed, can be taken to be *the* curriculum for citizenship education. In any event, as pointed out by Schugurensky (2002), several variants of every curriculum are performed simultaneously in classrooms. He lists *the prescribed, the taught, the tested, the reported, the hidden, the missing, the external* and *the learned curricula*. This holds for citizenship education as well, and the complex mix of curricula has barely been touched on in research. While for educators it has been important to track the extent to which the *prescribed*, the *taught* and the *learned* curricula coalesce, research tends to focus narrowly on measurable learning outcomes.

2. When specific learning is expected, it is not clear whether lessons in citizenship education are designed so as to ensure maximum learning.

Insofar as specific goals can be formulated, it is rare that findings from a wide range of research on learning are applied to improving citizenship education. When asked, students have shown that they are conscious of reaping benefits from performance-based learning, learning by doing rather than from direct instruction (Carter, 2007; DeCampli, Kirby and Baldwin, 2010; Gordon, Kane and Staiger, 2008; see also Dewey, 1922). Moreover, among the learning experiences students regard most highly are those they derive from classes based on discussion (Galston, 2007; Kahne et al., 2006). It is not surprising that the combination of performance-based classrooms with discussion has been most effective in promoting achievement in various subjects (Carter, 2007). Applying a multifaceted conceptualization of effective learning (Dahlberg and Moss, 2005; Hatch, 2010; Olsson, 2009) in citizenship education is important, especially since such conceptualization is appropriate to understanding of democracy as individual and collective engagement and participation, and with a definition of government as 'deliberative democracy' (Gutmann and Thompson, 2004).

Support for the indications that performance-based classrooms and courteous discussion are effective in developing active engagement is found in new studies of learning throughout life. Beginning very shortly after birth, learning is *social* and supported by brain circuits that link *perception* and *action*. According to innovative research, people at all ages, including infancy, learn effectively through imitation, shared attention and empathetic understanding (Meltzoff et al., 2010; see Mead, 1934). Yet, programmes for citizenship education are often dedicated to teaching students to *be* what is expected of them instead of teaching them how to *act* in order to realize the ongoing project of democratic citizenship. Far too many programmes for citizenship education neglect the conditions of 'doing' and fall into the trap of modelling passivity rather than action. Instruction without performance and discussion, with little opportunity for shared attention and empathetic understanding cannot counter the felt trends of civic indifference that theoreticians decry.

3. What is missing in almost all the definitions of citizenship education is the realization that in sharing the status of citizens, people have real-life interests and problems that involve others. Since different interests may be at cross-purposes, solutions have to be found collectively. Such issues are inevitably part of children's school life, and ignoring the realities of children's social life is a sad mistake.

Reading the classroom as a 'society' in which children undoubtedly have different interests is an important first step in furthering citizenship education. So far, prepared curricula have tended to deal with topics and materials that are far from the everyday experience of students in schools. Teaching the formal frameworks of citizenship, encouraging service to the community and developing a favourable disposition toward carrying out duties imposed by the state, can be endorsed as relevant. But for students these facets of citizenship education are related to the lives of 'other people' and not to their own lives in schools.

For the children, the classroom is a society that maintains itself by implementing functions. Children's society has to *adapt* to the environment in and out of the school (an *economic* function); it has to be *integrated* by means of a shared language and sets of shared symbols (a *cultural* function); it has to pass on behaviours and values from day to day (function of *pattern maintenance*); and, when problems arise in relation to any of the functions, society has to set goals and make decisions on how to accomplish them (the function of *polity*) (Parsons, 1960). The polity is, of course, the institution that runs society. A fully capable citizen learns to participate in all the functions, including the central requirements of the polity and this includes participating in complex series of procedures that have to be learned through practice. After all, issues that require collective decision-making are part of the scene at all levels of formal education.

4. Even though researchers are agreed that citizenship education must begin at an early age (Keeter et al., 2002), little attention has been paid to how citizenship education can be made meaningful for students in kindergarten and the early years of primary school.

Instead of deliberating on which items of knowledge and which presumed civic orientations and skills can be adapted to the needs of the kindergarten, there should be recognition that citizenship is part of the *hidden curriculum* in every educational institution; it is constantly being taught even when no thought is given to the form or the content. This is done in the mode of establishing relationships to authority, in the uses of time and space, in the language and symbols of the classroom, in the materials that are compiled to serve students in the school situation, and in the opportunities, or lack of opportunities, for practising collective decision-making. The configuration of all the elements in children's society, the classroom and perhaps the school, convey the extent to which citizenship is indeed substantive – inclusive and egalitarian, or merely formal – restricted and suppressive.

Defined as relations between the individual in the group and the state, citizenship education is a lifetime project that is disrupted in schools by mistaken definitions and inattention to the messages that are conveyed. The interpretation of government as deliberative democracy (Gutmann and Thompson, 2004; Habermas, 2006) provides guidelines for a pedagogy of truly active citizenship which can assure social inclusion for all. And this is possible from the earliest stages of formal education.

Pedagogy in schools – what is to be done?

I suggest that rather than 'knowledge' of the existing political system and 'attitudes' that are appropriate to reinforcing the status quo in existing political and social institutions, the quintessential expression of citizenship, *civic action as participatory behaviours*, is the most important focus of citizenship education from early childhood on. Such behaviours have to be initiated in ways that enable collective decision-making as early as age five – in kindergartens. The philosophy that governs such a programme is a compound view of the nature of democracy, the significance of fairness in social process, the nature of the classroom as an operative society, and the importance of student participation in learning. This grounding of social inclusion implies that in school classes there is no need to simulate representative democracy. Everyone in the class can be involved in learning by realizing the duty and the right to contribute to the collective. Since the context of citizenship education is different in different states, I will restrict my proposal to guidelines that can be adapted to each locale.

Following on the conceptualization of the class as a society, and on the understandings of the nature of learning throughout the life course, there are strong arguments for basing school pedagogy on *deliberative democracy* as a core educational process rather than as a distant goal. Following Gutmann and Thompson, we propose to adopt procedures of deliberation related to the real-life concerns of students in order to make democratic activity an ongoing classroom event. Here, the steps can be noted schematically:

- Defining a common problem;
- Suggesting possible solutions;
- Weighing consequences of each suggested solution;
- Deciding on the solution most likely to satisfy all the needs;
- Dividing the tasks among small groups of children;
- Reporting to the class on the outcomes of each task;

- Synthesizing the outcomes in order to reach an agreed upon solution to the defined problem that is best for the time.

The process begins with the teacher as listener, for the first step is to help students *discover* a problem that is of common concern and requires that the group as a whole make a decision. In this connection teachers must be careful not to suggest problems, but indeed to note what issues trouble the children and are of interest to them. Given an issue, it has to be defined in open discussion with the children. In discussions, children can suggest how the problem can be solved, and each suggested solution is examined in light of its probable *consequences*. After weighing the consequences, the group can come to a *collective decision* about the best way to go about reaching a viable solution. This is the stage at which it becomes possible to carry out a '*division of labour*'. Sub-tasks are defined in collective discussion and assigned to students. The distribution of tasks has to include all the students and the teacher who has to be on guard to act as no more and no less than *prima/us inter pares*. When implemented, the *outcome of each sub-task is reported to the group*. After all the tasks have been completed, the groups can decide on whether their decision was effective, and whether the problem originally discussed has been solved.

Central to the scheme is the understanding that at each stage *every* student in the class is to be involved – in the discussions (even if several children say the 'same' thing) and in the assumption of responsibility (individual or group) for carrying out the tasks decided on, reporting on them and contributing to the solution. Every child is active in the political function of working out the attainment of a goal to solve a problem that the collective has located. Throughout, deliberations, discussions and tasks are carried out with a view to a desirable end (as it appears at the time) through procedures based on mutual respect for the rights of all the individuals involved, with every phase grounded in equality, and in fair terms of cooperation. Justice, avoiding mishaps of injustice, is a primary consideration (Rawls, 1999).

Clearly these steps cannot be carried out within pre-set time limits; they are not a 'unit of study', but can, and must, be a long-term course of action. Moreover, the scheme is not designed to replace any part of the curriculum. It is rather an ongoing process that is interwoven with learning activities, one that is, so to speak, carried on 'in the seams' of the regular class proceedings. Because the core of the process is the understanding that issues are raised by the students themselves, *deliberative democracy* can be integrated in all classes of formal schooling (in kindergartens, and successively in classes in elementary school and in secondary school) as education for habits of active citizenship through acquaintance with inclusive democratic procedures.

Conclusions

Citizenship is a relational process and therefore citizenship education has to be undertaken as a process throughout the school career. Education for democratic citizenship can be implemented by allowing children to *practise* deliberative democracy from kindergarten on. Practising collective democratic decision-making is key to secure learning as well as to the acquisition of orientations to lifetime engagement. Knowledge of citizenship is not advanced by contact with the political questions that concern the adult community, issues that are likely to be irrelevant to pupils' perceptions of their own lives. It can be cultivated only by working through questions about problems which are meaningful for students while they are at school, and in which personal responsibility is called for. In the concepts of Westheimer and Kahne (2004), the person who completes a school education with long-term experience in deliberative democracy as described in the scheme proposed here can be active in community organizations, becomes accustomed to organizing for advancing collective projects, and is in command of appropriate strategies for contributing to the common good. People oriented to habitual participation in 'political' action in schools will also be acquiring 'personal responsibility' and an 'orientation to justice', two additional qualities of 'the good citizen' (Westheimer and Kahne, 2004). The realization of democracy and of the meaning of citizenship in a democratic state is, like the vision of a utopia, 'an endless process, an endless proliferating realization of Freedom, rather than a convergence toward an already existing Truth' (Rorty, 1989, p. xviii). Making sure that every student learns how to realize Freedom is the crux of the meaning of citizenship education and the gate to comprehensive social inclusion.

Bibliography

Ahmad, I. (2004). Islam, democracy and citizenship education: An examination of the social studies curriculum in Pakistan. *Current Issues in Comparative Education*, 7(1), 39–49.

Benhabib, S. (2004). The rights of others: Aliens, residents, and citizens. Paper presented at a Conference on 'Migrants, Nations and Citizenship', July 5–7. www.crassh.cam.ac.uk Retrieved: 2 November, 2010.

Billig, S. H. (2000). Research on K-12 school-based service learning: The evidence builds. *Phi Delta Kappan*, 81(9), 658–664.

Bowles, S. and Gintis, H. (1987). *Democracy and Capitalism*. New York: Basic Books.

Carter, N. (2007). *The Politics of the Environment: Ideas, Activism, Policy* (2nd edition). Cambridge, UK: Cambridge University Press.

Castells, M. (2000). *End of the Millennium*. Hoboken, NJ: Wiley.

Castles, S. and Davidson, A. (2000). *Citizenship and Migration: Globalization and the Politics of Belonging*. New York: Routledge.

Chhokar, J. S. (2006). Education for citizenship. *The Times of India*, March 17. Retrieved: 28 October, 2011.

Dahlberg, G. and Moss, P. (2005). *Ethics and Politics in Early Childhood Education*. London: Routledge.

Debord, G. (1967). *The Society of the Spectacle*. trans. D. Nicholson-Smith. New York: Zone Books.

DeCampli, P., Kirby, K. K. and Baldwin, C. (2010). Beyond the classroom to coaching: Preparing new nurse managers. *Critical Care Nursing Quarterly*, 33(3), 132–137. doi: 10.1097/CNQ.0b013e3181d913db. Retrieved: 31 October, 2011.

Delanty, G. (1997). Models of citizenship: Defining European identity and citizenship. *Citizenship Studies*, 1(3), 285–303.
Department for Education and Skills, UK. (2007). *The National Curriculum: Handbook for Secondary Teachers in England*. www.nc.uk.net. Retrieved: 31 July, 2016.
Dewey, J. (1922). *Human Nature and Conduct: An Introduction to Social Psychology*. New York: The Modern Library.
Dobson, A. and Bell, D. (2006). *Environmental Citizenship*. Cambridge, MA: MIT Press.
Enjolras, B. and Sivesind, K. (eds). (2009). *Civil Society in Comparative Perspective*. Bingley UK: Emerald Group Publishing.
Etzioni, A. (1997). *The New Golden Rule: Community and Morality in a Democratic Society*. London: Profile.
Etzioni, A. (1995). *The Spirit of Community: Rights, Responsibilities and the Communitarian Agenda*. London: Fontana.
Galston, W. A. (2007/1993). The promise of communitarianism. *National Civic Review*, 82 (3), 217–220. DOI: 10.1002/ncr.4100820303. Retrieved: 31 July, 2016.
Giddens, A. (1990). *The Consequences of Modernity*. Stanford, CA: Stanford University Press.
Gordon, R., Kane, T. J. and Staiger, D. (2008). Identifying effective teachers: Using performance on the job. In: J. Furman and J. Bordoff (eds), *Paths to Prosperity* (pp. 189–226). Washington, DC: The Brookings Institution.
Gutmann, A. and Thompson, D. (2004). *Why Deliberative Democracy?* Princeton, NJ: Princeton University Press.
Habermas, J. (1998). *On the Pragmatics of Communication*. Cambridge, MA: MIT Press.
Hahn, C. E. (1998). *Becoming Political: Comparative Perspectives on Citizenship Education*. Albany: State University of New York Press.
Hart, R. (2008). Stepping back from 'the ladder': Reflections on the model of participatory work with children. In: A. Reid, B. B. Jensen, J. Nikel and V. Simovska (eds), *Participation and Learning: Perspectives on Education and the Environment, Health and Sustainability* (pp. 19–31). Berlin: Springer.
Hatch, J. A. (2010). Rethinking the relationship between learning and development: Teaching for learning in early childhood classrooms. *The Educational Forum*, 74(3), 258–268. Retrieved: 25 April, 2011, from ProQuest Education Journals. Document ID: 2107145451.
Holston, J. (ed) (1999). *Cities and Citizenship*. Durham and London: Duke University Press.
Ichilov, O. (ed) (1998). *Citizenship and Citizenship Education in a Changing World*. London: Woburn Press.
Janoski, T. (2010). *The Ironies of Citizenship*. Cambridge: Cambridge University Press.
Janoski, T. (1998). *Citizenship and Civil Society*. New York: Cambridge University Press.
Joppke, C. (2005). *Selecting by Origin: Ethnic Migration in the Liberal State*. Cambridge, MA: Harvard University Press.
Kahne, J., Chi, B. and Middaugh, E. (2006). Building social capital for civic and political engagement: The potential of high-school civics courses. *Canadian Journal of Education*, 29(2), 387–409.
Kalekin-Fishman, D. (2004). *Ideology, Policy and Practice: Education for Immigrants and Minorities in Israel Today*. New York: Kluwer Academic Publishers.
Kalekin-Fishman, D. and Pitkänen, P. (eds). (2007). *Multiple Citizenship as a Challenge to European Nation-States*. Rotterdam: Sense Publishers.
Kan, W. (2010). *Education and Citizenship in a Globalising World*. Beijing Normal University, China. www.ioe.ac.uk/about/documents/aboutOverview/Kan_W.pdf. Retrieved: 28 October, 2011.

Keeter, S., Zukin, C., Andoline, M. and Jenkins, K. (2002). The civic and political health of the nation: A generational portrait. Center for Information and Research on Civic Learning and Engagement. www.civicyouth.org. Retrieved: 30 September, 2014.

Kennedy, K. J. (ed) (1997). *Citizenship Education and the Modern State.* London: Routledge Falmer.

Koopmans, R., Statham, P., Giugni, M. and Passy, F. (2005). *Contested Citizenship: Immigration and Cultural Diversity in Europe.* Minneapolis, MN: University of Minnesota Press.

Langton, K. and Jennings, M. K. (1968). Political socialization and the high school civics curriculum in the United States. *American Political Science Review,* 62, 852–867.

Lefebvre, H. (2003). *The Urban Revolution.* Minneapolis, MN: University of Minnesota Press.

Li, D. (2002). A summary of the Fifth National Working Conference of minority education. http://www.mne/edu.cn/minority/. Retrieved: 31 October, 2015.

Litt, E. (1963). Civic education, community norms, and political indoctrination. *American Sociological Review,* 28(1), 69–75. Retrieved: 22 October, 2010.

Marshall, T. H. (1949). *Citizenship and Social Class and Other Essays.* Cambridge: Cambridge University Press.

Mead, G. H. (1934). *Mind, Self, and Society.* Chicago: University of Chicago Press.

Meltzoff, A. N., Kuhl, P. K., Movellan, J. and Sejnowski, T. J. (2010). Foundations for a new science of learning. *Science,* 325(5938), 284–288. DOI: 10.1126/science.1175626. Retrieved: 31 October, 2011.

Mohanty, R. and Tandon, R. (2006). *Participatory Citizenship: Identity, Exclusion, Inclusion.* London and New Delhi: Sage.

Mossberger, K., Tolbert, C. J. and McNeal, R. S. (2007). *Digital Citizenship: The Internet, Society, and Participation.* Cambridge, MA: MIT.

Nurturing Youth. (2009). Active citizenship in India: Report on a stakeholder consultation. New Delhi, 3–4 March, 2009.

OFSTED. (2005). Subject reports 2002/03: Citizenship in secondary schools: HMI2335. www.ofsted.gov.uk/publications. Retrieved: 28 October, 2011.

Olsson, L. M. (2009). *Movement and Experimentation in Young Children's Learning.* Abingdon, Oxon: Routledge.

Parsons, T. (1960). *Structure and Process in Modern Societies.* New York: Wiley.

Rawls, John (1999). *A Theory of Justice* (revised edition). Cambridge, MA: Harvard University Press.

Rorty, Richard (1989). *Contingency, Irony, and Solidarity.* Cambridge, UK: Cambridge University Press.

Schröter, Y. and Jäger, R. (2007). Multiple citizenship in Germany. In: D. Kalekin-Fishman and P. Pitkänen (eds), *Multiple Citizenship as a Challenge to European Nation-States* (pp. 81–120). Rotterdam: Sense Publishers.

Schugurensky, D. (2002). The eight curricula of multicultural citizenship education. Eric Document EJ654873.

Smith, L. and Verma, G. (2007). Dual citizenship: The British position. In: D. Kalekin-Fishman and P. Pitkänen (eds), *Multiple Citizenship as a Challenge to European Nation-States* (pp. 39–58). Rotterdam: Sense Publishers.

Soysal, Y. (1994). *Limits of Citizenship: Migrant and Postnational Membership in Europe.* Chicago: University of Chicago Press.

Sünker, H. (2009). Democratic education – Educating for democracy. In: E. Ropo and T. Autio (eds), *International Conversations on Curriculum Studies. Subject, Society and Curriculum* (pp. 89–108). Rotterdam/Taipei: Sense.

Sünker, H. and Swiderek, T. (2010). Forschungslagen, politische Praxis und Perspektiven politischer Bildung in Deutschland. Hans-Böckler-Stiftung, Arbeitspapier 184. Düsseldorf.

Thapan, P. M. (2008). Schooling, identity and citizenship education in contemporary India. Lecture at the Fondation Maison des Sciences de l'Homme, 16 April. Retrieved: 28 October, 2011.

Torney-Purta, J. (2002). The school's role in developing civic engagement: A study of adolescents in twenty-eight countries. *Applied Developmental Science*, 6, 203–212.

Torney-Purta, J. and Lopez, S. V. (2006). Developing citizenship competencies from kindergarten through Grade 12: A background paper for policymakers and educators. Denver, Colorado: Education Commission of the States. www.ecs.org. Retrieved: 21 January, 2010.

Turner, B. S. (2001). The erosion of citizenship. *British Journal of Sociology*, 52(2), 189–209.

Walzer, M. (1998). The civil society argument. In: G. Shafir (ed), *The Citizenship Debates: A Reader* (pp. 291–310). Minneapolis, MN: University of Minnesota Press.

Westheimer, J. and Kahne, J. (2004). What kind of citizen? The politics of educating for democracy. *American Educational Research Journal*, 41(2), 237–269.

Yates, M. and Youniss, J. (1999). *Roots of Civic Identity: International Perspectives on Community Service and Activism in Youth*. New York: Cambridge University Press.

Yuval-Davis, N. (2010). *Intersectional Politics of Belonging*. London: Sage.

3

PEDAGOGIES AND PARTNERSHIPS FOR EDUCATING THE WHOLE CHILD

Carl A. Grant and Elisabeth Zwier

Introduction

Major changes are taking place in *what* democratic societies teach the young, *how* they teach the young and *which* of these young matter (Grant and Lei, 2001; Nussbaum, 2010). Currently, there is a bifurcation in the primary aim of education. Some argue that schools need to focus on the teaching of science and mathematics in order to facilitate economic development in a competitive global society (Hanusheck et al., 2008; Zuckerman, 2011). Others argue that schools need to pay attention to the teaching of the whole child for life in a democratic society (Biesta, 2006; Brighouse, 2006, 2008; Nussbaum, 2010). Some within this second group contend that particular attention needs to be given to children who may experience social exclusion; for example, Roma or Traveller children in Europe, street children in large cities in Latin America, children living in refugee camps in Africa and Dalit children in India. According to the Centre for Human Rights Research (CIDH, 2012),

> Social inclusion refers to a policy designed to ensure that all people are able to participate in society regardless of their background or specific characteristics, which may include: race, language, culture, gender, disability, social status, age, and other factors. Compared to the general population, groups with such special characteristics are much more likely to face low education, unemployment, homelessness – and resulting poverty and social exclusion.
>
> *(n.p.)*

Many scholars, including the authors of this chapter, contend that the primary aim of education should stem from the first line of Article 26.1 of the Universal Declaration of Human Rights, 'Education shall be directed to the full development of the human personality and to the strengthening of respect for human rights and fundamental freedoms' (UDHR, 1948). For students to develop their full personalities, we argue that parents and community members should be involved in students' education alongside teachers. Additionally, we contend that educators should use culturally responsive approaches to educating students and work in partnership with families and community members. We draw on educational literature to examine what these pedagogies and partnerships look like in practice and consider how such approaches seek to educate the whole child. Taken together, the educational approaches we suggest seek to promote social inclusion and may serve to counter social exclusion in schools. We recognize that schools, both historically and presently, have served to empower some students and their families, while simultaneously marginalizing others on the basis of race/ethnicity, social class, gender, etc. (OEI and UNESCO, n.d.). Rather than a panacea for all social ills, education is but one element among a range of social, economic and political dimensions of social inclusion which need to be advanced systematically (Americas Quarterly, n.d.). The question is whether education emphasizing economic development or children's holistic needs best meets the aims of social inclusion.

The bifurcation

The current emphases on global markets, economic competition and preparing students for a twenty-first century workplace has misplaced richer and more appropriate aims of education and schooling, namely commitments to citizenship and adequate attention to issues regarding quality of life and the pursuit of a flourishing life and, consequently, the full development of students' human personalities (Biesta, 2006; Brighouse, 2006, 2008; Nussbaum, 2010).

According to the philosopher Martha Nussbaum (2010), it is high time we recognize that there is a crisis in education throughout the world, which is detrimental to the future of democratic governments. Nussbaum (2010) argues that in a drive for national profit, nations and their systems of education are doing away with the skills necessary for keeping democratic societies alive. To Nussbaum's claims, we add that the problem is only made worse by the fact that most teacher education programmes fail to include a multicultural curriculum, and in particular, the teaching of the history and literature of groups of colour is weak or non-existent. We argue that this context and content is essential to prepare educators who can teach the whole child. Nussbaum (2010) contends that attention needs to be given to the humanities and the arts because the teaching and learning within these disciplines is the connective tissue of democracy. If the arts and humanities continue to be neglected, Nussbaum (2010) observes, 'Nations all over the world will soon be producing generations of useful machines, rather than complete citizens who can think for themselves, criticize tradition and understand the significance of another person's sufferings and achievements' (p. 5). Nussbaum (2010) argues that although science and technology are important for the health of nations, other equally crucial abilities are at risk of getting lost in the competitive flurry – abilities crucial to the health of any democracy internally, and to the creation of a world culture capable of constructively addressing our most pressing problems. These abilities are associated with the humanities and the arts: 'The ability to think critically, the ability to transcend local loyalties and to approach world problems as a "citizen of the world," and the ability to imagine sympathetically the predicament of another person' (Nussbaum, 2010, pp. 1–2, 7).

Political philosopher Harry Brighouse's (2006, 2008) writings on education are useful here, especially his observations regarding the tension between economics, education and schooling. Brighouse (2006, 2008) asserts that people need to earn a living and that economic achievement is a worthy goal for societies, and thus, should be supported by governments. Yet he questions whether these are *sufficient* ends for schooling (Brighouse, 2008, p. 58). Brighouse's (2008) answer to this inquiry is that an economic agenda is necessary, but not sufficient. That said, Brighouse (2006) points out that if the education system fails completely to consider the economy, it would be failing the children it claims to serve because schools have an obligation to prepare children for the society in which they live (p. 28). Brighouse (2006) contends that students should be prepared for the world of work because people need incomes, for most work takes up a sizeable portion of their lives and, finally, because people also need a sense of self-reliance.

Considering both philosophy and political philosophy, Brighouse (2006) argues that if quality of life is the basis of the concern for economic stability and growth, but this concern does not improve the quality of life, then education should not be guided primarily by economic considerations. To do so, Brighouse (2006) declares, is inappropriate, for 'in pursuing relevance to the child's immediate surroundings and to the economy's short-term demands, we steer education away from the life-enhancing mission it could have' (p. 4). He further claims that while economic achievement, stability and growth are important, this is true only insofar as they promote full human flourishing (Brighouse, 2008, p. 60). Therefore, Brighouse (2006) contends that the principle of flourishing is one which schools need to emphasise and it is that primary intrinsic value that schools should serve (p. 4). As major contributors to the aim of education, schools should facilitate students' present and future flourishing. Brighouse (2006) asserts: 'We owe a duty to children that their childhood be rich and enjoyable, but we also owe them a duty to prepare them so that they can have a significant range of opportunities to lead a flourishing life in adulthood' (p. 9).

Gert Biesta's scholarship about the relationships between education, lifelong learning and democratic citizenship is significant to our argument about teaching for the 'full development of the human personality'. In *Beyond Learning: Democratic Education for a Human Future*, Biesta (2006) forges a tight connection between education/educators and the need to prepare students for more than mathematics and science in this time of crisis. Biesta calls attention to students' uniqueness and their 'coming into the world', elements which are critical to the development of a full personality and achieving a flourishing life. Biesta argues:

> It is immediately clear that educators carry an immense responsibility. This responsibility is more than a responsibility for the 'quality' of teaching or for successfully meeting the needs of the learner or the targets of the institution. If education is about creating opportunities for students to come into the world, and if it is about asking the difficult questions that make this possible, then it becomes clear that the first responsibility of the educator is responsibility for the *subjectivity* of the students, for that which allows the student to be a unique singular being.
>
> *(p. 30)*

Biesta (2006) further adds,

> Teachers and other educators not only have a crucial task in creating the opportunities and a climate in which students actually respond, they also have a task in challenging their students to respond by confronting them with what and who is other and by posing such fundamental questions as 'What do you think about it?', 'Where do you stand?', and 'How will you respond?'
>
> *(p. 28)*

In response to Nussbaum's argument concerning a crisis in education where science and mathematics drive the curriculum and drive out the arts and humanities, Brighouse's attention to a flourishing life and Biesta's argument about the uniqueness of students, we strongly believe that educators in PK-college educational institutions should employ culturally responsive pedagogies and promote school-home-community partnerships. We champion these ideas as a way for educators to push back against the bifurcation in education and to promote the development of citizens who are independent thinkers, but seek to understand and care for the 'other' (Nussbaum, 2010). Such citizens are essential for the changes at both the personal and institutional/structural levels that must be undertaken in order to meet the needs of students who are different from those in the mainstream and may experience social exclusion for a variety of reasons.

The approaches

There are several approaches that schools of education may take to prepare teachers that are inclusive of the arts and humanities but also provide them with the pedagogical tools to meet the needs of students who are 'othered' (Nussbaum, 2010). One such approach is 'multi-cultural democratic education', articulated by Gibson and Grant (2010). Gibson and Grant (2010) locate the approach within the context of a human rights philosophy, with special attention to Article 26.1 of the Universal Declaration of Human Rights that references the 'full development of the personality'. Three components are significant to the approach: culturally responsive teaching, school-home-community partnerships and constructive pluralistic engagement. The concept of 'intersectionality' is also significant because it provides teachers with a lens of analysis to better understand their students by taking into account students' intersecting identity axes (e.g. race, class, gender, religion) and the implications of these intersections for interpersonal and institutional power relationships (Grant and Zwier, 2012). Taken together, multicultural democratic education and intersectionality theories seek to further the goals of social inclusion by 'identifying strategies for overcoming or eliminating the barriers to full participation in quality education for individuals and groups which experience discrimination, marginalisation and exclusion or which are particularly vulnerable' (OEI and UNESCO, n.d., p. 10).

Multicultural democratic education

1. Culturally responsive teaching

Culturally responsive teaching is an approach to education that advocates teachers, administrators and school staff should respond to the needs of the students. The National Center for Culturally Responsive Educational Systems (NCCRESTT, 2008) contends, 'Culturally responsive teaching is the valuation, consideration, and integration of individuals' culture, language, heritage and experiences leading to supported learning and development' (p. 4). Gay (2010) argues that the purpose of culturally responsive education is to develop intellectual, social, emotional and political learning by 'using cultural referents to impart knowledge, skills, and attitudes' (p. 382). She notes, 'Culturally responsive instruction employs culturally mediated cognition, culturally appropriate social situations for learning, and culturally valued knowledge in curriculum content' (Gay, 2010, p. 382).

Culturally responsive teaching is validating, comprehensive, multidimensional, empowering, transformative and emancipatory (Gay, 2010). This type of instruction is validating because it uses cultural knowledge, prior experiences and performance styles of diverse students to make learning more appropriate and effective for them and it teaches to and through the strengths of students. It acknowledges the legitimacy of students' cultural heritages both as legacies that affect students' dispositions, attitudes and approaches to learning, and as worthy content to be taught in the formal curriculum. There are strong connections between home and school experiences and academic and socio-cultural realities. For example, using literature that reflects multiple ethnic perspectives and literary genres; incorporating everyday-life mathematics concepts, such as the economics, employment and consumer habits of various ethnic groups. In order to teach to the different learning styles of students, activities reflect a variety of sensory opportunities – visual, auditory and tactile.

2. School-home-community partnerships

To develop the knowledge base and skills necessary for instruction to be culturally responsive, there are numerous models for school-home-community partnerships.

We present a brief overview of four models and frameworks that are currently being explored and implemented in schools throughout the United States. Each model identifies ways for families, communities and schools to become partners with the goal of increasing student achievement. Models feature many positive elements (e.g. specific types of involvement to implement and the acceptance of parents as intellectual resources and as proponents of curriculum transformation). Yet, in some models, the demographic diversity of students and their families are ignored and culturally responsive teaching is often not assertively put into practice. Consequently, there are many missed opportunities to benefit students and parents who are ethnically and racially diverse.

One. The most popular partnership model used in US schools is one developed by Joyce Epstein (2004). Epstein's School-Family-Community Partnership model features six types of involvement:

- *Parenting:* Help parents learn parenting skills, create home conditions to support their child's progress and help schools to better understand families.
- *Communicating:* Carry out effective communication from school-to-home and from home-to-school.
- *Volunteering:* Organize volunteers to support the school and students.
- *Learning at home:* Engage families in helping their children with homework and other curriculum-related activities.
- *Decision-making:* Encourage parent leaders and include families as participants in school decisions.
- *Collaborating with the community*: Organize services and resources from the community, and provide services to the community.

Each of these types of involvement, Epstein argues, is to be developed and nurtured by schools in order to effectively create partnerships and ultimately impact the achievement of students.

Two. Project MAPPS (Math and Parent Partnerships in the Southwest) was developed by Civil and Bernier (2006). The MAPPS model of parent involvement views parents, particularly 'minority' and working-class parents, as intellectual resources. The aim of the model is to help parents become community leaders in order to promote their participation in school activities.

Three. The Curriculum Enrichment Model aims to enhance the school curriculum by incorporating the contributions of families by opening lines of communication between parents and teachers (White-Clark and Decker, 1996). The rubric of success for this model is the connection established between parents and what and how their children learn. Schools that adopt this model believe that parents can make a significant contribution to their children's achievement.

Four. Transformative Education Context (Olivos, 2006) is a model that sets out to transform not only the curriculum but also all aspects of education. Advocates of this model are inspired by the work of Brazilian educator Paulo Freire. Freirean principles of dialogue and problem-posing education are two major components of the model. The use of these principles facilitates critical reflection and dialogue about education for parents. Also, the principles support parents having equal voice in the decision-making process. In addition, the Transformative Education Context model argues that since knowledge is socially constructed, all participants should have voice. Accordingly, curriculum knowledge is constructed out of the history and culture of the different racial and cultural groups in the school and a balance of power exists between parents, schools and students.

3. Constructive pluralistic engagement

Carl Grant and Aubree Potter (2011) advocate the implementation not only of culturally responsive teaching but also of constructive pluralistic engagement. These authors borrow from the work of Eck (2006) to argue that constructive pluralism is a form of pluralism which pays particular attention to 'minority and marginalized groups' in that it needs, seeks and acts upon their active participation. It is 'constructive' because it is built through the participation of groups with one another. It goes beyond the awareness and acceptance of diversity, contending that 'diversity' falls short of authentic (structured) engagement among groups of people, and therefore is not pluralism. Constructive pluralism requires that groups strive to see each other through the perspectives of other groups. Grant and Aubree (2011) write that:

> The development of a democratic community is not about minority groups being assimilated into mainstream culture, completing adopting mainstream values and only using mainstream language. Instead, constructive pluralism strives toward cultural groups' claims for 'special' rights/social justice (e.g. recognition) in cultural, educational, religious and linguistic matters over and above those of equal citizenship.
>
> (p. 78)

Diana Eck (2006), Director of the Pluralism Project at Harvard University, argues that pluralism is not an ideology, but rather a dynamic process through which people engage with one another in and through their very deepest differences. Eck (2006) contends that pluralism is not just another word for diversity. It goes beyond mere plurality or diversity to active engagement with that plurality. She contends that diversity – religion, ethnicity and race – is an observable fact of American life today. Eck (2006) adds that diversity alone is not pluralism; it requires pluralism to be created. She further states, 'Pluralism requires participation, and attunement to the life and energies of one another... It goes beyond mere tolerance to the active attempt to understand one another' (Eck, 2006, p. 70).

We firmly believe that applying constructive pluralism in education involves engaging parents, community members and school staff in order to bring about a more democratic and socially just education, and jointly advocate for the full development of students' personalities and promote flourishing lives. The argument for constructive pluralism is built upon the following rationales: it meets the demands of a global society, illuminates global, national and local discussions on minority rights, acts as glue for alliances of different ethnic and social groups, and increases social capital. Constructive pluralistic engagement will be better served, we argue, if the concept of intersectionality is used to help promote the 'engagement'.

Intersectionality

Grant and Zwier (2012) argue that by integrating intersectionality as a concept and tool into educational practice, including into teacher education programmes, teachers will be better prepared to promote all students' development and enhance the conditions for them to lead flourishing lives. Their work on intersectionality draws on Ritzer's (2009) definition of intersectionality as:

> [A] theory which seeks to examine the ways in which various socially and culturally constructed categories interact on multiple levels to manifest themselves as inequality in society. Intersectionality holds that the classical models of oppression within society, such as those based on race/ethnicity, gender, religion, nationality, sexual orientation, class or disability do not act independently of one another; instead, these forms of oppression interrelate creating a system of oppression that reflects the 'intersection' of multiple forms of discrimination.
>
> *(p. 1)*

In addition, Grant and Zwier (2012) are of the opinion that it is important to understand that there is not one theory of intersectionality, but different conceptualizations and theorizations of it, including different terms/phrases such as 'multiple jeopardy' (King, 1988, p. 47); 'vectors of oppression and privilege' (Ritzer, 2009, p. 204); and 'interlocking system' (Razack, 1998, p. 10).

Recent studies suggest that because socially constructed categories of difference influence student outcomes – academic, inter- and intra-personal (Chapman et al., 2010), pre-service teachers should be prepared to strategically consider students' identity axes in their curricular and pedagogical decisions (Allard and Santoro, 2008; DiAngelo and Sensoy, 2010; Heilman, 2010). Research on intersectionality and education suggests students' achievement can be addressed through intersectional curricula, teaching, assessment and relationships (Allard and Santoro, 2008; DiAngelo and Sensoy, 2010; Irizarry, 2007) that take an asset-based view of students, their families and communities (Camarrota, 2007; Chapman et al., 2010).

When thinking intersectionally, teachers must be careful to consider students' identities flexibly, work at unlearning their stereotypes and assumptions, and reflect on their own identities (Allard and Santoro, 2008; DiAngelo and Sensoy, 2010; Heilman, 2010; Irizarry, 2007). Another common issue is deficit theorizing, where teachers assume there is little they can do to help students achieve and fail to ask students and their parents for advice (Grant and Sleeter, 2007). However, by examining the processes of teaching and learning through an intersectional lens, we can better support a holistic range of student outcomes and counter oppressive power structures and relationships in schools.

By integrating approaches from multicultural democratic education (culturally responsive teaching, school-home-community partnerships and constructive pluralistic engagement), as well as viewing our students and ourselves intersectionally, we believe teachers can better respond to the whole child and, in particular, the needs of marginalized students.

The everyday practices

What happens when teachers, families and communities work together to support the whole child through culturally responsive pedagogies and partnerships?

Culturally responsive pedagogies

Culturally responsive teaching ensures that *curriculum*, *instruction* and *pedagogy* are designed to connect with students and empower them through their school experience. It replaces an 'at-risk' and 'otherness' ideology with an ideology of providing opportunities for students to learn (Gay, 2010; NCCRESTT, 2008). This approach to education necessarily begins with eliciting and responding to the pedagogies that students consider culturally responsive (Gallagher-Geurtsen, 2009; Gay, 2010; Gay, 2007). Moreover, culturally responsive pedagogy encompasses 'what teachers need to know about a specific group of students, who they need to be, and who they need to continuously become' (Irizarry, 2007, p. 27). Teachers, students, families and communities all have a role in making schooling culturally responsive. First, these educational actors must view each other as resources. Second, they should work at building connections across educational contexts, including schools, homes and community settings.

1. View each other as resources

Culturally responsive pedagogy requires teachers to develop an asset-based view of students and their families. Such an educational approach views students as resources, focuses on their lived experiences (Allard and Santoro, 2008) and values their culture and cultural practices as 'hybrid funds of knowledge' (Irizarry, 2007, p. 23). In order to be responsive to their students, teachers need to be aware of the history and cultures of the groups their students and their families may belong to (Heilman, 2010), connect to youth culture and pop culture (Irizarry, 2007) and be in tune with relevant technological and socio-political knowledge (Gallagher-Geurtsen, 2009). Several studies report students value pedagogies that incorporate multiple modes of expression including music; for example, writing raps about social justice issues (Irizarry, 2007), code-switching between standard English and vernacular (Irizarry, 2007) and educators' stories about their life experiences (Achinstein and Aguirre, 2008; Irizarry, 2007). Challenging curriculum rather than basic-skills instruction increases high school completion for students in remedial tracks (Camarrota, 2007). Students, their families and their teachers all have a role to play in communicating their knowledge and trying out new teaching and learning practices.

2. Build connections across educational contexts

Teachers' knowledge of and experience in their students' communities helps them become connected to the context and constantly work at making their pedagogies culturally responsive (Grant and Sleeter, 2007; Irizarry, 2007). Irizarry (2007) asserts community experience is valuable for all teachers, facilitating connections even for those who are not members of the same racial or ethnic group as their students. Pedagogy that is culturally responsive to students' intersectional identities fosters their critical consciousness and encourages engagement in activities that respond to social justice issues in their lived context (Camarrota, 2007; Gallagher-Geurtsen, 2009). Gallagher-Geurtsen (2009) argues, 'With a skilled teacher, able to help students identify the flows that students create and govern their lives, students will critically look at the rules of the game and institute change that is meaningful to them' (p. 202). Camarrota (2007) finds that critiquing the social injustices that constrain students' educational journeys helps clear emotional and intellectual space for engagement and learning. Teachers, students, families and community members must work at forging connections and raising awareness of social justice issues in their context.

School-home-community partnerships

Intersectional research urges schools, parents and/or other caregivers and community members to re-envision their roles and spheres of action as educational actors (Chapman and Antrop-Gonzalez, 2011; Grant and Sleeter, 1996; Howard and Reynolds, 2008; Kelly, 2009; West-Olatunji et al., 2010). These actors can better promote students' flourishing when they use intersectionality as a frame to understand students' learning experiences, whether they belong to majority or minority groups.

Research reports three approaches which schools, parents and communities can use to increase the development of students' full personalities through partnerships: first, analyse and take into account the interaction effects of school culture and student cultures; second, employ parenting strategies for academic success; and third, work as partners: school-home-communities.

1. Analyse the interaction effects of school culture and student cultures

School culture influences students' academic achievement, sense of academic efficacy and career plans (Grant and Sleeter, 1996; Watkins and Aber, 2009); and students' peer cultures influences students' schooling outcomes (Kelly, 2008). Grant and Sleeter (1996) assert that social context defined by race, social class and gender can produce a student culture in which students accept and live out their parents' place in a stratified society, in spite of the school's espoused mission as equalizer and escalator to a better life (p. 19). Watkins and Aber (2009) report that middle school students' race, class and gender influence their perceptions of their school's racial climate, academic achievement and school behaviours. Additionally, Kelly (2008) claims peer-group interaction and intra-group processes affect students' educational expectations, aspirations and outcomes. Students tracked into less demanding academic routes – predominantly students of low socio-economic status and/or students of colour – seek friendships based on similarity, develop new norms of success and sanction peers who seek to fit the school's norms (Kelly, 2008). However, Kelly (2008) finds that these students do not necessarily label academic behaviours as 'acting white', a common thesis in some of the early work on peer cultures (e.g. Fordham and Ogbu, 1986).

2. Employ parenting strategies for academic success

A second factor that shapes the full development of students' personalities is parenting that supports students at school and at home, fostering academic success (Chapman and Antrop-Gonzalez, 2011; West-Olatunji et al., 2010). These scholars describe how African American parents' authoritative parenting style couples firm discipline with demonstrative caring and encouragement to support their children's achievement (West-Olatunji et al., 2010). Chapman and Antrop-Gonzalez (2011) extend these notions to the school context, calling for teachers to teach with rigour and care in order to increase achievement for all, but particularly for African American students.

3. Work as partners

Several studies report that parents are eager to participate in schools but their participation depends on whether schools encourage or discourage their involvement (Howard and Reynolds, 2008; West-Olatunji et al., 2010). Moreover, research also suggests cultural differences between school and home may make some parents of colour reluctant to become involved either because they trust the 'experts' (Howard and Reynolds, 2008; Levine-Rasky, 2009); distrust schools to the point of limiting students' attendance, for example, Traveller families in the UK (Bhopal, 2004); or are excluded by White, middle-class parents (Levine-Rasky, 2009). These issues can be further complicated by teachers' stereotypes of parents of colour as incompetent, unfit, or lacking interest (West-Olatunji et al., 2010, p. 138). Howard and Reynolds (2008) asked parents of middle-class African American students in suburban schools how parent involvement influences students' achievement and what positive involvement might look like. They report that parents vary widely in the type of school-home partnership they seek, with some preferring backstage (at home) involvement and others engaging in frontstage involvement (volunteering, making decisions as part of a committee, etc.) (Howard and Reynolds, 2008). Levine-Rasky (2009) reports dynamics at a multi-racial school operate to privilege White, middle-class parents (who are engaged in close relationships with teachers and principals, active involvement in activities, fundraising) and exclude immigrant, non-English speaking, non-White parents (whose involvement is limited to special event attendance, one-shot volunteering, non-involvement). Though White, middle-class parents' actions appear individual, their effect is collective, reproducing social class advantage (Levine-Rasky, 2009). Bhopal (2004) details how schools in the UK successfully connected with Traveller parents by providing adult literacy programmes as a way to build relationships, understand parents' views and provide them with skills to support their children's achievement.

Challenges

In promoting school-home-community engagement Julie Carter (2007) reminds us of some challenges we will face. Carter (2007) states,

> In the growing trend toward urban school reform, especially within struggling urban contexts, vital educational stakeholders such as school boards, unions, parents, university and business interests often function at cross-purposes in determining the mode and trajectory of change. This tug-of-war is even more poignant in cities with racially charged public school histories, and where reform movements serve to bolster hopes for the rescue of ailing economies. In cases such as these, various constituents converge to fight for and claim credit for public school improvement and blame others when schools are underachieving.
>
> *(p. 68)*

Parent and community voices are vital to the implementation of meaningful school reform initiatives. As educators we should neither deny nor forget that we live in a world of rational communities, that these communities are important for specific purposes and that the main reason why we have schools, at least from a historical point of view is in order to reproduce the world of rational communities. Yet, we should not forget that this is not all that matters in life, and that perhaps what ultimately matters is not the reproduction of rational communities but bringing into being communities that can foster and support flourishing lives for all students, including those who experience social exclusion.

Conclusions

In this chapter we have argued for engaging educators in culturally responsive pedagogies and promoting school-home-community partnerships in order to work towards social inclusion. For students to develop their full personalities, parents and community members should be involved in their education alongside teachers. If all the actors involved in education work towards teaching the whole child, we will develop citizens who can think and care for themselves and others and who are prepared for life in a democratic society. Education for 'the full development of the human personality' (United Nations, UDHR, Article 26.1) requires pedagogies and partnerships that involve all educational actors – teachers, parents, students and community members – in a joint endeavour.

Bibliography

Achinstein, B. and Aguirre, J. (2008). Cultural match or culturally suspect: How new teachers of colour negotiate sociocultural challenges in the classroom. *Teachers College Record*, 110(8), 1505–1540.

Allard, A. C. and Santoro, N. (2008). Experienced teachers' perspectives on cultural and social class diversity: Which differences matter? *Equity & Excellence in Education*, 41(2), 200–214.

Americas Quarterly. (n.d.). *The Social Inclusion Index*. Retrieved: 10 November 2010 from http://www.americasquarterly.org/Charticle-The_Social_Inclusion_Index.html.

Bhopal, K. (2004). Gypsy travellers and education: Changing needs and changing perceptions. *British Journal of Educational Studies*, 52(1), 47–64.

Biesta, G. J. J. (2006). *Beyond Learning: Democratic Education for a Human Future*. Boulder, CO: Paradigm Publishers.

Brighouse, H. (2006). *On Education*. London: Routledge.

Brighouse, H. (2008). Education for a flourishing life. *Yearbook of the National Society for the Study of Education*, 107(1), 58–71. DOI: 10.1111/j.1744-7984.2008.00130.x. Retrieved: 31 July 2016.

Camarrota, J. (2007). A social justice approach to achievement: Guiding Latina/o students toward educational attainment with a challenging, socially relevant curriculum. *Equity & Excellence in Education*, 40, 87–96.

Carter, J. (2007). The challenge of parent engagement in urban small schools reform. *American Educational Research Association 2007 E-Yearbook of Urban Learning, Teaching, and Research*. Retrieved from http://www.aera-ultr.org/.

Centro de InvestigaciónenDerechosHumanos (CIDH). (2012). *What Is Social Inclusion?* Retrieved: 19 November 2012 from http://www.cidh.es/en/social-inclusion.html.

Chapman, T. K. and Antrop-Gonzalez, R. (2011). A critical look at choice options as solutions to Milwaukee's schooling inequities. *Teachers College Record*, 113(4), 787–810.

Chapman, T. K., Lamborn, S. D. and Epps, E. (2010). Educational strategies for children of Milwaukee: A critical race theory analysis. *Multicultural Learning and Teaching*, 5(2), 4–27.

Civil, M. and Bernier, E. (2006). Exploring images of parental participation in mathematics education: Challenges and possibilities. *Mathematical Thinking and Learning*, 8(3), 309–333.

DiAngelo, R. and Sensoy, O. (2010). "OK, I get it! Now tell me how to do it!" Why we can't just tell you how to do critical multicultural education. *Multicultural Perspectives*, 12(2), 97–102.

Eck, D. L. (2006). *From Diversity to Pluralism*. Pluralism Project at Harvard. http://www.pluralism.org/pluralism/essays/fromdiversitytopluralism.php.

Epstein, J. (2004). School, family, and community partnerships link the plan. *Principal*, 69(6), 19–23.

Epstein, J. (2005). Attainable goals? The spirit and letter of the No Child Left Behind Act on parental involvement. *Sociology of Education*, 78(2), 179–183.

Fordham, S. and Ogbu, J. U. (1986). Black students' school success: Coping with the burden of 'acting white'. *The Urban Review*, 18(3), 176–206.

Gallagher-Geurtsen, T. (2009). Inspiring hybridity: A call to engage with (in) global flows of the multicultural classroom. *Multicultural Perspectives*, 11(4), 200–203.

Gay, G. (2010). *Culturally Responsive Teaching: Theory, Research, and Practice*. New York: Teachers College Press.

Gibson, M. and Grant, C. (2010). 'Working in the small places': A human rights history of multicultural democratic education. In: R. Hoosain and F. Salili, *Democracy and Multicultural Education*. Charlotte, NC: Information Age Publishing.

Grant, C. A. and Lei, J. L. (eds). (2001). *Global Construction of Multicultural Education*. Mahwah, NJ: Lawrence Erlbaum.

Grant, C. A. and Potter, A. (2011). Models of parent-teacher/school engagement in a time of educational reform, increased diversity, and globalization. In: E. M. Olivos, O. Jimenez-Castellanos and A. Monroy Ochoa (eds), *Bicultural Parent Engagement: Advocacy and Empowerment*. New York: Teachers College Press.

Grant, C. A. and Sleeter, C. E. (1996). *After the School Bell Rings*. London: Falmer Press.

Grant, C. A. and Sleeter, C. E. (2007). *Doing Multicultural Education for Achievement and Equity*. New York: Routledge.

Grant, C. A. and Zwier, E. (2012). Intersectionality and education. In: J. A. Banks (ed), *Encyclopaedia of Diversity in Education*. New York: Routledge.

Hanusheck, E. A., Jamison, D. T., Jamison, E. A. and Woesssman, L. (2008). Education and economic growth. *Education Next*, Spring 2008, 62–70.

Heilman, E. E. (2010). Hoosiers, hicks, and hayseeds: The controversial place of marginalized ethnic whites in multicultural education. *Equity & Excellence in Education*, 37(1), 67–79.

Howard, T. C. and Reynolds, R. (2008). Examining parent involvement in reversing the underachievement of African American students in middle-class schools. *Educational Foundations*, Winter-Spring 2008, 79–98.

Irizarry, J. G. (2007). Ethnic and urban intersections in the classroom: Latino students, hybrid identities and culturally responsive pedagogy. *Multicultural Perspectives*, 9(3), 21–28.

Kelly, S. (2009). Social identity theories and educational engagement. *British Journal of Sociology of Education*, 30(4), 449–462.

King, J. (1988). Multiple jeopardy, multiple consciousness: The context of a Black feminist ideology. *Signs*, 14(1), 42–72.

Levine-Rasky, C. (2009). Dynamics of parent involvement at a multicultural school. *British Journal of Sociology of Education*, 30, 331–344.

McCauley, M. (2012). The world economy is in crisis because no one has any idea how it really works. Retrieved: 11 October 2012 from www.stirringtroubleinternationally.com/2012/09/27/economics-is-in-crisis-because-it-cannot-explain-how-an-economy-works/.

National Center for Culturally Responsive Educational Systems (NCCREST). (2008). Culturally responsive pedagogy and practice. Retrieved: 12 May 2011 from http://www.nccrest.org/professional/culturally_responsive_pedagogy-and.html.

Nussbaum, M. (2010). *Not for Profit: Why Democracy Needs the Humanities*. Princeton, NJ: Princeton University Press.

Olivos, E. M. (2006). *The Power of Parents: A Critical Perspective of Bicultural Parent Involvement in Public Schools*. New York: Peter Lang.

Organización de EstadosIberoamericanos and UNESCO. (n.d.). *Workshop 2: Quality Education and Social Inclusion*. Retrieved: 19 November 2012 from http://www.ibe.unesco.org/International/ICE47/English/Organisation/Workshops/Workshop2CompENG.pdf.

Razack, N. (1998). *Looking White People in the Eye*. Toronto: University of Toronto Press.
Ritzer, G. (2009). *Intersectionality 101: Sexism, Racism, Speciesism, and More*. Retrieved: 17 Sept. 2010 from http://animals.change.org/blog/view/intersectionality_101_sexism_racism_speciesm_and_more.
United Nations. (1948). *Universal Declaration of Human Rights*. Retrieved: 18 October 2012 from http://www.un.org/en/documents/udhr/index.shtml.
Watkins, N. D. and Aber, M. S. (2009). Exploring the relationships among race, gender, and middle school students' perceptions of school racial climate. *Equity & Excellence in Education*, 42(4), 395–411.
West-Olatunji, C., Sanders, T., Mehta, S. and Behar-Horenstein, L. (2010). Parenting practices among low-income parents/guardians of academically successful fifth grade African American children. *Multicultural Perspectives*, 12(3), 138–144.
White-Clark, R. and Decker, L. E. (1996). *The hard-to-reach parent: Old challenges, new insights*. Retrieved: 8 October 2012 from http://eric-web.tc.columbia.edu/families/hard_to_reach/.
Zuckerman, M. B. (2011). Why math and science education means more jobs. *US News & World Report*. Retrieved: 12 October 2012 from http://www.usnews.com/opinion/articles/2011/09/27/why-math-and-science-education-means-more-jobs.

4

BROADSTREAMING THROUGH CREATIVE LEARNING

An approach towards educational inclusion

Vijoy Prakash

Context

Educational inclusion has been one of the most important challenges of modern times. This chapter discusses various approaches to inclusion and argues in favour of broadstreaming in contrast to the approach of mainstreaming. Broadstreaming can be developed as the 'natural process of learning'. One such model is 'creative learning'.

The model has been applied to find a new approach to identifying learning difficulties. The chapter also suggests a framework for diagnosis of strengths and weaknesses of an individual child, and methods of planning for their remedial action. This is instrumental in the identification and monitoring of learning difficulties in the case of dyslexia, dyscalculia, dyspraxia, attention deficient hyperactivity disorders (ADHD), autism and other learning difficulties that are related to the improper processing and management of the flow of information. In fact, the learning difficulties can now be seen as difficulties in terms of 'core creative competencies' such as concentration, memory, thinking, imagination, emotional management, power of observation and power of communication. Based on the diagnosis, the model is used for pointing out the exact deficiency or nature of the problem in information flow and management. Thus proper remedial action can be immediately planned on the basis of the natural process of learning or natural learning style.

Introduction

Educational inclusion has been one of the most important challenges of modern times. The World Declaration on Education for All, adopted in Jomtien, Thailand (1990), called for universalisation of access to education for all children, youth and adults, and promoting equity. This implied being proactive in identifying the barriers that many encounter in accessing educational opportunities and identifying the resources needed to overcome those barriers. The need for inclusive education was further stressed at the World Conference on Special Needs Education: Access and Quality, held in Salamanca, Spain (June 1994). The Dakar Framework for Action also clearly paved the way for inclusive education as one of the main strategies to address the challenges of marginalisation and exclusion in response to the fundamental principle of Education for All, namely that all children, youth and adults should have the opportunity to learn. In both developed and developing regions, there is a common challenge as to how to attain high-quality equitable education for all learners.

Inclusive education is a process of strengthening the capacity of the education system to reach out to all learners and can thus be understood as a key strategy to achieve Education For All. As an overall principle, it should guide all education policies and practices, starting from the fact that education is a basic human right and the foundation for a more just and equal society.

According to the EFA Global Monitoring Report 2005, one way to move towards a relevant, balanced set of aims is to analyse the curriculum in terms of inclusion. An inclusive approach to curriculum policy recognises that while each learner has multiple needs – even more so in situations of vulnerability and disadvantage – everyone should benefit from a commonly accepted basic level of quality education. This underlines the need for a common core curriculum that is relevant for the learner while being taught according to flexible methods.

The social composition of schools and classrooms is changing with more learners entering schools. Multi-grade, multi-age and multi-ability classrooms are the reality in most places. It is essential that alternate frameworks for imparting learning in varying contexts be analysed and better understood. Greater attention is also needed to investigate unique contexts and settings – schools that promote active learning and inclusion, provide multicultural settings, and function in refugee and emergency situations.

There is need to work out a comprehensive model for curricular reforms, which can provide the framework for ensuring not only an access but also 'success to all children'.

Mainstreaming versus broadstreaming

There can be two approaches to inclusive curricula. One prevalent approach is the traditional approach of mainstreaming. It is used to refer to the selective placement of all in one or more 'regular' education classes. Proponents of mainstreaming generally assume that a student must 'earn' his or her opportunity to be placed in regular classes by demonstrating an ability to 'keep up' with the work assigned by the regular classroom teacher. Thus, the same curriculum is applied to all. It is assumed by giving equal opportunity, one is able to achieve a similar result.

Mainstreaming allows children with disabilities to be placed in regular schools, but only if they can follow the mainstream curriculum academically. Mainstreaming occurs mostly for children suffering from illnesses that have no impact on cognitive abilities and for children with a sensory impairment (having the necessary assisting devices such as hearing aids or Braille books) and those who have only a physical impairment. Mainstreaming does not require the teacher to adapt the curriculum or change their teaching methods. It does not take care of the existing strengths and weaknesses of the group or community or take into account any individual special requirement.

Broadstreaming attempts to broad-base the components of curricula so as to take care of the individual requirements of all children. It takes into account the strengths and weaknesses of the community and builds upon it. It tries to build the existing environment so that it grows to the level of the mainstream. The concept of broadstreaming respects individuality, promotes dignity of labour and provides a base for an equitable society. The mainstream approach mainly takes care of the similarity in inputs, whereas a broadstream approach takes care of the similarity in outputs. It is not only being together that is important; it is equally rather more important to create an enabling environment to learn together. But merely being placed in the same school is not sufficient to ensure that an environment is there to enable learning for all. Mainstreaming mainly caters to the needs of the mainstream children.

A broadstream approach means taking into account the differential requirements of all children by the pedagogy. It is based on the concept that children learn differently. Each child has a different natural learning process. It means creating a learning environment in such a way that all types of children, either with a learning difficulty or coming from an excluded socio-economic community, get a teaching method which is suited to their method of learning and are suited to their context. In this context, it means giving equal importance to the lifestyle practices, habits, language, vocation, etc. of underprivileged and marginalised communities as compared to that of the mainstream system (Table 4.1). The concept of broadstreaming requires development of a pedagogy which can ensure the equal development of all.

Creative learning

Understanding of the 'natural process of learning' has undergone a big change in the last few decades. Earlier, we had research on the behavioural dimensions of learning, but now with the advancement of science and technology, we have a better understanding of the functioning of the brain. This has resulted in new understanding of the learning system. Prakash (2007) has prepared a model of 'creative learning' based on a new understanding of the natural process of learning. He has defined creative learning as *a type of learning, which makes a person creative*. It means a *changed way of observation, thinking, feeling and doing things through the process of inquiry and exploration*. He has also suggested a systems model of creative learning based on information processing through the brain. The basic features of the model are as follows:

TABLE 4.1 Comparison of mainstreaming and broadstreaming

	Mainstreaming	*Broadstreaming*
1	Mainstreamed assumed to be better than others.	Broadstream emphasises on equality (all are equal).
2	Underprivileged should learn the standard language. Their language is of no value.	Include language of underprivileged in teaching process and gradually shift to standard language.
3	Knowledge is created by mainstreamed population and underprivileged are the recipients.	All are equal participants in the creation of knowledge.
4	Food habits, family traditions and culture of underprivileged are of no value. They should gradually adopt food habits, family traditions and culture of the mainstream. Hence, curricula emphasise the mainstream values only at times denigrating values of other communities.	Give importance to food habits, family traditions and culture of all including the underprivileged in the curricula.
5	Mainstreamed skills and work are considered more dignified than that of marginalised group.	All skills and work are considered equal. Working for dignity of work becomes easy. All works are considered equal.
6	Based on strengths of mainstream population.	Based on the strengths of all persons and communities.
7	Common curricula and common evaluation system based on mainstream requirement.	Broadstreamed curricula and evaluation system with due flexibility to suit the needs of different types of children.

1. Rational and emotional brain
2. Multiple intelligence and learning styles
3. Symbolic system in the context of multiple intelligence
4. Systems model of creative learning

Rational and emotional brain

One of the startling revelations of the last few decades is that our mental life consists of two types of mind. One is the *rational mind*, which is the mode of comprehension we are typically conscious of. It is more prominent in awareness, thoughtful, able to ponder and reflect. Then we have another system of knowing, impulsive and powerful, at times even illogical. It is referred to as the *emotional mind* (Goleman, 1996, p. 9). *Rational mind thinks, while emotional mind feels* (ibid.).

It has been found that sensory signals from the eye or ear travel first in the brain to the thalamus and then – across a single synapse – to the amygdala, the emotional brain. The second signal from the thalamus is routed to the neocortex, the thinking brain. This kind of branching allows the amygdala to respond before the neocortex, which mulls information through several levels of brain circuits before the full perception is complete and a final response is prepared. As a result, anatomically emotional systems can act independently of the rational thinking system. Some emotional reactions and memories can be formed without conscious, cognitive participation at all (ibid., p. 20).

So far, our main emphasis in the educational field has been on the development of the rational mind only. But Daniel Goleman (1996) has highlighted that *it is not only just IQ that matters for success in life. Intellect cannot work at its best without emotional intelligence. A person with high IQ may fail, if he/she does not have proper emotional intelligence.* We have many instances where very bright people could not succeed in life because they could not maintain proper emotional control. *The complementarity of limbic system and neocortex, amygdala and pre-frontal lobes are full partners in mental life. When they interact well, emotional intelligence rises, as does intellectual ability* (ibid., p. 32).

This new research asks us to harmonise what is traditionally understood as head and heart. In the educational field, this has serious implications. *We have to develop our education system in such a way that it takes care of developing intellect as well as emotions. We have to develop not only thinking faculties but feeling also.*

Multiple intelligence and learning styles

The concept of intelligence has also undergone a big change. Howard Gardner (1983), a psychologist and professor of education at Harvard University, suggested in his book, *Frames of Mind: The Theory of Multiple Intelligences*, that there are several kinds of intelligences or '*multiple intelligences*', which help people communicate, problem-solve and create. Gardner (ibid., p. xiv) defined intelligence as the 'ability to solve problems or to create products, that are valued within one or more cultural settings' – a definition that says nothing about either the sources of these abilities or the proper means of testing them. Multiple intelligences are different ways to demonstrate intellectual ability. These intelligences form the base for identification of the nature of the learning process of a person. In fact, these intelligences provide the framework of the natural process of learning, which can be a base for individual pedagogic designing.

One of the important conclusions of the multiple intelligence theory is that *every child has a unique learning style*. Within the education community, Gardner's theory of multiple intelligences have been translated into a recognition that children excelling in certain 'intelligences' learn best in one of these multiple different styles of learning. Although the list of intelligences is still growing, generally the following eight intelligences are used for teaching and learning purposes. They also refer to different types of learning styles.

- Verbal
- Logical
- Spatial
- Rhythmic
- Kinaesthetic

- Interpersonal
- Intra-personal
- Natural

Enhancing learning ability

Every person has different intelligence in different measures. This determines the capacity for handling information in the brain. Since these filters are developed in different measures in different persons, each person has a unique learning style. Such learning styles are a combination of one or more such filters. For example, we may have persons who are more familiar and efficient in learning through spatial and kinaesthetic methods. Such persons are learners through pictures and body language. If such persons were given instructions through pictorial and activity methods, they would have better receptivity than when they are instructed through verbal or logical methods.

Learning style also refers to the potentiality of a child to present his/her ideas in a creative way. Multiple styles also refer to the multiple ways of presenting ideas for communication to others. A child of spatial learning style would find it easy to make a painting or draw a sketch to present his/her ideas.

It would be interesting to note that logical/mathematical and verbal/linguistic intelligence forms the basis for most systems of modern education and all kinds of standardised testing programmes. As a result, only a part of our intelligence system is developed in the process. The creative learning process requires development of all types of intelligence to the optimum level.

In view of the multi-intelligence concept, a person's learning will depend on the information being received through different intelligence channels. Here information may basically be conceived as the set of stimuli being received through different sensory organs related to the particular intelligence channel. As the brain is capable of processing information received through different intelligence channels simultaneously, the total information reaching the brain which is ultimately responsible for any learning would depend on the information reaching the brain through different intelligence methods. In other words, the total information received by a person can be expressed as

$$L_o = F(L_V, L_L, L_R, L_S, L_K, L_{Intra}, L_{Inter}, L_{Nat})$$

Where,

L_o = Total information received in the brain

F = Denotes the functional relationship between information received through different intelligence methods and the total information received in the brain

$L_V, L_L, L_R, L_S, L_K, L_{Intra}, L_{Inter}, L_{Nat}$ = Information received through Verbal, Logical, Rhythmic, Spatial, Kinaesthetic, Intra-personal, Interpersonal, Natural methods

So, total learning of a person depends on the functioning of various intelligence channels. In this sense information through various sensory organs is received and communicated in the brain through different ways, leading to different ways of knowing and communicating, which can be identified as the learning style.

Once learning style is identified, it would be easier for us to select the learning methods and materials a child will enjoy using because it 'fits' with his or her way of learning. *Learning style means the method by which a person acquires and communicates knowledge.* It explains why some children learn '1,2,3s' by looking at a book, others by singing a song about numbers and some by manipulating objects. Children fit into several of these categories of learning styles. Teachers should use a wide variety of teaching approaches in presenting new subject matter in the hope of sparking interest in a variety of different learners.

Symbolic system of learning in the context of multiple intelligence

Verbal intelligence has led to the development of language as a system of transaction through symbols. Similarly, other types of intelligence also provide a framework for symbolisation of experiences, which forms an independent set of symbol systems. Each intelligence has its own mode of communication as we have languages in verbal learning. Spatial intelligence leads to development of a symbol system in which experiences are presented, codified and communicated in the form of pictures. Rhythmic intelligence helps us in the formulation of a set of rhythmic symbols for presentation of our experiences.

Information is said to be received and transmitted in the brain in the form of symbols and patterns. Every intelligence leads us to the development of its own system of symbols and patterns. We can understand any real or imaginary experience in terms of these symbols and patterns only. These symbols provide a method of comprehension of experiences, storage and processing leading to their problem-solving and manipulation, and communication to others.

In this generalised sense, *symbols may be defined as a set of information in terms of any of the intelligible modes having a definite prescribed and identifiable meaning. It may be a set of sound waves such as voices, a set of visuals such as scenes or pictorial letters like alphabets, a set of spatial representation in terms of pictures, a set of kinaesthetic activities like signals of traffic constables, etc.* (Prakash, 2007).

In this context language becomes one of the sets, and not the only one, to comprehend, manipulate and communicate experiences, or talking in a plain sense. We may have a different language system for a different intelligence mode. We shall have a set of symbols too for a language system pertaining to spatial intelligence, another set for kinaesthetic intelligence, still another for interpersonal intelligence, and so on. Each of these mutually exclusive and independent sets provide a different framework for codification, storage, processing and transmission of information pertaining to human experiences.

Verbal intelligence has words as its symbols. Numbers, lines, etc. are again symbols related to logical intelligence. Musical notes become the symbols for rhythmic intelligence. Similarly, spatial intelligence has its own symbols in the form of pictorial representations. A flower is written in a particular way. A meaning has evolved through the ages for various kinds of pictorial representation for the pictorial and written word, which is acceptable to society. A pair of spectacles drawn in a particular way represents *Gandhi*. A cartoonist develops his own pictorial symbols to represent his ideas.

Interpersonal intelligence requires symbolic structures in the form of social etiquettes and manners and other forms of social interactions. We have different ways to greet each other, different ways to express happiness and grief and so on. There are symbolic ways to understand our inner environment also. The symbolic structure of intra-personal intelligence is highly individualistic.

Each intelligence mode has certain advantages over others. A pictorial symbol may depict experiences which a thousand words cannot. We communicate through facial expressions what can never be effectively communicated in verbal structure. This concept has given us a broader tool for communication which can be taken to be complementary and supplementary. The same human experience can be codified through multiple means and ways. So, multiple intelligence provides multiple ways of handling, storing and communicating experiences.

Logical intelligence received a boost with the development of mathematics, which provided a framework for symbolisation of logical relationships. They were also developed, as they could be converted to written symbols, which facilitated their preservation.

Kinaesthetic intelligence pertaining to technological intelligence also developed as they could also be preserved. Symbolic structure of other intelligence modes could not be developed to that extent, as they did not have technological support for proper preservation. They had to take recourse to a language system for their preservation. If kinaesthetic expressions as codified in the form of various *Mudras* had to be preserved, they could be done only with the help of words and sentences. This definitely diluted the real purport of the symbolic kinaesthetic representation. Real kinaesthetic symbols were preserved only through human memory and transmitted through direct human interaction.

The availability of multimedia presentations has facilitated a plethora of alternatives for the observation, storage, manipulation and communication of ideas and experiences. Earlier we had only language based on a verbal system for communication of our experiences. The statement of people can be recorded in the form of a written note or speech on an audio or visual recorder. There is a need to use symbols of different intelligence modes in order to have an effective and accurate presentation and communication of ideas.

In the context of a symbolic method of learning, education can be reduced to learning about symbols and the art of their manipulation. Different symbolic structures are now developing at a faster rate and we have a better opportunity to select a symbolic base pertaining to one's own physical, mental and psychological requirement.

Symbolic patterns

Another dimension of learning is that the symbols are generally received and communicated in the form of patterns. *Patterns are a spatial and/or temporal arrangement of a set of symbols following certain relationships* (Prakash, 2007). These patterns provide the framework for receiving and conveying information. Hence, learning the art of identifying patterns is an essential competency for the learning process. In mathematics, we learn various types of such patterns in arithmetic, geometry and algebra. They are in the form of formulae, rules, theorems, etc. Similarly, we have various matrices, set representations, etc. to facilitate manipulation of patterns. In languages, we have patterns in the form of phrases, sentences, paragraphs, etc. We also have rules of grammar for these patterns. Dance forms have different patterns of displaying emotions and expressions.

Prakash (2007) has given detailed mathematical formulation of symbols into patterns. In a pattern, the arrangement among symbols may be spatial, temporal or mixed.

When a child plays with words orally to create a new sentence formation, he/she is playing with the temporal pattern of words. However, if he/she writes words in different forms, he/she tries to make a spatial pattern of words.

Activities have to be designed for the learner to master the art of pattern recognition and pattern creation through their own learning style. A verbal child may find it easier to learn the pattern of spoken or written words, whereas a spatial child would easily find patterns in paintings and art forms.

If we give a brush to a child, he/she would paint here and there. It may not have any meaning to us. But, he/she may say, 'This is a picture of a happy man.' This is his/her own symbolic representation of ideas. He/she may also make a representation of those patterns of ideas in the form of scenery. *So, one of the objectives of the learning system should be to encourage children to identify existing patterns and create new patterns.*

Mathematical analysis of the symbolic method of learning

A learning system consists of symbols, rules of symbolic arrangement, and patterns, which may be mathematically represented as (Prakash, 2007):

$$L = L(S, R, P)$$

Where,

L = Total learning of a person

$L(S, R, P)$ = Learning function of symbols (S), Rules of symbolic arrangement (R) and Patterns (P)

Symbols involved in the learning process for a learner are really a collection of symbols of all available areas of intelligence.

$$S = \sum S_i$$

Where,

S_i = Symbols pertaining to a particular area of intelligence

$\sum$ = Summation over all areas of intelligence

A normal person, generally, receives information in all areas of intelligence. For him/her symbols of all areas of intelligence are involved in the learning process. Blind people are not able to receive information through visual observation. So, they cannot participate in the normal learning activity as our learning sessions are mostly dependent on writing skills. For these people a major breakthrough in learning was made when symbolic codification was done using touch sense in the form of Braille script. Then, they could easily participate in the normal learning activity.

Symbols of one area of intelligence are also related to the symbols of other areas. The word '*tree*' is related to the picture 'tree', a spatial symbol, and kinaesthetic representation of tree through body language.

Hence, we see that symbols are related to each other in two ways:

- **intra-intelligence relationship** (relationship among symbols of inside one area of intelligence) and
- **inter-intelligence relationship** (relationship among symbols of different areas of intelligence).

Understanding of such relationships of symbols is of paramount importance in the context of learning.

The meaning of the collection of symbols

The meaning of a set of symbols changes by simple addition of new information or their new arrangement. The meaning of a set of symbols in a pattern would depend upon the contextual situation.

Let x be the meaning of symbol A and y be the meaning of symbol B. Then the meaning of AB may be:

- $x+y$ as in '*good girl*'
- $x-y$ as in '*a great man*' (used contextually to denote an idiot)
- z (different from both x and y as in '*run down*')

Symbols and commutative law

Some of the symbols follow commutative law, i.e., xy is equal to yx. For example, 'fruit and vegetables' and 'vegetables and fruit' would have similar meanings.

Some symbols may not follow commutative law, i.e., xy is not equal to yx. '*He is*' and '*Is he*' may have different meanings.

Symbolic patterns

We have seen that symbolic patterns are a spatial or temporal arrangement of symbols, i.e.

$P = P(x,t)$
Where,
P = Pattern function
$P(x, t)$ = A function of symbols in space and time

Based on the arrangement of symbols there would be three types of patterns:

- *Spatial* – arrangement of symbols in space. For example, written words, pictures, posters, etc.
- *Temporal* – arrangement of symbol in time and space. For example, spoken words, audio presentation, rhythmic (musical) presentation etc.
- *Mixed* – both spatial and temporal. For example, TV presentation, cartoon show, facial expressions, drama, etc.

Unit patterns

Big patterns are, generally, a replication and combination of smaller patterns. A book is divided into pages, chapters, etc. An article is divided into various paragraphs, a paragraph in sentences. A sweater or textile design is divided into smaller patterns that are replicated to generate the bigger pattern. These smaller units of pattern are referred to as *unit patterns*.

The knowledge of the nature of the unit pattern and the rules of their replication is crucial for the understanding of pattern learning process. Internally, unit is an arrangement of symbols. These arrangements may be spatial or temporal. In a textile cloth, arrangements of symbols are spatial and the unit is, thus, spatial. In a song, the verse is divided into units of rhythms. Such rhythms are temporal in nature.

Rules of pattern making

Pattern making rules are an extremely important area of learning. Unit patterns have their own intrinsic or *intra-unit pattern rules*. The unit patterns are connected with each other by a separate set of rules, which may be called *inter-unit pattern rules*.

Intra-unit pattern rules

Unit patterns are composed of symbols. The basic arrangement of symbols in a unit pattern may be of the following kinds:

- **Spatial arrangement**: These unit patterns follow certain spatial arrangement or distribution of symbols, i.e., they observe an explicit spatial relationship among themselves. A sweater or a cloth has a simple replicable relationship of knots. In writing, we arrange our thoughts in terms of simple words. These words follow certain definite spatial rules of arrangement or distribution, which are spatially replicable and are, thus, identified as unit patterns. Since space is three-dimensional, we may have various kinds of unit patterns based on the nature of relationships followed by them. Engineering drawing, the language of engineers, is an extremely good example of spatial arrangement.

a **Uni-dimensional**: These are rules pertaining to the spatial distribution of symbols in one dimension. Some of the uni-dimensional arrangements may be as follows:

- Linear forward. For example, Hindi and English script.
- Linear backward. For example, Urdu script.
- Linear disordered. For example, Woodroffe (1954) in his famous book on Tantraraj Tantra gives a beautiful example of disordered placing of symbols. He has given examples of nineteen verses from the book. These verses follow a cryptic style where content can be concealed and which can be read by only those who have the secret code. One such verse is:

shu te sa shve re tu va vet tta kam rvva pi pa ra sa
jaa dhaa hi na poo vi bru tu jncha va lpa sya na sa ka

This cannot have any meaningful construction in normal reading. However, if the secret code, 8, 4, 6, 2, 7, 3, 5, 1 (which indicates the order of placing of the letters in above placement) is known, the verse actually reads as follows:

Vasreshu tu teshvevan sarvapattarkam pivet
Broohi poojavidhanaya kalpanajnchasavasya cha

- Vertically upward. For example, posters, magazine cover, etc.
- Vertically downward. For example, book cover, posters, etc.

b **Two-dimensional**: These are rules pertaining to the distribution of symbols in a plane involving two dimensions. Some such arrangements may be as follows:

- Linear
  - Diagonal. For example, book covers, magazine covers, yantras, etc.
- Non-linear
  - Circular/semi-circular. For example, yantras, seal, badge, monogram, etc.
  - Triangular. For example, yantras.
  - Rectangular. For example, yantras, tombs, coffins.
  - Square. For example, *Garbha Grih* of deities.
  - Steps. For example, minarets.
- Two-dimensional graphs
- Irregular

c **Three-dimensional**: There are certain arrangements, which follow a three-dimensional structure. Some such regular arrangements may be identified as follows:
- Cubical
- Parallelepiped
- Spherical
- Three-dimensional graphs

- **Temporal arrangement**: The arrangement of symbols may also be defined in terms of time. In music the time relationship is used to great advantage. To make the composition aesthetically pleasing, the symbols of voices, tones and intensity are varied in the moving time.
- **Spatio-temporal arrangement**: Both spatial and temporal arrangements can be fruitfully utilised for effective presentation. In TV shows, this can be easily seen where symbols are arranged in space and time simultaneously.

Inter-unit pattern rules

Units are replicated following certain rules. There are two types: regular and irregular.

Regular patterns

These patterns follow certain fixed rules, such as,

- **Identical/similar replication**. For example, in textiles, knitwear, etc. In Border designs, the same design is replicated again and again. In plants, leaves of similar pattern appear at regular intervals.
- **Replication with periodical change**

    a *Spatial periodicity*. For example, in textiles, knitwear, mathematical addition or multiplication tables, etc. In plants, leaves appear at a periodical angular distribution.
    b *Temporal periodicity*. For example, TV or radio programmes.

- **Replication with fixed boundary parameters, but free content**. For example, in classical poetry or songs the metres are fixed, but the content is different. The same metres are repeated again and again, but wordings are different. In books, pages follow a fixed format like paragraphs, headings, sub-headings, etc., but the contents are different. In languages, words are linked together by certain grammar rules like tense, conjunctions, verb patterns, etc. to form sentences. Sentences become another unit pattern for the generation of paragraphs. Paragraphs become a further unit pattern for the generation of essays, notes, etc.

Standardisation of symbols and patterns

Historically, various symbols and patterns have evolved in all societies. They form the acceptable base of a communication system. Society members, experts, academicians collectively decide the nature of the set of the symbols and patterns. These standard sets of symbols and patterns are, then, used for a common communication system. If a new symbol or pattern has to be introduced, it must be acceptable to the experts of the area or general society members. The acceptable patterns become the acceptable format for communication.

In the contemporary education system, we generally confine ourselves to imparting education of the standard symbols and patterns with little scope of innovation regarding creation and use of new symbols and patterns. In the context of inclusion one of the major challenges before us is to broaden the base of symbols used by different social groups in different contextual conditions. It should also include symbols and patterns pertaining to different intelligence in the learning system. Children should also be taught the art of using existing standard symbols and patterns in a creative way and of developing new acceptable symbols and patterns.

Systems model of creative learning

In the last few decades, our understanding of the workings of the mind and learning has undergone large-scale changes. One approach to understand the natural process of learning is to see the flow of information through the brain. The **information processing theory** approach to the study of cognitive development has proposed that like a computer, the human mind is a system that processes information through the application of logical rules and strategies. Just like a computer, the mind has a limited capacity for the amount and nature of the information it can process. Just as the computer can be made into a better information processor by changes in its hardware (e.g. circuit boards and microchips) and its software (programming), so do children become more sophisticated thinkers through changes in their brains and sensory systems (hardware) and in the rules and strategies (software) that they learn.

Atkinson and Shiffrin (1968) presented the 'information processing' model of memory. It was improved and extended by Prakash (2007) through the model of 'creative learning' to include comprehensive processing of information in the learning process.

Based on information flow through the brain, three phases of learning can be identified (Figure 4.1):

- Receptive phase (observation phase)
- Processive phase
- Productive phase.

Receptive phase (observation phase)

Here a learner receives information using his/her sensory organs. *If the system is efficient, one can receive more and more information, and thus, can have a better power of*

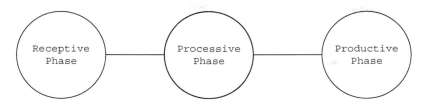

FIGURE 4.1 Three phases of learning

observation. A person with a deficient receptive system would, however, be handicapped from the beginning and he/she will not be able to receive adequate information required for making him/her creative. It should be emphasised that efficiency of organs is not a pre-condition for becoming creative. *Beethoven* was functionally deaf, when he composed some of his great works. *Soordas*, one of the greatest Hindi poets of all time, was blind. Hence, sensory advantage is not a pre-condition for creativity. But sensory organs should not be seen in isolation. *Although these creative people were deficient of one or other sensory organ, they had other fully developed sensory organs, which they used, to maximum extent. Hence, their entire receptive system was quite efficient.*

Processive phase

The second stage of learning is the processing in the brain of information received through various sensory organs.

Memory

Once the information has been received, it goes to memory, where it is stored either temporally or on a long-term basis (Figure 4.2). We can remember this information, whenever we require it for use. We remember much of the information we learnt in school, many scenes we saw in childhood, songs we have heard and various tastes, smells, touch sensations, etc.

However, it is not necessary that all information received will be stored in the brain. We retain some of this information, but forget much of it. The information retained can be recalled later as per requirement. We may recall all or part of the

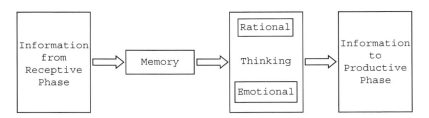

FIGURE 4.2 Processive phase of creative learning

information. Weak recall may be tested by recognition. We may not recall the face of a person, but we may recognise him, when we meet the person.

Even though computer memory and human memory perform similar tasks, they are different in their operations (Baron, 1995, p. 217). We can remember a fact or part of it at one time and may fail to do so at another time. However, the computer either gives the information or does not (Lewandowsky and Murdock, 1989).

Richard Atkinson and Richard Shiffrin (1968) suggested a model based on information processing, often referred to as **modal model**. It suggested that memory starts with a sensory input from interactions with the environment. This input is held for a brief period of time, say for several seconds at most, in a sensory register that is associated with the sensory channels: vision, hearing, touch, taste and smell. From the **sensory register**, information may be passed on to the **short-term store (memory)**, where it is held for 20–30 seconds. This depends upon attention. When we observe through our senses, we pay attention to some of the information. The information attended to is passed on to the short-term memory, others are lost. Experiments suggest that the capacity of sensory memory is quite large – indeed, it may hold fleeting representatives of virtually everything we see, hear, taste, smell or feel (Reeves and Sperling, 1986). These representations are retained for very brief periods. Visual sensory memory lasts for less than a second, while acoustic sensory memory lasts for not more than a few seconds (Cowan, 1984).

Different learners will have different memory in different areas as per their learning styles. A child having a spatial learning style will have good memory pertaining to pictures and picture-related matters. They can easily recognise and retain any information in pictorial forms. Similarly, a verbal child would have better memory of words. A rhythmic child has better memory of rhythm and rhymes.

Thinking

Information retrieved from memory is then subjected to processing, popularly known as thinking. Thinking is generally defined as the cognitive rearrangement or manipulation of information from the environment and symbols stored in long-term memory (Morgan, King and Robinson, 1979). As we have already seen, a symbol represents, or stands for some event or items in the world of images. The processing of information in terms of symbolic manipulation is done at this stage. The manipulation may be of two types: one type may be private where the symbols created and their meaning is personal, such as in dreams. This is often referred to as autistic thinking. The other type depends on direction either for solving certain problems or creating something new. This is called directed thinking.

Thinking classification

Thinking may be thought of in terms of convergent and divergent questioning (Guilford 1956).

Convergent thinking Convergent means coming to a point. A convex lens converges light rays to a particular point. Similarly, thinking, which has the result of having only one set of results of a set of stimuli is called convergent thinking. For example, if we ask the question, 'What is your name?' it will have a unique answer. So, thinking must converge to produce the answer. Similarly, if we ask the question, 'What is 2+2?' it will have a unique answer, i.e., 4.

Convergent thinking focuses on an answer, a solution. It is used when solving problems such as long division and calculating income tax. Convergent thinking techniques eliminate uncertainty, simplify complexity and enhance decision-making ability. Convergent questions seek to ascertain basic knowledge and understanding.

Divergent thinking Divergent thinking refers to an individual's ability to generate multiple solutions to a problem. It is typically measured by presenting individuals with an open-ended stimulus problem to which they are required to generate as many solutions, ideas, concepts and approaches as possible. The greater number of alternatives generated results in a greater probability of a better, more creative solution.

If we ask the question 'What are the names of your friends?' it will have unlimited answers. The person will have to scan all friends and suggest different answers. This takes us to the concept of divergent thinking which means having unlimited responses to a single stimulus. The question, which we asked earlier, will have answers like Rohan, Sohan, Shyam, Gita, Sita, etc. Similarly, if we ask the question 'Which two numbers add to ten?' we will have unlimited answers, i.e., 1 +9, 2+8, 3+7, 4+6, 5+5, −2+12, etc.

Production phase

After the processive phase comes the production phase, in which the information processed in the processing phase works as stimuli for activating different locomotor systems. This leads to the performance of various activities by a person. For example, a person starts writing on paper using his/her fingers or starts walking on a road.

A group of people consisting of a poet, an artist, an agriculturist and a musician are taken to a garden. All observe the same set of trees, water and landscapes. The poet will express his view in terms of poems. The artist may like to draw a picture to give expression to his ideas. The agriculturist may look into the garden to explore the possibility of raising an orchard and express his views orally or through farming models. The musician may get the same information converted to stimuli to generate a new song or music.

In the same way, in a class of children having different learning styles the same set of observations may lead to different ways of communication. If children are asked to visit a fair, individuals would remember different aspects of it. They may also prefer to make their communication in different ways. A rhythmic child may like to recite an interesting tune which he/she might have heard there. A kinaesthetic child may like to mime how salesmen were trying to advertise their products. A verbal child may make a detailed description of various activities happening in the fair ground. A spatial child might have noticed the detailed layout of the exhibitions. He/she may take special notice of the designs of textiles or paintings on display in the field and may like to express his/her views through paintings or a clay model of the fair ground. An interpersonal child may have noticed how people were using the occasion for social interaction or he/she may like to use the time spent there for meeting friends or making different arrangements for the group.

The productive phase of learning is highly need-based. A child needs to learn the art of production or communication of ideas from the point of view of the user. A writer may like to convey his/her ideas in the form of written matter to be read by readers. One may like to speak one's thought and ideas to others. One may also present one's ideas in pictorial form or compose a song to be listened to by others. One may enact a drama or perform a dance to convey his/her ideas to viewers.

Hence, at the elementary stage of learning, children should be exposed to various kinds of communication. This requires:

- Developing mastery over accepted standard patterns of communication.
- Learning the art of creating new patterns of communication.

Children need to be made proficient in these communication and presentation skills. Communication skills are also essential for developing proper interpersonal interactions. At the elementary level, more emphasis needs to be given to developing communication skills like speaking, writing etc.

Importance of concentration

Concentration is one of the important factors in the learning process. *Concentration is sustained focused attention at a particular point, idea or activity.* Each of the phases of learning involves different types of concentration. The concentration needed in the receptive phase is known as receptive concentration, in the processing phase as processive concentration and in the production phase as productive concentration. When we listen to music, we exercise our receptive concentration and are, thereby, able to receive more information. When we think on a particular idea, we exercise our processive concentration. Thereby, we are able to generate and process more ideas. When a farmer ploughs a field or when we play music, we have to maintain productive concentration, when we concentrate on performance.

Concentration should be developed in all phases by choosing an activity pertaining to one's learning style and trying to focus on it for longer periods of time.

Core Creative Competencies

Based on the above analysis, Prakash (2007) has identified the *core creative competencies* which can form the basis of all learning activities and evaluation.

- Concentration
- Power of observation
- Memory
- Thinking

    a   Convergent
    b   Divergent

- Emotional management
- Power of expression/communication

Special features of the systems model of creative learning

1. Learning being dependent on the individual learning style, the new model suggests that the natural learning process should be **totally learner-specific**. Each learner should follow a strategy for learning to suit his/her natural learning process. Thus, the school system having uniform curricula and syllabi for all children needs a fresh approach.
2. The primary objective of any learning method should be to maximise the availability of relevant information to the brain for processing and to ensure smooth transmission until presentation into a useful form. So, *the learning programme should ensure the smooth flow of relevant information at an enhanced rate and quantum*. The learner should be made *proficient in all phases of learning that is* receptive, processing and productive or communicative. However, there should be an attempt to maximise the competency pertaining to all sensory organs of the receptive and processive phases in all children. But, the productive phase should be developed only with reference to one's individual and societal needs. This would require development of all core creative competencies (CCC) to the optimum level.
3. The learner should learn how to *synchronise all phases of learning*. This would facilitate the functioning of learning process at optimum efficiency.
4. The learning method should try to make learners learn the art of maximising the availability of information in the brain. Any equipment or appliances which enhance the availability of information should find a prominent place in the learning schedule. Some of the learners, such as those who are blind or deaf, may have deficient sensory organs. So, they should either use additional appliances to enhance the availability of information to the brain or try to use other developed sensory organs to their full extent so that information flow to the brain can be maximised.
5. The model also suggests the important role of *curiosity* in the learning process. Sufficient curiosity helps in sustaining and maintaining the self-learning

process, as it helps to receive more and more information and motivates the learner to pursue the learning process more vigorously. Learning should be *discovery-based and should promote curiosity*. In other words, the learner should learn the *art of questioning from early childhood*.
6. *Learning efficiency* can be increased only by receiving information in all available learning intelligence areas. Learners must be given the opportunity to develop all intelligence areas to their optimal level. A child of spatial learning style may have spatial intelligence which is more developed so he/she can receive and transmit more information in an effective way through spatial methods.

Applications of the model of creative learning in managing learning difficulties

Special children are those who are either physically challenged due to the absence of any organs or their sensory or loco-motor system is less developed because of some malfunctioning. It is also interesting to note that if one or more sensory organs are deficient either in physical or in operational terms, it will affect the total quantum of information received in the brain.

All senses act simultaneously, but to receive information about a certain object/thing, we have to concentrate only on some of these senses depending upon the situation and object about which we are gathering information. When we look at a flower, all sensory organs work simultaneously to make different observations. With eyes, we observe its outer details and our nose examines the quality of smell. Similarly, when we touch the flower, we feel its texture.

Hence, we find that the learning processes involved in receipt of information sometimes work as complementary, sometimes supplementary and sometimes independent of each other. *However, since all these variables are interdependent, even if one or more of these are non-functional or less efficient, other methods may be used to gather more and more information so that the total quantum of information available for processing in the brain is maintained at optimum level*. This way deficiency in one can be compensated by the better efficiency of the other. *A blind person may not be able to use spatial techniques for gathering information, but he/she can use his/her auditory senses to the maximum extent to compensate through verbal and logical intelligence methods*. A blind person can receive more information by listening and touching than a common person. Similarly, for a deaf and dumb person the entire transmission of information has to be through touch, movement of limbs and facial expressions.

For production of information we also have to use the remaining part of the loco-motor system. A child without hands may use his feet to write or even paint.

There is another kind of special children who have a highly accentuated learning style. They may be typically categorised into one of the learning styles. These children need a special type of treatment in the form of teaching, development of teaching learning materials and evaluation system.

If a child has only one or two intelligences developed, he/she needs materials and a method of teaching which will suit his/her learning style. Such children should not be considered learning deficient. A painter like *M.F. Hussain* or a singer like *Lata Mangeshkar* would have learning styles pertaining to spatial or rhythmic fully developed, but they may not have other intelligences developed to that level. Hence, if they are tested on the intelligences pertaining to verbal or logical intelligence, they may not succeed or show their full worth. For them, full potential can be realised only by channelling the learning activities through their own particular learning styles. That is why many outstanding sports players may not have outstanding academic careers.

For such special children entire learning material can be designed for the child in that learning style. For example, if the child learns in a spatial way or his/her spatial learning is more prominent, we should have more pictorial learning matter for him/her. He/she can be shown learning matter through visual media like TV, video, etc. This way, she/he would be able to receive more information. Be it science, mathematics or social studies, all subjects would have to be covered through pictures and visual presentations.

For a rhythmic child, the learning matter should be designed in terms of songs, music, etc. For such children background music, even in the classroom, would be of great help in the transmission of information.

Identifying learning difficulties

When children do not get good grades in any subjects, we often goad them to work harder in the subject. Is it the right way to assess and motivate the child? Experiences at the School of Creative Learning have shown that the issue of failure in the examination may be a product of various external factors like physical ailment or social distraction. However, even if there is no such problem, a child may not do well in the examination due to lack of proper core creative competencies. For example, if the child is not doing well in mathematical competencies, one must look whether the child is deficient in:

- Concentration
- Memory
- Rational thinking

If the child is really deficient in these competencies, they should be asked to perform exercises to develop those competencies. For example, if the child does not have good concentration, he/she should do exercises to develop it. Once developed, some hard work may improve their grades.

Similarly, if the child is not doing well in languages, one should look for deficiencies in mental competencies in:

- Concentration
- Memory

- Thinking
- Power of observation

    a   Listening
    b   Reading

- Power of communication

    a   Writing

If the child is not doing well in science subjects, one must look into competencies like:

- Concentration
- Memory
- Thinking
- Power of observation

    a   Listening
    b   Reading

- Power of communication

    a   Technological skills
    b   Writing

If child is able to develop these competencies and even then he/she is not performing well, then he/she should be motivated to do hard work to acquire the necessary information pertaining to that subject.

In this context there is no need to categorise learning difficulties for any child as dyslexia, dysgraphia, dyscalculia, ADHD, dyspraxia, autism, etc. Such classification is stigmatic and does not help in remedial action. The holistic model based on identification of the exact nature of the learning difficulty in the information processing system will help us in designing a correct programme of action for handling different learning difficulties. Deficiency in concentration in core creative competencies is present in different measures in all learning difficulties. So based on proper diagnosis the activities and exercises for improvement in concentration and memory would have a favourable impact on all these cases.

In light of the above analysis, it is clear that in the context of the creative learning model there is no need to classify learning difficulties in terms of traditional learning difficulties. In fact, the learning difficulties can now be seen as difficulties in terms of core creative competencies such as concentration, memory, thinking, imagination, emotional management, power of observation and power of communication. In this context the remedial action can easily be related to interventions to develop the difficulties being faced in terms of the said core creative competencies.

Bibliography

Atkinson, A. W. and Shiffrin, R. M. (1968). Human memory: A proposed system and its control processes. In: K. W. Spence (ed), *The Psychology of Learning and Motivation: Advances in Research and Theory*, 2, 89–195. New York: Academic Press.

Baron, R. A. (1995). *Psychology*. Upper Saddle River, NJ: Prentice Hall.

Cowan, N. (1984). On short and long auditory stores. *Psychological Bulletin*, 96, 341–370.

Gardner, H. (1983). *Frames of Mind: The Theory of Multiple Intelligences*. New York: Harper and Row.

Goleman, D. (1996). *Emotional Intelligence*. New York: Bantam Books.

Guilford, J. P. (1956). The structure of intellect. *Psychological Bulletin*, 53, 267–293.

Lewandowsky, S. and Murdock Jr., B. B. (1989). Memory for serial order. *Psychological Review*, 96, 25–57.

Morgan, C. T., King, R. A. and Robinson, N. M. (1979). *Introduction to Psychology* (6th ed). New Delhi: Tata McGraw-Hill.

Prakash, V. (2007). *Creative Learning*. New Delhi: VIVA Books.

Reeves, A. and Sperling, G. (1986). Attention gating in short-term retention of individual verbal items. *Psychological Review*, 93, 180–206.

UNESCO. (2005). *Education for All, 2005: The Quality Imperative*. Paris: Global Monitoring Report.

Woodroffe, J. (1954). *Tantraraj Tantra*. Madras: Ganesh and Co.

PART II
Perspectives on policy and practice

5

INCLUSIVE EDUCATION AND SOCIETAL DEVELOPMENT

An Indian perspective

Ran Bijay N. Sinha and Rupa Lakshmi

Context

India stands at 135th on the Human Development Index (HDI) out of 187 countries (Human Development Reports, 2014). At 135, India's position is the same as it was in 2010 and 2012. However, it has been doing well in increasing its purchasing power parity (PPP) claiming 4th rank in the world, next only to the USA, China and Japan (World Bank, 2011). India has the second largest education system in the world, with 200 million children aged between 6 and 14, around 25 million of whom are out of school (World Bank, 2004). India's 1.3 billion people speak 18 different languages (GOI, 2002), and 844 dialects (Singal, 2005). The diversity is also reflected in disparities of educational achievement. For example, in Kerala, the literacy rate recorded in the 2001 census was 90.92% while in Bihar it was 47.53% (GOI, 2002). As a result, the overall average literacy rate for India was 65.38%. The above figure reflects the complexity of context (Govinda and Biswal, 2006). A study by Hulme, Moore and Shepherd (2001) reports that almost one-third of the world's chronically poor live in India and they remain disadvantaged not only economically but also in terms of education and health. This chapter examines how educational and social exclusion affects children and young people in India, the challenges facing inclusive education there and the societal response to overcoming those challenges.

Role of education

The critical role of education in societal development emphasizes that a society cannot develop fully unless most of their children are getting a good education. Initially, development was mainly confined to economic growth. The expression of 'social development' was introduced in 1960 in UN reports. According to

UNDP (1997), societal development is reflected in levels of literacy and schooling, gender equity, health, personal empowerment and so on. Kamin (1988) stresses about societal development and notes 'three components of societal development, economic, political, and socio-cultural-psychological, are inter-penetrable'. However, Sinha (1990) commented that the universal model of development cannot guarantee societal development because of cultural uniqueness and variation in socio-cultural dimensions. More recently, Alkire and Santos (2010) considered development as multidimensional and includes factors such as education, health, gender parity and political participation.

According to Pareek (1988), creation of a sense of power in individuals and collectives in a society and its use by them in solving their problems may be termed as societal development. The underlying concept of societal development is a concern for human well-being, quality of life, adaptability, social change and enlarging options, opportunities and choices. In fact, the concept of societal development is inseparable from the characteristics of individuals living in a given society or culture. Thus societal development includes people as well as the culture and heritage of that society in which they belong. According to a report by the World Bank (2011), India's underperformance in the HDI was due more to inequality in education (43%) than in health (34%) or in income (16%). Thus it is clear that societal development is possible only when the majority have access to a good inclusive education.

Many Indian thinkers (Fagg, 2001) have questioned the relevance of modern schools imparting education. Gandhi's ideas about a basic education requiring a synthesis of body, mind and spirit were reflected in his belief that 'a proper and harmonious combination of all three is required for the making of the whole man and constitutes the true economics of education'. He proposed an 'alternative pedagogy' based upon learning through the application of a variety of crafts, such as carpentry or agriculture, so relevant for India's contemporary agrarian economy. He also believed that sound education should produce a useful citizen – a whole man and woman with harmonious development of all the four aspects of human life – hand, head, heart and spirit. His educational philosophy stresses 'service to humanity' irrespective of caste, creed, colour, religion or nation. It emphasizes the promotion of everlasting world peace.

Rabindranath Tagore, a Nobel Laureate, developed an alternative approach to education by setting up Shantiniketan, West Bengal, in 1921, a co-educational school with progressive features which was a radical step at the time. In that school classes were held in the open air and children learnt by engaging themselves in nature study and craft work. It is important to mention that Tagore had dropped out of school early. Yet he considered education the most important tool for nation-building. At Shantiniketan, the emphasis was given on self-motivation rather than on discipline and on fostering intellectual curiosity rather than competitive excellence. The contribution of education, according to Tagore, was incomplete if the economic aspect of education was neglected. He also advocated that educational institutions should keep harmony with their surroundings.

In order to understand the concept of inclusive education within the Indian context, one needs to reflect on the history of special education. The formal education of children with disabilities began in India in 1869 when Jane Leupot started a school for 'blind students' in Benares, Uttar Pradesh (Miles, 1997). Miles has also reported that the first formal school for children with intellectual and physical disabilities was established in the eastern part of India in Kurseong in 1918. Aggarwal (1994) reported that by 1966 there were 115 schools for students with a visual impairment, 70 schools for students with a hearing impairment, 25 schools for students with an orthopaedic disability and 27 schools for students with an intellectual disability. According to Pandey and Advani (1997), by 1991 there were about 1,200 special schools in India for students with various types of disability.

In recent years the explosive growth of private schools in India is seen by many to be a result of dissatisfaction with the poor quality of the education provision in government schools (Nambissan, 2003; Singal and Rouse, 2003). The role and function of all schools should be determined in the light of the needs of the specific community. A comparative study of government, government aided and private schools of Delhi by Qamar and Zahid (2001) came to three major findings. First, private schools enrol students with higher socio-economic status than the other schools. Second, private schools impose more rigorous screening at the time of admission and allow only selected students to appear at the board examinations. Third, government-aided schools showed a value addition of 22% and the private-aided school showed an addition of 19%, so the private schools did not make any value addition despite their screening bases.

Concept of inclusive education

The question is often raised why inclusive education is necessary as a new educational strategy particularly in those countries that have a commitment to and apparent existing policies on education for all. UNESCO (1994) states that,

> All children learn together, wherever possible, regardless of any difficulties or differences they may have. Inclusive schools must recognize and respond to the diverse needs of their students, accommodating both different styles and rates of learning and ensuring quality education to all [in approaching] curricula, organizational arrangements, teaching strategies, resource use and partnerships with their communities.

Thus, inclusive education emphasizes child-to-child learning and the participation of parents and community in the planning and execution of services for children in general and disabled children in particular.

The term 'inclusive education' has a different meaning for developed and developing countries (Tha, 2008). In developing countries, a large number of children are 'excluded' from the schooling process due to social, economic and physical disability factors. There are an estimated 25 million children out of school in India due to factors such as, poverty, gender disability and caste (World Bank, 2004). It is sometimes used in the UK to describe practices within special schools (Spurgeon, 2007). Further, in the context of the UK, it is no longer associated with disability or special needs, but rather with school attendance or behaviour (Ainscow et al., 2006). Ainscow et al. developed a typology of six ways of thinking about inclusion:

- Inclusion as a concern with disabled students and other categorized as 'having special educational needs'
- Inclusion as a response to disciplinary exclusion
- Inclusion in relation to all groups seen as being vulnerable to exclusion
- Inclusion as developing school for all
- Inclusion as 'Education for All'
- Inclusion as a principle approach to education and society.

According to UNESCO (2001), inclusive education is seen as 'a process of addressing and responding to the diversity of the needs of all learners through increasing participation in learning, cultures and communities, and reducing exclusion from education and from within education'. In fact, the purpose is that the entire education system will facilitate a learning environment where teachers and learners embrace and welcome the challenge and benefits of diversity.

Inclusion means not only the inclusion of those with disabilities, but also socially and economically disadvantaged children belonging to diverse, cultural and linguistic groups. It is used normally in the context of the education of children with disabilities resulting mainly due to physical and sensory impairments. Singal (2005) perceives inclusive education as 'a concept that has been adapted from the international discourse, but has not been engaged with in the Indian scenarios'. According to Mastropieri and Scruggs (2004), inclusive education means 'that students with disabilities are served primarily in the general education settings, under the responsibility of (a) regular classroom teacher when necessary and justifiable, students with disabilities may also receive some of their instruction in another setting, such as (b) resource room'. In fact, the concept of inclusive education has been originated in Europe and taken a 'whole school' approach to institutional change and also influenced by the social model of disability (Peters, 2004). The Indian Parliament passed the Persons with Disabilities (PWD) Act of 1995, which grants legal opportunities, protection of rights and full participation to persons with disabilities. The Act provides to 'ensure that every child with disabilities has access to free education in an appropriate environment till he attains the age of eighteen years'. In addition, the Act also provides for the reservation of 3% of seats in admission into higher and professional institutions.

The issue and context of exclusion in India is different in some aspects, but not in all, from other developed countries. For example, in the UK, exclusion from schools normally refers to 'disciplinary exclusion' arising due to the conduct of children or behaviour that does not conform to school rules. In India, three broad categories of exclusion can be identified: first, exclusion as understood in the UK; second, exclusion as a consequence of social and economic factors; and third, exclusion due to internal or cultural and curricular factors. More recently, Sayeed (2008) discusses a social inclusion perspective which holds that education makes it possible to prevent individuals from getting marginalized and socially excluded from the mainstream of society.

Inclusive education may be organized at three levels in India: at national or state level, at the individual school level and at the teacher or classroom level. At the national level, the Indian Constitution states that 'free and compulsory education should be provided to all children until they complete the age of fourteen years'. The first Education Commission in India, popularly known as the Kothari Commission, 1964–66 addressed the issues of access and participation by all. It commissions a 'common school system' open to all children irrespective of caste, creed, community, religion, economic condition and social status. For inclusive education, a school can take initiative through a shared vision by members of school management, teachers and staff. The school needs to examine its admission policy and the composition of its student population. This would seem to be the most essential factor for making a school successfully inclusive. Some children may not be able to cope with the school-level curriculum and they may need it to be individualized. Thus, the individual-level curriculum based on the abilities of the child would focus on larger objectives of education.

Inclusive education differs from commonly held notions of 'integration' and 'mainstreaming', which tend to be concerned principally with disability and special educational needs. By contrast, inclusion is about the child's right to participate and the school's duty to provide education to the child. Inclusion rejects the use of special schools or classrooms to separate students with disabilities from those without. Julka (2005) reported that recommendations to send children with disabilities to mainstream schools were first made in the Sargent Report in 1944 and again in 1964 by the Kothari Commission.

Ainscow (1999) explained different perspectives on inclusive education on the basis of the understanding of 'educational difficulties'. According to him, educational difficulties experienced by a child could be attributed to the disabilities within the child. Second, they might be construed as due to a 'mismatch' between the characteristics of a child and the organizational and curricular arrangements available in the school. Third, difficulties may result from the limitations of the curriculum referred to in a broader sense to include all the planned and unplanned experiences offered by schools. Oliver (1996) highlighted that traditionally discussions of inclusive education are concerned with disabilities. There are different models and definitions of 'disability' which are in common use. For example, the medical model defines disability as a physical, medically diagnosed deficit which handicaps. In the UK, the medical model is reflected in the psycho-medical dominance of segregated education for children with disabilities in the 1950s (Clough and Corbett, 2000). In India, the Ministry of Social Justice and Empowerment, which is responsible for people with disabilities, has a medically inspired classification system whereby one's disability is categorized as loco motoric, visual, hearing, speech or mental (GOI, 2005).

The World Health Organization estimates that 10% of any population are disabled (Thomas, 2005; Bagley, 2000). It is also felt that with disability or impairment, both being a cause and consequence of poverty, the Millennium Development Goals cannot be achieved without a specific disability focus (DFID, 2000). Some writers are of the opinion that disability is not only closely related to poverty, but also becoming widely recognized as a cross-cutting development issue that bears relevance to all dimensions of social exclusion (Thomas, 2005); although, social exclusion is not necessarily the opposite of inclusion (Kabeer, 2000).

In fact, it is widely believed that inclusive education has the potential to improve teaching processes for all children as well as fulfilling their rights. According to Gardner (1993), inclusive education does not believe in the individualistic form of learning primarily based on linguistic and logical-mathematical intelligence. It explores the abilities and potentials of children in other areas of intelligence such as spatial, musical, kinaesthetic, interpersonal and intra-personal.

Challenges

As briefly stated, there are three kinds of inclusion facing different kinds of challenges:

a   Physically handicapped children, besides suffering economic disadvantages, may also have to suffer a social stigma. Many people might perceive them as worthless for society and hence subject them to at best sympathy and at worst neglect. In addition, the schools may not have adequate infrastructure or amenities or technical support for taking up their challenges.
b   Socio-economically disadvantaged children, besides facing socio-economic constraints, suffer because of the concept of development in terms of gross domestic product (GDP) which is basically a structural factor that defines exclusiveness rather than inclusiveness. This is precisely the reason that the public schools, despite rhetoric, are neglected and the policy makers talk of the public private (PP) model for allowing the privatization of education.
c   Getting alienated children involved in their schooling requires changing the traditional approach to teaching and the world view of teachers in favour of child-centric education, and parents who are in favour of genuine education for self-development rather than rote learning for passing examinations. They also recommend social incentives in the job market to those who develop their whole personality rather than focusing on those who have achieved higher marks. Social and economic exclusion resulting in children's non-enrolment and non-completion of school years remains a major hurdle as well as a major challenge for policy makers and educational practitioners in India.

In summary, the challenges of inclusion in India are at three different levels such as first, the inclusion of children with disabilities; second, inclusion of children from socially and economically disadvantaged groups who earlier have not attended school or have dropped out after only a few years of schooling; and third, the inclusion of children who are in classrooms but feel alienated due to non-relevant curriculum and teacher-centred pedagogy. Daniels and Garner (2000) list six challenges of the 'new' pedagogy for inclusive education. Three of them relate to the special education needs (SEN) policies which are not relevant for the Indian context. The other three relate to the national curriculum, teachers' training and information and the uses of communication technology in education.

The National Policy of Education (1986) recommended as a goal 'to integrate the handicapped with the general community at all levels as equal partners to prepare them for normal growth and to enable them to face life with courage and confidence'. Further, the Delhi Declaration on Education for All (1994) pledged that 'we will ensure a place for every child in a school or appropriate education programme according to his or her capacities'.

Societal responses

The media has always played an important role in providing information to the public. There is no department in education which is not influenced by information technology and the news media. Different mediums such as print, radio, television, internet, etc. play a vital role in the education sector. They also play an important role in forming public opinion in modern society which is clearly shown in the inclusive education debate.

Researchers have shown that inclusive education results in improved social development and academic outcomes for all learners (Rustermier, 2008). It leads to the development of social skills and better social interaction because learners are exposed to a realistic environment in which they have to interact with other learners, each one having unique characteristics, interest and abilities. The purpose of development is to offer people more options. One of their options is access to income not as an end in itself but as a means to acquiring human well-being. But there are other options as well, including lifelong learning, knowledge, political freedom, personal security, community participation and guaranteed human rights. People cannot be reduced to a single dimension as economic creatures (UNDP, 1990, p. iii).

Reflections

The fundamental principle of inclusive education is that all children should have the opportunity to learn together. Diversity is characteristic of all children and youth. Diversity is to be found within each individual child. Children are the future of any country. There is a noticeable dearth of empirical and academic research on inclusive education in India. Dyer (2000) suggests that there is a need for more research into both the implication and impact of inclusive education in India. Actually, there is an urgent need to develop a long-term strategy in which every step taken adds to the sound base for inclusive education. The interventions for inclusive education include early detection and identification, functional and formal assessment, appropriate educational placement, preparation for an individualized educational plan and a special focus on girls. A zero rejection policy has been adapted under *Sarva Shiksha Abhiyan* (SSA, i.e., Education for All) of the Ministry of Human Resource Development, which ensures that every child with special needs, irrespective of the kind, category and degree of disability, is provided with meaningful and quality education. It is also important that teachers, principals and others maintain a positive attitude to inclusion. They must be convinced of the benefits that inclusive practices bring to all children. Inclusive education needs to be seen in context of general problems that education systems face around the world. UNESCO (2008) states that the world needs to recruit 18 million new teachers by 2015 if it is to fill the teacher gap. Verma's (2002) study found the following: social and cultural inclusion involves recognition, respect and acceptance of minorities, and also co-operation, solidarity and participation. Inclusive societies and governments promote a system in which all their members can fully participate and share its welfare provision, irrespective of social origin, gender or ethnicity. Inclusion covers other things such as education, employment, social security, health, culture and political activity.

Bibliography

Aggarwal, R. (1994). India. In: K. Mazurck and M. A. Winzer (eds), *Comparative Studies in Special Education*, 179–203. Washington, DC: Gallaudet University Press.

Ainscow, M. (1999). *Understanding the Development of Inclusive School*. London: Falmer.

Ainscow, M., Booth, T. and Dyson, A. (2006). *Improving Schools, Developing Inclusion*. Abingdon: Routledge.

Alkire, S. and Santos, M. E. (2010). *Acute Multi-Dimensional Poverty: A New Index for Developing Countries. Working Paper 38*. Oxford: OPHI, University of Oxford.

Bagley, C. (2000). Temperament. In: M. Davies (ed), *Encyclopaedia of Social Work*, 64. Oxford: Blackwell.

Clough, P. and Corbett, J. (2000). *Theories of Inclusive Education*. London: Paul Chapman Publishing, Sage.

Daniels, H. and Garner, P. (2000). Inclusive education: Challenges for the new millennium. In: H. Daniels and P. Garner (eds), *World Yearbook of Education 1999: Inclusive Education*. London: Kogan Page.

Department of Education. (1986). *National Policy on Education 1986*. New Delhi: Ministry of Human Resource Department, Government of India.

DFID. (2000). *Disability, Poverty and Development*. London: Department for International Development.

Dyer, C. (2000). *Operation Blackboard: Policy Implementation in Inclusive Elementary Education*. Oxford: Symposium Books.

Fagg, H. (2001). Back to the Sources: A Study of Gandhi's Basic Education. Dissertation submitted to the Department of Educational Studies, University of Oxford.

Gardner, H. (1993). *Frames of Mind: The Theory of Multiple Intelligence*. London: Fontana Press.

GOI. (1964–66). Report of the Education Commission: Education and National Development. New Delhi: Ministry of Education.

GOI. (2002). India 2002: A Reference Annual. Publication Division, Ministry of Information and Broadcasting. New Delhi: Government of India.

GOI. (2005). Ministry of Social Justice and Empowerment Annual Report 2004–05. New Delhi: Government of India.

Govinda, R. and Biswal, K. (2006). *Access to Elementary Education in India: Identifying Issues, Gaps and Priorities*. India Country Analytical Report, Chapter I, Consortium for Research on Educational Access, Transitions and Equity.

Hulme, H., Moore, K. and Shepherd, A. (2001). *Chronic Poverty Meanings and Analytical Frameworks*. Manchester: IDPM, University of Manchester (CPRC-Working paper 12).

Hum Dev Report. (1990, 1997, 2014). United Nations Development Programme (UNDP). New York: Oxford University Press.

India, Ministry of Human Resource Development. (1986). National Policy on Education 1986; Program on Action 1992. www.Mhrd/gov/in/sites/upload_files/mhrd/files/uploa d_document/upe.pdf.

Julka, A. (2005). Educational provisions and practices for learners with disabilities in India. Paper presented at the Inclusive and Supportive Education Congress, University of Strathclyde, Glasgow.

Kabeer, N. (2000). Social exclusion, poverty and discrimination: Towards an analytical framework. *IDS Bulletin*, 31(4). Falmer: Institute of Development Studies.

Kamin, S. (1988). The value system and its implication for development in Thailand. In: D. Sinha and H. S. R. Kao (eds), *Social Values and Development: Asian Perspectives*. 152–174. New Delhi: Sage.

Mastropieri, M. A. and Scruggs, T. E. (2004). *The Inclusive Classroom: Strategies for Effective Instruction*. 7. New York: Pearson.

Miles, M. (1997). Disabled learners in South Asia: Lessons from the past for educational exporters. *International Journal of Disability, Development and Education*, 44(2), 97–104.

Ministry of Law, Justice and Company Affairs. (1996). *The Persons with Disabilities (Equal Opportunities, Protection of Rights and Full Participation) Act, 1995*. New Delhi: Government of India.

Nambissan, G. (2003). *Educational deprivation and primary school provision: A study of providers in the city of Calcutta*. IDS Working Paper 187, Social Policy Programme, June 2003. Falmer: Institute of Development Studies.

Oliver, M. (1996). *Understanding Disability: From Theory to Practice*. London: Macmillan.

Pandey, R. S. and Advani, L. (1997). *Perspectives in Disability and Rehabilitation*. New Delhi: Vikash Publishing House.

Pareek, U. (1988). Culture and development: The case of Indonesia. In: D. Sinha and H. S. R. Kao (eds), *Social Values and Development: Asian Perspectives*. 175–196. New Delhi: Sage Publication.

Peters, S. (2004). *Inclusive Education: An EFA Strategy for All Children*. Washington, DC: World Bank.

Qamar, F. and Zahid, M. (2001). Cost, equity, quality and resource use efficiency in senior secondary schools: Some policy imperatives. In: *National Conference: Focus Secondary Education*. New Delhi: NIEPA.

Rustermier, S. (2008). Inclusive education: A world wide movement. http://inclusion.uwe.ac.uk/Inclusion week/articles/Worldwide.htm. Retrieved: 1 August, 2016.

Sayeed, Y. (2008). Education and poverty reduction/eradication: Omission, fashions and promises. In: S. Maile (ed) *Education and Poverty Reduction Strategies: Issues of Policy Coherence*. Cape Town: HSRC Press.

Singal, N. (2005). Responding to difference: Policies to support 'inclusive education' in India. Paper presented at the Inclusive and Supportive Education Congress, University of Strathclyde, Glasgow.

Singal, N. and Rouse, M. (2003). 'We do inclusion': Practitioner perspectives in some 'inclusive school' in India. *Perspectives in Education, Special Issue: The inclusion/exclusion debate in South Africa and developing countries*, 21(3), 85–98.

Sinha, J. B. P. (1990). Role of psychology in national development. In: G. Misra (ed), *Applied Social Psychology in India*. 177–199. New Delhi: Sage Publication.

Spurgeon, W. (2007). Diversity and choice for children with complex needs. In: Cigman (ed), *Included or Excluded? The Challenge of the Mainstream for Some SEN Children*. London: Routledge.

Tha, M. (2008). From special to inclusive education. In: C. Bagley and G. Verma (eds), *Challenges for Inclusion: Educational and Social Studies from Britain and the Indian Sub-Continent*. 1–20. Rotterdam: Sense Publisher.

The Delhi Declaration. (1994). As a Part of the Report on Education for All summit of Nine High-Population Countries: Final Report New Delhi, 12–16 December, 1993, UNESCO, Paris.

Thomas, P. (2005). *Disability, Poverty and the Millennium Development Goals: Relevance, Challenges and Opportunities for DFID*. London: Disability Knowledge and Research.

UNESCO. (1994). *The Salamanca Statement and Framework on Special Needs Education*. Paris: UNESCO.

UNESCO. (2001). *The Open File on Inclusive Education*. Paris: UNESCO.

UNESCO. (2008). *EFA Global Monitoring Report – Education for All by 2015, Will We Make it?* Paris and Oxford: UNESCO and Oxford University Press.

Verma, G. K. (2002). *Migrants and Social Inclusion: Lifelong Learning and the New Europe*. University of Malaya, Asia-Europe Institute.

World Bank. (2004). Project Appraisal Document on a Proposed Credit of the Amount of SDR 334.9 million to the Republic of India for an Elementary Education Project (Sarva Shiksha Abhiyan). Hum Dev Sector Unit, South Asia region.

World Bank. (2011). *World Development Indicators Database*. Washington, DC: World Bank.

6

THE FIELD OF EDUCATION IN NEW ZEALAND

Inclusion/exclusion in schooling

Charles Crothers

> Inclusivity involves 'How groups are privileged, marginalised, judged, included etc. through everyday languages and practises and also the frameworks in which these practises are embedded'
>
> Gordon-Burns (2012: p. xx)

Introduction

The sociology of education has always been concerned with various dimensions of inclusion and exclusion and their effects on the distribution of achievement in the education systems of different countries. This interest has led to studies of access to education more generally, and especially access to education of high quality. In the 'new sociology of education' there is a focus on the content of subject-matter in schooling and how this is framed and delivered for different social groupings (Moore, 2007). Beyond this, the focus is on how the social organisation of education is intertwined with wider economic, social, political and cultural factors, as well as with the processes by which educational experiences and credentials are drawn on in the construction of identities and collectivities. While there does seem to be some social mobility between generations, it has repeatedly been shown that most education systems emphasise the reproduction of class and of material relations, which best serve those whose social background is highly attuned to the prevalent criteria for privilege. Like its organisation and the curriculum, the conduct of education tends to be subtly shaped by biases of gender and class (Moore, 2007). These processes are reinforced by the fact that teachers tend to emphasise static cultural values.

This chapter describes the interplay of inclusion and exclusion in the education system of New Zealand. First it will look at key policy decisions, then at research findings and finally at inclusivity and its problems in practice.

Policies of inclusiveness

The ideology of the education system in New Zealand has been dominated by a concern for inclusiveness. In the early decades of the colony (from the 1840s on), schooling (at least of some sort) was determinedly pushed out across the country, including to the then-tribal Maori. A major extension of education was the provision of free secondary schooling in the late 1930s by the reforming Labour Party which mobilised around the ringing statement by then Education Minister Peter Fraser:

> The Government's objective is that every person whatever his level of academic ability, whether he be rich or poor, whether he live in town or country, has a right, as a citizen, to a free education of the kind for which he is best fitted and to the fullest extent of his powers.

This quote is very often seen as foundational; see Minto, 2004 for assessment of the New Zealand education system against the standard set by Fraser. The next wave of development in New Zealand's education system was the massive expansion of low-cost tertiary education in the 1960s which extended opportunities to school-leavers and people in late teenage years. Moreover, these steps have been encouraged by prevailing educational philosophies which emphasise a broad approach to a liberal general education facilitating citizenship and producing graduates who are 'good persons' – people who enjoy good physical and mental health. While the 'liberal' ideology of education has held widely within New Zealand, it has been supported particularly by teachers who remain heavily unionised and vigorously led. More generally, until the most recent decades these effects have been reinforced by traditional New Zealand culture which has emphasised egalitarianism and inclusiveness, at least in social class terms, and to a large extent in the bi-cultural framing of Pakeha (non-Maori New Zealanders) relationships with Maori.

However, at every stage 'countervailing forces' have pushed back against these tendencies under various banners: particularly those of effectiveness, efficiency and mono-culturalism. Secondary schooling, and even more so tertiary education, were for many decades the preserve of the wealthy. Despite the liberal discourse, the secondary education system from World War II on cast school-leavers into two roughly equally sized groups of goats and sheep with only the latter allowed to go on to the higher levels of secondary schooling, let alone higher education. Ironically, in the 1980s, a Labour government instituted general state reforms which were the scourge of New Zealand during the 'Rogernomics' decade. (This period is commonly named after the neo-liberal reforming Minister of Finance Roger Douglas.) The entire education system was forced into considerable alignment with neo-liberal ideologies.

Since then there has been some reversion to the ideological centre under 'third way' government, most recently succeeded by a lurch again to the right (this time from a National Party-led government). A range of critics and many members of the wider public are concerned either that all students achieve at least minimal levels of performance by national standards and/or that well-established Euro-centric notions of educational process and subject-matter content are adhered to. Endeavouring to meet the goals of various cultural subgroups is seen at best as diverting from these more worthy educational goals and at worst crippling the entire educational system (or vulnerable groupings within it). 'Politically correct' emphasis on participative, culture-friendly education processes (e.g. the learning of Maori language and culture) are seen as diversionary and probably harmful, and likely to undermine the possibility of the disadvantaged rallying against their disadvantage. The confusion accompanies demographic changes, as New Zealand has, in recent decades, become far more ethnically differentiated where more open displays of class and a range of other social differences have been valorised (Crothers, 2013, 2014).

New Zealand is an interesting 'research laboratory' for the investigation of these complexly intertwined themes as the country is small and highly integrated organisationally. Once objectives are set, they can be speedily achieved. Moreover, national affluence affords the investment of considerable resources. Indeed, the New Zealand education system often achieves considerable international recognition for the quality and the vigour of its ability to adapt.

This capacity for adaptive-ness has facilitated inclusiveness; for example, Gordon-Burns (2012: 156) argues that 'Several developments in Aotearoa New Zealand have advanced change towards an inclusive education system faster than has occurred in many other countries' and then cites several policy documents. Drivers of adaptability include:

- active advocacy by parents and educational interest-groups;
- the development and implementation of appropriate central government strategies;
- collaboration on UN conventions and statements;
- research highlighting advantages of particular approaches.

At an abstract level, policies of inclusivity can be seen as honouring the country's constitutional foundation: the Treaty of Waitangi. (The Treaty – in Maori 'Te Tiriti' – was signed in 1840 between a representative of the British Crown and Maori chiefs.) There is considerable consensus about the various axes of inclusiveness, but unclear rankings of their differential importance, as the following statement by Gordon-Burns shows. Inclusiveness, for example, is not just about economic disadvantage but also about 'the perspectives of Maori and cultural responsiveness, Te Tiriti o Waitangi and bi-culturalism, inter-culturalism, gender, sexualities, economic disadvantage, age, religion and disability'. However, major problems still arise in actually enacting inclusion in practice.

Research findings on New Zealand education

International and national contexts

New Zealand has usually scored well in early rounds of international comparisons in the well-known International Association for the Evaluation of Education (IAE) studies. However, more recently the results have been less positive. The gap between high and low performing students remains one of the widest in the Organisation of Economic Cooperation and Development (OECD). These low performing students are likely to be Maori or Pasifika (New Zealanders born in (mainly Polynesian) Pacific countries such as Samoa, Tonga, Cook Islands and their New Zealand-born descendants) and/or from low socio-economic communities. (For a more specific comparison of UK versus New Zealand approaches to educational reform see Thrupp, 2004.)

Data sources and educational research in New Zealand

Statistical information is extensive, and much has been available in official reports housed on the 'Education Counts' website (www.education.counts.nz). The backbone of the information is collected through a variety of (often annual) surveys of schools and other authorities: covering student characteristics, school characteristics, such as the physical plant, characteristics of school-leavers, characteristics of school trustees, etc. Some of these include important 'supplementary' information which allows investigation of the influence on student achievement by a school's characteristics and the characteristics of the surrounding area. The construction of decile ratings of schools in terms of parental occupations, for example, has been a lever for improving the allocation levels of funding support as well as for monitoring school performance in relation to socio-economic status. In addition, in recent years, national standards have been configured as a neo-liberal strategy to ensure that as many students as possible receive a sufficient education. There have, therefore, been standards testing at least for primary schools, which provides (hotly contested) information on both individual and school performances. It is feared that teachers then teach 'to test' – setting objectives that are too narrow and failing to educate their students in the vast range of materials that they should be exposed to. Until the 1980s an inspectorate, made up of professionals who were both advisor-mentors and assessors of teaching quality, were available to teachers at both primary and secondary levels. This aspect of the system was replaced in the 1980s by the Education Review Office (ERO). Although ERO staff are available less to give advice, they are in a better position to make formal and public assessments.

Thus, there are large and sophisticated statistical and research apparatuses devoted to recording and studying educational processes in New Zealand. The system is heavily invested in monitoring and feedback as mechanisms for improvement and in evidence-based approaches to providing high-quality education. However, the socio-demographic data which is routinely collected is limited and this restricts the extent to which particular axes of inclusiveness are able to be monitored and studied.

The New Zealand education research system has heavily invested in an array of significant research projects, with the Ministry of Education funding research programmes, and the New Zealand portions of several important international projects. These provide information and knowledge essential for assessing how inclusiveness is working in New Zealand, and results of research studies can have major impacts on the concerns of policy-makers (and to some extent the public).

Other research comes from the angle of children and youth and has generated much information about the wider spectrum of their attitudes and behaviours.

The New Zealand system of education: schools, students and their characteristics

The backbone of this chapter is a portrait of the numbers and types of schools in New Zealand and some of their key student and other characteristics. From this skeletal description some of the structure and operation of these schools can be inferred and used as a foundation for adding further information. Furthermore, much of the history of schooling in New Zealand is inscribed in the present structure. The range of types available also affects the extent to which inclusion is possible.

Free primary and secondary education is a right for all New Zealand citizens and permanent residents from a student's 5th birthday until the end of the calendar year following the student's 19th birthday, and is compulsory for students between the ages of 6 and 16 (15 with parental and school permission). (A recent proposal by the New Zealand government, called Schools Plus, would see students required to remain in some form of education until age 18. Disabled students with special educational needs can stay until the end of the calendar year they turn 21.)

In 2011 there were:

- 211,000 enrolments in over 5,100 licensed or licence-exempt early childhood education services, employing 19,800 teachers;
- 762,683 students in 2,543 primary and secondary schools, employing 52,000 teachers;
- 466,000 enrolments in tertiary education providers and 195,000 enrolments in industry-based training in 29 public institutions and nearly 700 private training establishments.

The New Zealand education system is organised in four fairly distinct levels: pre-primary, primary, secondary, tertiary (or post-secondary) and 'after study'. At each level schools can be distinguished according to whether they are public or private, by ownership, whether they are co-educational or single-sex, to religious orientation and so on.

The transition points between the different levels of schooling are important as it is particularly in transitioning between levels that family/community effects are highlighted.

Pre-school

Many children, and the policy aim is to provide for all, attend some form of early childhood education (ECE) before they begin school at age 5. The pre-school sector is state-supported but not provided by the state, and is subdivided into different types of learning arrangements which are shaped by the purpose of the organisation. The distribution of children in these frameworks is as follows:

- 9% Play centre (birth to school age)
- 21% Kindergarten (ages 3–5)
- 5% Kohanga Reo (ages 0–5, state funded Maori language nest)
- 65% Chartered Early Childhood Centres (ages 0–5; licensed and state funded, usually privately owned).

The various forms of pre-school education differ in the requirements and in their effects. For example, since play schools require parental attendance, working parents (and some single parents) can seldom use this approach.

Recent international testing data show that a learner's participation in ECE will have a significant impact on their subsequent educational achievement at age 15, with the benefits being particularly significant for children from disadvantaged backgrounds. Following these findings, government expenditure on ECE has tripled in the last ten years, with 87.5% coming from the Ministries of Education and the rest from the Ministry of Social Development. The next task in ECE needs to ensure that it makes the difference it is capable of making, particularly for Maori and Pasifika learners, and children from low socio-economic backgrounds, who do not access as much education in early childhood as others, and who when they do participate have, so far, not benefited as much.

Primary (and intermediate)

Although many children did not attend school – particularly in rural areas where labour was more important in the earliest days of Pakeha settlement, those who did go to school went to schools governed by the provincial government or a church or a private organisation. Since the population was small and thinly scattered with poor transport networks in the many isolated areas, many tiny schools were set up so that children had only to travel short distances to school. The quality of education and the physical school varied widely. The first free national system of primary education was established by the Education Act 1877. This sought to establish standards of quality of education, and to be 'free, compulsory and secular'. Today 85% of the children attend a state school (government owned and fully funded); another 11% study in state-integrated schools (many formerly schools of the Roman Catholic Church); 4% are enrolled in private schools; 1% in kura (Maori language immersion); 1% in correspondence schools; and 0.5% in schools for children with special needs. Community and family influences on children's achievement are considerable but variable (Biddulph et al., 2003).

Secondary

There are three types of secondary school:

- state (government funded) – serving 82% of the students;
- state integrated schools (former private schools which are now '"integrated" into the state system on a basis which will preserve and safeguard the special character of the education provided by them') – 12.4%; and
- private (approximately 25% government funded, supplemented by tuition fees) – 5.6%.

Historically, access to secondary schooling was far more limited than access to primary schools. In 1900, less than 10% of New Zealand's population went to fee-paying secondary schools, with the aim of going on to university education and then to careers in the professions. The Education Act 1914 required all secondary schools to offer free education to all those who passed a Proficiency examination and by 1917, 37% of the population went to secondary school. Secondary schools were run along the lines of the English grammar school system, offering a traditional curriculum which was suitable only for those able to attend university. This curriculum approach continues to exert a strong influence on secondary schools today.

An attempt to address this limited curriculum was made early in the twentieth century by introducing technical high schools which offered a more 'practical' and 'relevant' curriculum, but these had limited success, and the dual system was strongly class-based. There was also a growth in numbers of district high schools (to suit small centres) from the early twentieth century. From the 1930s on, other attempts were made to reform secondary schooling. The Thomas report of 1944 examined alternatives to the unpopular technical high schools and its approach to the curriculum was to remain in place for the following fifty years. A School Certificate exam, at the end of the fifth form, was implemented while the Matriculation exam was replaced by a University Entrance exam. A common core curriculum provided material drawn from both practical and academic strands, with the aim of catering for students of widely differing abilities, interests and backgrounds. But schools resisted the full impact these reforms might have had by streaming students into different ability classes (often as measured by IQ tests), and giving these classes different versions of the core curriculum.

Early in the 1980s another round of reform began (amongst a wide array of neo-liberal changes in New Zealand during the period of 'Rogernomics'), particularly addressing the administration of education. *Administering for Excellence* was written by a group drawn from industry. Termed the *Picot Report* after its chair (a supermarket magnate), the report provided a business model of education management. *Tomorrow's Schools*, the programme which implemented the recommendations, involved replacing the Department of Education with a Ministry with a focus on policy rather than delivery. Schools were turned into formally autonomous entities managed by boards of trustees. Curriculum reforms were finally completed in the 1990s and are currently still in force. In 1989, the school leaving age was raised to the present age of 16. Finally, the School Certificate examination was eased out.

The most recent secondary school assessment system is the National Certificate of Educational Achievement (NCEA), which has been planned, implemented and operated in schools under a cloud of controversy. NCEA is a standards-based assessment which measures pupils on whether or not they can perform a task or possess a skill by breaking subjects down into discrete parcels of knowledge that are tested in chunks throughout the year. Alternative international examinations are also being used by some schools – the Cambridge International Examinations (CIE), and the International Baccalaureate (IBO) Diploma Programme. At least in principle, these examinations use various assessments, including high-stakes exams, to assess pupils at the end of a course of study on how well they have mastered all the learning materials relevant to a given secondary school subject. (For an overview of teenagers and their educational experiences see e.g. Wylie et al., 2009.)

In addition to the general state schools, there is a range of other state-funded options for secondary schooling, all of which teach the New Zealand curriculum. These include:

- kura kaupapa Maori, state schools catering for Years 1–8 or Years 1–13 where teaching is in the Maori language and is based on Maori culture and values;
- special schools for students with disabilities;
- integrated schools – schools that used to be private, and that keep their special character, which receive government funding supplemented by charging attendance fees (since they own their own buildings and land);
- designated character schools, which have been allowed to develop their own objectives to reflect a particular set of values (e.g. Maori immersion teaching);
- the Correspondence School, which provides distance education for children who have medical or other problems or live too far from a school.

Tertiary

Since the nineteenth century, the New Zealand university system has expanded dramatically. In 2010 there were 466,000 students enrolled in formal study programmes with tertiary education providers including 8 universities, 18 polytechnics, 3 wananga (Maori-framed universities), 36 Industry Training Organisations and around 700 private training establishments (as of 1 November 2011).

In June 1869 the Otago Provincial Council passed the Otago University Ordinance, creating the University of Otago which opened in 1871 with a staff of three professors. In the meantime, the University of New Zealand was created by Act of Parliament in September 1870 and became the examining and degree-granting body for all New Zealand university institutions. Constituent Colleges were established in Christchurch (Canterbury College, 1873), Auckland (1883) and Wellington (Victoria University College, 1897). In 1962 the University of New Zealand was disestablished and the four university colleges became full universities in their own right. In 1964 two new universities were created: the University of Waikato to cater for the needs of the area around Hamilton and the fast-growing Waikato region, and Massey University in Palmerston North was founded as the New Zealand (later Massey) Agricultural College in 1926. In 1990 Lincoln University was established. Originally set up as a School of Agriculture in 1878, it was renamed Canterbury Agricultural College in 1896, became Lincoln College in 1961 as a constituent college of the University of Canterbury before it became a full, self-governing university. Finally, begun as the Auckland Technical School in 1895, the Auckland University of Technology was established in 2000.

Funding for tertiary education organisations is through a component of the Parliament-approved overall government budget termed 'Vote Tertiary Education' and is administered by the Tertiary Education Commission. Funding for student support is largely through 'Vote Social Development' with policy and administration shared between the Ministry of Education (policy lead), StudyLink (loan and allowance grants) and Inland Revenue Department (collection of loan repayments). (For a general discussion of investment in education see e.g. Nair et al., 2007.)

Both participation in tertiary education and its costs have increased over recent decades. This has led to a stronger emphasis on ensuring the quality and value for money of tertiary provision. Improved information provision and stronger performance incentives for students and providers are resulting in a stronger focus on qualification completions and progression to higher levels. However, older images of quality education (often stressing the learning of an Anglo-European cultural canon) are under threat.

Although the tertiary sector was one of the last areas in New Zealand government services to fall prey to Rogernomics, the effect of neo-liberalism on it has been considerable. Universities have been encouraged to develop a wide array of courses, to be as commercial as possible while university teaching and especially research have been made tightly accountable. A wide range of studies have investigated the reforms and their effects. Strathdee (2011) argues that reducing access to higher education and concentrating funding for research in the universities has created a more elitist system of higher education. Because the attention of most staff is on their research performance, which is now measured at 6 yearly intervals, it is likely that teaching standards will drop. Moreover, economic pressures push universities into offering tuition through large classes where contact with academic staff is minimal.

Access is considerable and patterns complex. Strathdee and Engler's study (2012) draws upon a national data set of over 45,000 young people to assess their propensity to progress to bachelor level study, while controlling for their ethnic backgrounds, their socio-economic status (as measured by the decile of the last secondary school they attended), their gender and their school achievement. The results are complex – with low achieving Asians in high ranked schools less likely to proceed along with low achieving Maori in lower ranked schools, but there is no difference overall between continuing to further education between those Maori and those Pakeha with similar levels of educational performance.

Axes of inclusion/exclusion

Keys to inclusion or exclusion in institutions of education at different levels are social class, streaming and zoning as well as ethnicity, location, age, family situation, disability, family type, home schooling and alternative education and country of birth.

Social class

Although the ideology of New Zealand education has often confronted head-on the effects of social class, it has more often been handled obliquely. New Zealand's education system is middle-class friendly, especially in relation to the fraction Bourdieu termed high in cultural capital, and even supportive of the thin layering of upper class. It has been less supportive of the business component of the middle class, at least in the eyes of some commentators (Crothers, 2013), by not sufficiently promoting the values and skills which are suitable for business people. The upper working class has varied historically in its interest in and need for education, with a concern for upward mobility being stressed at some historical periods such as during the period of the reforming Labour Party at mid-century (and also earlier). Technical education and apprenticeship systems have been provided for this grouping but the ways of doing so has varied over time. Some reaches of the working class have regularly been ill-served by schooling, and the situation is aggravated by a misfit between some working-class culture values and the predominantly middle-class ethos of schooling.

Upper class interests have been served through a small set of elite secondary schools (many of which are boarding schools and many which are 'private') and which serve as a conveyor belt through to the senior professions such as medical practice and law. These schools emphasise a mix of high academic standards and involvement in a range of other activities including elite team sports and general acquisition of cultural and social capital.

In general, one can say that schooling has been captured by cultural capital-rich fractions of the middle class and serve their interests best, while other groupings receive less consideration. Many schools heavily subscribed to by working-class children flounder and founder under the weight of educational difficulties, although some are able to rise above their challenges. Recently, child poverty – exhibited, for example, in children coming to school without lunch and/or not having eaten breakfast – has been repaired through a government-supported food-in-school scheme.

'Technical education' in the zone of the highly skilled upper working class generally had been provided by secondary-level technical colleges (although these were phased out as not providing a sufficiently general education), and later by the establishment of polytechnics. A whole structure of apprenticeship education and night classes for adults is provided at many secondary schools. However, there have been difficulties in maintaining a good service which links vocational education back to families and forward to employers. Opportunities for apprenticeships were reduced during the 1980s and 1990s but were reconstituted in a more limited form in the 2000s. On the one hand, universities have reached out in this direction by including more vocational areas (e.g. taking on the education of teachers and nurses), but they have tended to withdraw from pre-degree teaching. On the other hand, in their quest for 'upward social mobility' some (former) technical institutes have jettisoned lower-level courses in favour of professional reaches. This area of education provision has also been affected by changes in the economy and in society, among them the much-eroded employment conditions in the youth labour market and the decline in the market value of semi- and unskilled labour. A variety of mechanisms endeavour to reduce social exclusion through reconnecting young people to the labour (and training) market (Strathdee, 2011; and as one example of a study of social origins of a particular profession: Heath et al., 2002).

Streams/Tracks

Learning differences are often handled by schools *internally* through tracking/streaming systems which can reinforce social class differences. For many decades these were explicit usually with an alphabetical numbering system indicating the ability levels of students. A school's third form class would, for example, be divided into 3A, 3B, 3C, etc. Although these systems have been abridged over time, they have also reappeared under the drive of neo-liberal inter-school competition.

Zoning/Property

Geographically based state school enrolment schemes were abolished in 1991. Although this opened up the choice of schools for students, it had undesirable consequences with popular high-decile schools experiencing large roll growths, while less popular low-decile school experienced roll declines. The Education Amendment Act 2000 partially solved this problem by putting in place a new 'system for determining enrolment of students in circumstances where a school has reached its roll capacity and needs to avoid overcrowding'. Schools which operate enrolment schemes have a geographically defined 'home zone'. Residence in this zone gives right of entry to the school in the area. Students who live outside the school's home zone can be admitted, if there are places available, in the following order of priority: special programmes; siblings of currently enrolled students; siblings of past students; children of past students; children of board employees and staff; all other students. If there are more applications than available places, then selection must be through a randomly drawn ballot.

The system is complicated by some state schools having boarding facilities for students living beyond the school's zone. Typically these are students who live in isolated farming regions in New Zealand, or whose parents live or work overseas. Many secondary schools, in imitation of private school practice, offer limited scholarships to their boarding establishment to attract particularly valued students, such as rugby players from Fiji!

Critics have suggested that the system is fundamentally unfair as it restricts the choice for parents to choose schools and schools to choose their students. Although the system does allow all students living in the community to have entry, as of right, regardless of their academic or social profile, the ability of groups of lower socio-economic status to purchase a house in the zone of a desirable school is often restricted. There is evidence that property values surrounding some more desirable schools become inflated; this is offset somewhat by the fact that students are accepted from rental accommodation or from homes where they are boarding. Some parents have purposely flouted zone boundaries by giving false addresses or by renting homes in the zone only through the enrolment process and moving out before the student commences school. Some schools now request rates invoices, tenancy agreements or power and telephone bills from parents to prove their residential address (Pearce and Gordon, 2006).

In a range of papers, Thrupp (e.g. 2005, 2008) has argued that schooling is geared to the concerns and interests of the middle classes. Predominantly middle-class school settings set the norm for the system with the middle classes targeting such schools for their children. He argues that those who work in the education sector help to perpetuate middle-class advantage in education: teachers, principals, policy makers, politicians and some academics provide support for these inequitable stances, instead of challenging them and providing support for alternatives which reflect wider interests.

Ethnicity

New Zealand is internationally prominent in its development of ethnically appropriate education, especially for the Maori. Separate schooling for Maori and Pakeha long prevailed. During the early decades of missionary schooling this was necessitated by language limitations. For many years separate schooling for Maori did not encourage maintenance of the Maori language and culture. On the contrary, maintenance of the culture was actively discouraged and use of the language was punished. Maori children in these schools were taught an 'inferior' curriculum designed to train them as domestics and farm labourers (Barrington, 2008).

Although Maori are now heavily urbanised, they remain overly represented amongst the ranks of the under-performing at all levels of the education-system compared to non-Maori. It must be realised that the non-Maori category has been ever-changing as both more Pacific and more Asian 'new settler' migrant children have come into the system in recent decades. Attempts to tackle this deficit have been launched from time to time with the most recent approach casting Maori education as a priority area which emphasises realising potential, understanding and accepting that culture counts.

The approach to education draws on a broader cross-government policy framework: the 'Maori Potential Approach' was developed by Te Puni Kokiri (the Ministry for Maori Development). This emphasises partnership, working together and sharing power. Emphasising the importance of discovering opportunities and realising potential, it represents a move away from focus on deficit, failure, problems and risks. Some 85% of Maori children are included in mainstream education, with the remainder in Maori-language-medium sector.

(There is much discussion of the socio-economic and cultural factors shaping school outcomes (and their inter-relations), e.g., Nash, 2004; Strathdee and Engler, 2012; Tunmer et al., 2004.)

Gender

Primary schools have almost all been co-educational. However, in earlier decades, because allowing boys and girls to mix freely was treated with suspicion, they were often kept apart, sitting on different sides of the room or even in separate classrooms, playing on opposite sides of a divided playground and sometimes entering and leaving school through separate gates. This form of segregation occurred in some co-ed secondary and technical schools as well. Single-sex secondary schools took this a step further, although their establishment from the 1940s on was generally not influenced by philosophical arguments over the supposed benefits and disadvantages of co-education, but merely the most cost-effective option for a small town or a city suburb.

Given the difficulties faced by boys in schools that have been disclosed recently, there has been increasing concern about their falling behind girls. Some of these difficulties are attributed to different lifestyles in terms of physicality, acceptance of schooling disciplines and perhaps facility with language. However, little seems to have been done to repair such deficits, beyond some attempts to recruit more male teachers.

Location

The far-flung nature of the New Zealand rural settlement system led to large numbers of small schools, often with one or two teachers who therefore have to cope with a very wide range of ages. There is also an extensive correspondence school set-up, and New Zealand held, for much of the previous century, an international reputation for expertise in this circumstance of education. However, over time the number of smaller schools has steadily been whittled down and it is seen as an area where costs can be saved, over the objection of local parents who see the closeness of their attachment with schooling dissolving.

Disability

There is no longer a separate *special education* system in New Zealand for disabled learners. The Ministry of Education provides services to about 7,000 students with high or very high needs each year, and funds schools to provide support to other students with more moderate needs. Additional support from Ministry of Education 'Special Education' in terms of additional funding or help from specialists is provided to schools which have such students. For issues affecting the younger disabled see Turnock (2011).

Alternative education

'Alternative education' is practised in some schools where teachers have to cope with many difficult children as well as in schools where middle-class parents want a more relaxed 'liberal' alternative education. Small groupings of schools provide for these categories of student. Most recently, the government has been propelled (through its co-governance agreement with the right-wing ACT Party) to consider setting up 'charter schools' which would be relieved of many of the regulations supposedly afflicting state and private mainstream schools. Such a major breech in the schooling system has led to marked concern from teachers, especially given the uneven record of such schools in other jurisdictions.

Sexuality

Decades ago same-sex attractions were not very apparent amongst school-age children – although, especially in boarding schools, it was recognised that traditional initiation pranks had some strange sexual connotations. Same-sex attractions can be a trigger for bullying (and especially cyber-bullying) and this is built into school-level preventative strategies.

Age

When exam results are taken as rigid entry requirements, age-inappropriate placements can occur, but this has been eased through 'social promotion' which target keeping age-grades of children together. Another age issue is seen in the continued presence of much older youth in secondary schools, some encouraged to stay by schools keen to bolster the prowess of their sporting teams.

Other (birth order, family type, family size)

A range of other characteristics might be relevant but are seldom addressed (Alton-Lee, 2003; Biddulph et al., 2003). Children labelled as deviant often face longer-term problems (Towl, 2013) – including students who become parents (Waterhouse, 2015). As beneficiary rolls continue to grow, there has been concern that children from one-parent homes might be disadvantaged. Very recent government moves to require single parents to carry out paid work might well exacerbate difficulties.

Nationality/country of birth

International students make up 9% of all students in public tertiary education institutions. The five main source countries for international students in New

Zealand were: China (22%), South Korea (16%), India (12%), Japan (10%) and Saudi Arabia (6%).

Country of birth, especially where the native tongue is not English, can exacerbate other ethnic differences. On the other hand, New Zealand has projected itself as a major source for export education with schooling at secondary and especially tertiary levels chasing the international student dollar. This industry, born during a period of high neo-liberalism and therefore a light regulatory regime, has been tarred by some major difficulties. There have even been a few scandals which might have been avoided had there been greater central controls. A range of skews afflicting domestic students can also result as the more needy 'international' students crowd out teacher resources which domestic students would like to access. (For studies into educational issues concerning 'non-New Zealand' students see e.g. Humpage, 2009.)

Private schools and home schooling

Private schools charge fees and are governed by independent boards, but must meet standards to be registered and receive government subsidies (Wane, 2012). Many private schools have boarding facilities with boarding fees paid by parents and scholarships (but then so do some state schools). Some parents and caregivers also choose to educate their children at home, but must provide an equivalent education. Some 1% of New Zealand school children (the majority Pakeha) are home-schooled, often with several children in each family. The numbers have steadily grown over time. Clearly, a major motivation for many involved is to provide Christian (or other culture-specific) education.

Conclusions

New Zealand education can be seen as a field or domain in which crucial societal tendencies are playing out variously over time. The general direction of New Zealand's education, which is to take a middle path between a mono-cultural approach (which inevitably excludes some) and a pluralism (which offers everyone a place in the sun). The extent to which there is deviation from this general path is complex and changing in detail, but while educational research has spurred various efforts for change, public discussion has yet to measure what the degree of variation is, let alone what might be appropriate. This may be because the extensive discussion in favour of inclusion has not been accompanied by a comprehensive theoretically focused analysis.

Bibliography

Alton-Lee, A. (2003). *Quality Teaching for Diverse Students in Schooling: Best Evidence Synthesis Iteration (BES)*. Wellington: Ministry of Education.

Barrington, J. M. (2008) *Separate but Equal? Maori Schools and the Crown, 1867–1969*. Wellington, NZ: Victoria University Press.

Biddulph, F., Biddulph, J. and Biddulph, C. (2003). *The Complexity of Community and Family Influences on Children's Achievement in New Zealand: Best Evidence Synthesis Iteration (BES)*. Wellington: Ministry of Education.

Crothers, C. (ed) (2013). Special issue on class/inequality. *New Zealand Sociology*, 28.

Crothers, C. (2014). Social class in New Zealand: A review based on survey evidence. *New Zealand Sociology*, 29(3), 90–127.

Gordon-Burns, D. et al. (eds) (2012). *Te Aoturoa Tataki: Inclusive Early Childhood Education (Perspectives on inclusion, social justice and equity from Aotearoa New Zealand)*. Well: New Zealand CER Press.

Heath, C., Stoddart, C. J. and Green, H. A. L. (2002). Parental backgrounds of Otago medical students. *New Zealand Medical Journal*, 115(1165), 7–14.

Humpage, L. (2009). A 'culturally unsafe' space? The Somali experience of Christchurch secondary schools. *New Zealand Geographer*, 65(1), 73–82.

Minto, J. (2004). Measuring current education policy and outcomes against the Beeby/Fraser quote of 1939. *Delta*, 56(1), 21–23.

Moore, R. (2007). *Sociology of Knowledge and Education*. London and New York: Continuum.

Nair, B., Smart, W. and Smyth, R. (2007). How does investment in tertiary education improve outcomes for New Zealanders? *Social Policy Journal of New Zealand Te Puna Whakaaro*, 31.

Nash, R. (2004). The association between social class and reading attainment: Is the most plausible explanation a 'deficit theory'? *Delta*, 56(2), 83–95.

Nash, R. (2004). The explanation of social differences in reading attainment: An inspection of the PIRLS New Zealand data. *Waikato Journal of Education*, 10.

Pearce, D. and Gordon, L. (2006). School zoning since 1990: A Christchurch study. *Delta*, 58(1), 41–54.

Strathdee, R. (2011). Educational reform, inequality and the structure of higher education in New Zealand. *Journal of Education and Work*, 24(1–2), 27–48.

Strathdee, R. and Engler, R. (2012). Who is missing from higher education in New Zealand? *British Educational Research Journal*, 38(3), 497–514.

Thrupp, M. (2004). 'Official school improvement' in England and New Zealand: A cautionary comparison. *New Zealand Annual Review of Education*, 14, 39–58.

Thrupp, M. (2005). School quasi-markets: Best understood as a class strategy? *Waikato Journal of Education*, 11(2), 137–149.

Thrupp, M. (2008). Education's 'Inconvenient truth': Part two. The middle classes have too many friends in education. *New Zealand Journal of Teachers' Work*, 5(1), 54–62.

Towl, P. (2013). Making opportunity from disappointment: Students, parents and teachers talk about stand-down. *New Zealand Journal of Educational Studies*, 48(1), 127–139.

Tunmer, W., Chapman, J. W. and Prochnow, J. E. (2004). Why the reading achievement gap in New Zealand won't go away: Evidence from the PIRLS 2001 international study of reading achievement. *New Zealand Journal of Educational Studies*, 39(1), 127–145.

Turnock, K. (2011). 'I'm scared of that baby': How adults and environments contribute to children's positive or negative understandings and experiences of disability in early childhood settings. *New Zealand Research in Early Childhood Education*, 14, 23–37.

Wane, J. (2012). The private school debate: Are they worth the money? *North and South*, 315, 32–41.

Waterhouse, S. (2015). The successful inclusion of pregnant and mothering students in New Zealand schools. *Set: Research Information for Teachers*, 1, 9–15.

Wylie, C., Hipkins, R. and Hodgen, E. (2009). *On the Edge of Adulthood: Young People's School and Out-of-School Experiences at 16*. New Zealand Council for Educational Research.

7

EUROPEAN UNION POLICIES FOR LIFELONG LEARNING

A 'portal' to social inclusion?

Eugenia A. Panitsidou

Context

Within a contemporary context of continuous technological evolution, the prevalence of neo-liberalism, internationalisation of economies and demographic transformations, the destabilisation of social environments along with increasing inequalities among regions, social groups or individuals have come to the fore. As pointed out by the European Council (Council of the European Union, 2010) in response to the economic crisis, recession has mostly plagued disadvantaged individuals and, at the same time, it has affected the welfare measures targeted for such groups. It is, therefore, suggested by the European Union (EU) that lifelong learning (LLL) policies should be extended, so that all citizens will have the chance to acquire new skills or upgrade existing skills (Commission of the European Communities, 2007a, 2007b). Such an initiative highlights the necessity to implement measures to ensure access to key competences demanded for living and learning within a knowledge society.

Political and economic integration of the European Union (EU), in addition to historical changes having occurred in the late twentieth century in the Balkan region and former Soviet countries, have resulted in massive population movements (Pitkänen, Verma and Kalekin-Fishman, 2002). Hence, demographic, social and cultural changes have taken place within EU countries, whilst socio-economic problems are intensified by a rapidly ageing population. Recent data show that 17.4% of the population are over 65 years old (Eurostat, 2011) and a high percentage are low skilled individuals (14.4% early school leavers [Eurostat, 2011]). Moreover, the present economic crisis has also resulted in the marginalisation of larger groups, while there has been a sudden increase in unemployment percentages (9.5% unemployed [Eurostat, 2011]).

Concepts and rationale

According to the Commission of the European Communities (2001, 2007b), LLL refers to all learning activity undertaken throughout life, with the aim of improving knowledge, skills and competence, within a personal, civic, social and/or employment-related perspective, in order to enable people at all stages of their lives to take part in stimulating learning experiences, as well as helping to develop the education and training sector across Europe.

Behrman, Crawford and Stacey (1997) have argued that adult participation in LLL can result in various benefits. The schema through which LLL may produce outcomes is threefold: a) by augmenting knowledge and information on which individuals' attitudes and values are based; b) by removing constraints limiting action through competence development; and c) by transforming behaviour, preferences and goals. Furthermore, subsequent benefits can be realised on multiple levels: individual, social and economic (Schuller et al., 2004), while all outcomes are initially deployable on an individual basis and are diffused into the social and economic spheres (Clemens, Hartley and Macrae, 2003).

The issue of accessibility to LLL is of paramount importance, so as to ensure inclusion of all citizens in the marketplace and society, whilst at the same time enhancing economic growth and social cohesion. However, socially vulnerable groups are often confronted with restricting factors inhibiting their participation in LLL courses such as:

- limited access to education and training, mainly due to organisational reasons;
- negative earlier experience from the educational system;
- lack of education and training courses to meet real needs and interests of these groups;
- lack of continuity in education and training programmes offered;
- lack of linking of education and training to a wider and more effective network, providing for psycho-social services that could help towards social inclusion;
- lack of support from the family environment of individuals experiencing social exclusion (e.g. prisoners, people with mental problems, etc.): either a) because there is no close family environment, or b) because of weak ties among members of close and wider family environment;
- limited employment prospects after completion of a training course.

(Cross, 1992)

Thus, taking targeted action to tackle exclusion of disadvantaged groups, through widening access and increasing participation in education throughout the lifespan has emerged as a major component of sustainable economic growth and social cohesion reinforcement, both globally as well as within the EU (Commission of European Communities, 2006a, 2007a, 2007b; Council of the European Union, 2002; Papastamatis and Panitsidou, 2009). It is widely accepted that ensuring equity and equal chances in LLL is a fundamental factor to provide all citizens with a wide range of basic skills, that is, a combination of broader knowledge, skills and attitudes in order to flexibly adapt to a rapidly changing and highly interconnected world (Commission of the European Communities, 2007a; Official Journal of the European Union, 2006).

On these grounds, European policy rhetoric has highlighted the socio-economic value of LLL and the benefits of investment in knowledge, stressing its effect on economic growth and social cohesion (Commission of the European Communities, 2003, 2005).

European policy for lifelong learning

According to Commission Communications (Commission of the European Communities, 2007a, 2007b, 2006a, 2009), social inclusion has become a challenge which should not be treated as subordinate to goals of competitiveness or economic growth. They also emphasise the complementarity between policies and strategies aiming for economic growth and social cohesion.

It is assumed that LLL policies entail significant economic and social outcomes, while, on the other hand, educational inequities are related to huge hidden costs. In order to tackle educational disadvantage, LLL could increase equity of outcomes and overall skill levels. As far as ethnic minorities and migrants are concerned, it has been pointed out that the focus should be mainly on the need for immigrants to adapt, most notably through support measures and training such as language courses (Commission of the European Communities, 2004, 2006b).

The decade of 2001–2010 found the EU amidst the worst economic crisis in decades, revealing strong interdependence among member states and highlighting close cooperation as a gateway to recovering from crisis. LLL is once again found amongst the priority areas, with the aim to raise participation of adults in LLL, especially the unskilled ones, to 15% by 2020. Grounded in the assumption that new skills and new trends of multiple entry and exit from the labour market will prevail, LLL is expected to provide for a framework to support such transitions. Hence, there is a greater need than ever before for LLL to become more accessible, in order to ensure a smooth transition between jobs and other activities, minimizing the loss of human capital due to long-term unemployment (Commission of European Communities, 2009; Council of the European Union, 2010).

Challenges

Research findings (Balatti, Black and Falk, 2007; Dymock and Billett, 2008; Preston and Feinstein, 2004; Preston and Green, 2003; Preston and Hammond, 2002; Schuller et al., 2004) have shown that participants in LLL courses are provided with a chance to acquire new knowledge and skills, and to develop understanding and self-confidence, parameters that induce changes in their personal lives, while enabling them to play a more active role in their family, community or work.

As far as the impact of LLL on disadvantaged groups is concerned, school drop-outs and the low skilled constitute a target group for several LLL programmes, such as literacy courses, while a great body of research builds on benefits deriving from adult participation in such courses (Dymock and Billett, 2008; Lance and Bates, 1998; Ward and Edwards, 2002). The areas in which substantial benefits have been recorded fall into improvement of educational level and basic skills, advancement of professional and financial status, increased participation in LLL, enhanced civic participation, as well as psychological (an increase in self-confidence and self-esteem) and health benefits.

There is some evidence to suggest that there is a close interrelationship between LLL and social capital enhancement (Falk and Kilpatrick, 2000). Falk, Golding and Balatti (2000) have highlighted the crucial role of social capital in generating social and economic benefits, arguing that strengthening of social capital at a mid-level (groups, networks, communities) and at the micro-level (individuals) is crucial for multiple socio-economic benefits, by the mediation of acquisition of knowledge and skills, as well as identity capital resources deployable on an individual basis, representing how people most effectively define themselves and how others define them in various contexts (Côté and Levine, 2002: 142).

Thus, existence of wider benefits as a result of adult participation in LLL courses is widely recognised, while the European policy rhetoric has highlighted its socio-economic value. However, extensive reference to private and social benefits of LLL is restricted to an abstract level, which, according to Schuller et al. (2004: 6), can be attributed to the lack of scientific research in the field, despite denoting LLL as a key component of European policies.

Adult Education Centres (AECs) were established in Greece in 2003, mainly under EU funding (75%), so as to enhance participation percentage of adult population in LLL, while they undertook targeted action to reach socially vulnerable groups. Altogether, 56 AECs had been put in operation since 2003, offering a wide range of courses. Due to the lack of relevant research in Greece, it was felt that a comprehensive study, investigating the wider impact of LLL courses, especially in cases of socially disadvantaged groups would throw some light on issues of LLL and its contribution to social inclusion. Findings would also provide practical information to be used in improving planning and delivery of LLL courses and promotion of LLL policies, and would serve as an incentive to increased citizen participation in LLL.

The study also aimed at a) identifying wider outcomes emanating from adult participation in LLL courses; and b) identifying and describing distinctive types of participants, through cluster analysis of the data, defined with respect to the benefits reported in the ten factors of the questionnaire. Additionally, resultant typologies were interrelated with demographic characteristics, aiming to provide an insight into interrelationships between LLL and wider outcomes, so as to identify areas of interest both for policy makers as well as for stakeholders.

The research strategies

The questionnaire,[1] which was selected as one of the most appropriate tools to address a wide statistical sample, was structured in three sections. The first comprised demographic data, while the second consisted of 48 closed questions/statements, asking to indicate degree of agreement/disagreement based on a five-point Likert scale, allocated in ten conceptual structures: work, qualifications and skills, attitudes and behaviour, self-concept, interests and leisure, healthy living, social relations, active citizenship and promotion of LLL. Finally, in the third section, an open question was included so as to record personal comments and views, which were subjected to content analysis.

To ensure internal consistency of the questionnaire, a pilot was conducted with an opportunistic sample of 30 individuals who attended LLL courses. Cronbach's alpha and corrected item-to-total correlation coefficients were estimated (Hair et al., 1995; Nunnally, 1978), far exceeding the minimum requirements for reliability and validity in all domains of the questionnaire (total reliability: 0.963, minimum value of the corrected item-to-total correlation ranging from 0.460 to 0.729).

Quantitative data was retrieved through questionnaires administered to a sample of 1,500 individuals who had participated in adult education courses at 24 AECs throughout Greece, operating in both urban and rural areas.

Analysis of the data from the questionnaires was carried out by descriptive statistical methods, as well as multidimensional, multivariate analysis (principal component analysis, reliability analysis and cluster analysis). In detail, to compare means and distributions, Dunnett T3 (Toothaker, 1993) and x^2 tests were applied, while to evaluate linear correlations between quantitative variables, the Pearson r correlation coefficient was used. In order to assess internal consistency, Cronbach's alpha coefficient was estimated for all items, while for construct validity, principal component analysis (direct oblimin) (Hair et al., 1995) was applied. To determine number of significant factors, the eigenvalue criterion (≥ 1) was used. For the statistical analysis SPSS v. 15.0 statistical package was used. The significance level of all statistical tests was predetermined at 0.05.

Qualitative content analysis of responses (Berelson, 1971) was conducted on the third part of the questionnaire using as units of analysis the conceptual structures identified through the quantitative data.

The majority of the participants in the sample belonged to the general population, were women, employed (with rather low wages), holding graduate level qualifications, aged 25 to 54, and married with a maximum of two children (Table 7.1). They had attended mainly foreign language and computer courses.

Respondents' perceived views on benefits that emanated from their participation in LLL courses were mostly neutral (means ranging from 2.7 to 3.3, characterisation: 'neither agree nor disagree') for most conceptual structures with the exception of qualifications and skills, self-concept and social relations. In detail, respondents agreed with the fact that the courses had enriched their professional qualifications (q1, mean = 3.5), having accrued more knowledge and skills (q6, mean = 4), which also facilitated them in carrying out activities they could not cope with before attending the course (q7, mean = 3.7). Additionally, they agreed to having developed communication skills, both written and oral (q10, mean = 3.5), and greater ability to experiment with new tasks or unfamiliar situations (q9, mean = 3.5). They also, admitted to having gained more self-confidence (q16, mean = 3.5), feeling more

TABLE 7.1 Profile of the majority of participants in the sample

Demographic characteristics	Profile	%
Gender	Female	72.3%
Social group	General population	88.3%
Age group	25–54 years	82.1%
Marital status	Married	56.8%
Number of children	0–2	85.1%
Education background	Higher education	52.0%
Employment	Employed	58.7%
Average monthly income	Up to €1,450	59.8%
Course field	Foreign languages and computers	89.4%

energetic and satisfied with themselves (q18, mean = 3.6) and having set new objectives (q19, mean = 3.5). As far as socialising is concerned, new friendships were reported to have been established through participation in the courses (q32, mean = 3.7), while moreover the feeling of being a member of a community/team was enhanced (q33, mean = 3.6). Finally, respondents acknowledged having developed meta-cognitive skills, knowing how and where to seek new knowledge and information (q44, mean = 3.6), while, additionally, members of their immediate environment were motivated to participate in LLL courses (q48, mean = 3.6).

Through cluster analysis five typologies were identified (Table 7.2), based on respondents' perceived views on the outcomes of their participation in LLL courses.

The typologies were assigned names according to degree of agreement with conceptual structures. In detail, the 'Hyper-beneficiaries' (T2) and 'Beneficiaries' (T4) acknowledged significant benefits as a result of their participation in LLL courses. On the contrary, the 'Pessimists' (T1) hardly recognised any positive returns from participation in LLL, while the 'Moderates' (T5) and the 'Reserved' (T3) tended towards a more neutral stance, being neither negative nor able to identify significant changes. It should however be noted that almost half of respondents fell into the clusters of hyper-beneficiaries and beneficiaries (42.4%).

The typologies identified were correlated with demographic characteristics, building an overall profile of respondents in the clusters. Perceived views along with special characteristics of each cluster are analytically presented in Table 7.3. It should be noted that secondary profile depicts particular demographic characteristics of respondents with higher values compared to sample means. For example, in the cluster of hyper-beneficiaries the characterisation 'Muslims' does not signify that the majority of respondents in the cluster were Muslims, but compared with sample mean (3.9%), there was greater representation of Muslims (11.2%) in the particular cluster.

TABLE 7.2 Primary profile of respondents

Conceptual structures	T1 Pessimists	T3 Reserved	T5 Moderates	T4 Beneficiaries	T2 Hyper-beneficiaries	Total	R^2	p
W – Work	1.7 **e**	2.7 **d**	3.1 **c**	3.7 **b**	4.4 **a**	3.2	0.667	<0.001
Q – Qualifications and Skills	2.0 **d**	3.2 **c**	3.1 **c**	4.0 **b**	4.5 **a**	3.5	0.647	<0.001
At - Attitudes and Behaviour	2.5 **d**	3.4 **c**	3.3 **c**	4.1 **b**	4.5 **a**	3.6	0.520	<0.001
sC – self-Concept	1.8 **c**	2.0 **c**	2.8 **b**	2.9 **b**	3.3 **a**	2.7	0.360	<0.001
Wl – Interests and Leisure	1.9 **e**	2.7 **d**	3.1 **c**	3.6 **b**	4.4 **a**	3.2	0.599	<0.001
Wh – Healthy living	1.4 **d**	1.9 **c**	3.0 **b**	2.9 **b**	3.9 **a**	2.7	0.570	<0.001
Sc – Social relations	2.1 **d**	3.2 **c**	3.3 **c**	3.8 **b**	4.5 **a**	3.5	0.573	<0.001
A – Active citizenship	1.6 **e**	2.3 **d**	3.1 **c**	3.2 **b**	4.1 **a**	3.0	0.640	<0.001
F - Family context	1.7 **e**	2.5 **d**	3.1 **c**	3.5 **b**	4.2 **a**	3.2	0.527	<0.001
L – Promotion of LLL	2.1 **e**	2.8 **d**	3.2 **c**	3.6 **b**	4.2 **a**	3.3	0.586	<0.001
N (%)	**116 (9.7%)**	**196 (16.3%)**	**379 (31.6%)**	**343 (28.6%)**	**166 (13.8%)**	**1200 (100%)**		

Note: For each conceptual structure, means followed by a different letter differ significantly at significance level. $p < 0.05$, according to Dunnett T3 test.

TABLE 7.3 Overall cluster profile

Cluster	Primary Profile	Secondary Profile
Pessimists (T1) (n=16, 9.7%)	Their views on returns of participation in LLL are negative. They do not acknowledge any benefits.	• Single • Men • Higher Education Graduates • Public Servants • Monthly income €1,451–1,800 • Attended European Languages and Greek Language and History
Reserved (T3) (n=196, 16.3%)	Their views on returns of participation in LLL are neutral in most conceptual structures.	• Single • No children • Attended European Languages
Moderates (T5) (n=379, 31.6%)	Their views on returns of participation in LLL are neutral in all conceptual structures.	• Higher Education Graduates • 55 to 64 years old
Beneficiaries (T4) (n=343, 26.0%)	Their views on returns of participation in LLL are positive. They acknowledge benefits in most conceptual structures.	• Married • Many children • Senior high school graduates • Unemployed and Housewives • Muslims • Attended Special Courses and Computers
Hyper-beneficiaries (T2) (n=166, 14.8%)	Their views on returns of participation in LLL are positive. They acknowledge benefits in all conceptual structures.	• Divorced • Primary school or high-school graduates • Attended < 2 courses • Muslims • Attended Special courses

According to our findings, it could be argued that what differentiates the clusters of 'Pessimists', 'Moderates' and 'Reserved' from those of the 'Beneficiaries' and 'Hyper-beneficiaries' is the fact that they comprise individuals with a good educational background (Moderates and Pessimists), without any particular family obligations, such as spouse or children (Reserved), with a steady job and rather high income (Pessimists). On the contrary, those who acknowledge significant changes as a result of their participation in LLL courses are 'disadvantaged' individuals, in need of greater support in personal, family, social or professional life. More specifically, among 'Beneficiaries' and 'Hyper-beneficiaries' are individuals with low educational background, belonging to ethnic minorities, unemployed, housewives, divorced or parents with more than three children, who attended special courses, such as literacy courses. (It should be noted that Muslim minority women in Greece are most often forced to leave school at an early age to get married, while their Greek is really poor since the language of communication in the family and in the local community context is Turkish.)

Findings from the content analysis of the open question in the questionnaire indicated increased benefits in relation to respondents' self-concept, especially for the retired and for the housewives. They commented that attendance on the courses helped them become more independent and efficient, increased their self-confidence and helped them set new goals. Moreover, new interests and creative use of leisure were identified among important benefits, while the enhancement of social relationships was described with enthusiasm. Respondents reported that, through LLL courses, they were given the chance to escape everyday life, socializing, as well as developing critical competences. Moreover, it is commonplace that relationships among trainees go beyond the classroom, enabling further social interaction and networking within the community.

Qualitative study

In an attempt to gain more meaningful insights into the situation (Cohen and Manion, 1994; Verma and Mallick, 1999), qualitative data were retrieved through 15 semi-structured interviews, conducted with selected individuals who had participated in AEC courses all over Greece.

Out of the 15 interviewees, the majority were women (11), three of them belonged to the Muslim minority, two were unemployed, four had a low level of education, and one had recently lost her husband, while four of them were over 55 years old. Moreover, the majority of the courses attended were on ICT and foreign languages, as well as literacy courses attended by three interviewees.

The data of the semi-structured interviews underwent a three-level qualitative analysis, following the 'grounded theory' methodology, proposed by Strauss and Corbin (1990), comprising 'open coding', 'axial coding' and 'selective coding'. Initially, constant comparative analysis was used to develop descriptive codes (Miles and Huberman, 1994), conceptualising and categorising the transcribed interview data. By comparing the codes (labels) that emerged across all interviews, five categories were identified: 'self-containment', 'functionality', 'social capital', 'leisure' and 'learning'.

At a second stage, by utilising a coding paradigm involving conditions, context, action/interaction strategies and consequences, an attempt was made to identify and define connections between categories and reach grounded conclusions. Finally, the core category, that is 'free access', was selected, systematically relating it to other categories, validating relationships and filling in categories that needed further refinement and development, so that recommendations could be formed.

All interviewees had a positive attitude towards perceived returns of their participation in AEC courses. However, those belonging to socially vulnerable groups, such as individuals with a low level of education, the elderly or people belonging to minorities, were really enthusiastic, admitting to having set new goals and developed new ambitions, comprising even enrolment in the university as in the case of an elderly woman.

Overall, the interviewees stated that their participation in AEC courses was a positive experience, which resulted in major wider benefits. The main categories under which significant benefits were recorded were as follows:

- *Self-containment.* The interviewees stated that they feel more active and self-satisfied following their participation in AEC courses, as the knowledge and skills they developed contributed to acquiring new interests and undertaking new activities.
- *Functionality.* The interviewees stated that they had acquired new knowledge and developed new competences such as ICT and communication skills, necessary for remaining functional within the contemporary socio-economic context.
- *Social capital.* It was stated by interviewees that by socialising during the courses with other people, often from different social or educational backgrounds, they had widened their networks of social relations, developing more understanding and respect towards 'difference' and establishing new friendships, which have been active even outside the courses' context. In addition, an important parameter, elicited from respondents' answers, was that social networking through relationships established during courses was not limited to strengthening of 'bonding ties', but of 'bridging ties' as well, which is crucial for social cohesion enhancement (Putnam, 2000).
- *Leisure.* The interviewees stated that creative use of leisure was made both during the courses, as well as after they were over, as the skills and knowledge acquired provided for motivation to undertake new interests or activities.
- *Learning.* A learning culture has been promoted. The interviewees stated that they wish to attend more courses in the future, while people from their close environment were motivated to participate in LLL courses, as well.

What was highlighted through axial coding of data was the fact that what is differentiated among individuals are the dimensions of structural transformations that could result into professional, family and social context, through participation in LLL courses. Taking into account that 'disadvantaged' individuals have increased quantitative and qualitative needs, data analysis indicated that they can respectively benefit most through participation in LLL courses. By contrast, for young people with a high educational background and a stable professional status, major benefits from LLL were restricted mainly to the fields of creative use of leisure and widening of social relations. They admitted, however, to having developed new knowledge and skills, valuable both on an individual as well as on a professional level.

Finally, through selective coding, the variable that was indicated to be systematically related to all categories and, thus, constitute the 'core category', was 'free access' to the courses. Given that individuals belonging to socially vulnerable groups are most often overwhelmed by financial difficulties, especially under the pressure of the present economic crisis, the AEC courses made a substantial contribution to the students' well-being, because they were provided without any cost. This particular finding entails political significance, as further targeted action and accompanying measures should be endorsed so as to raise participation of 'disadvantaged individuals' in LLL, while at the same time ensure that there is indeed 'free' access.

Discussion, reflections and implications

The present study attempted to identify perceived outcomes arising from adult participation in LLL courses. On a second level of analysis, it sought to identify and describe distinctive types of participants, while resultant typologies were interrelated with demographic characteristics.

What was striking among the findings was the fact that 'disadvantaged' participants reported increased benefits arising from their participation in educational courses. In detail, it was made evident that what varies among individuals are the dimensions of change that might occur through the learning process and structural transformations that could result for the professional, family and social contexts. Given that each person has different traits and needs, which also are in constant interaction with the environment and specific situations, cluster analysis and qualitative data demonstrated that disadvantaged individuals can benefit most through LLL courses.

Our findings were in line with previous research findings (Hammond and Feinstein, 2005; Lightfoot and Brady, 2005; Preston and Feinstein, 2004; Swain, 2006), highlighting that, for individuals with low education background, women or older people, participation in LLL courses can serve as a catalyst for personal development and overall welfare. More specifically, successful completion of LLL courses, offering a 'second chance', can be proven exceptionally beneficial for an improvement in self-esteem of individuals who had failed earlier in formal education (Preston and Feinstein, 2004; Preston and Hammond, 2002). Participants, for example, in literacy courses reported that they have changed in general, have renewed hopes and aspirations, as well as felt increased self-esteem and self-confidence, which enabled them to control and redefine their lives (Swain, 2006). It was found that women who participated in education courses went through a cyclical and reciprocal process of increasing self-efficacy, enhancing personal development, improving family and social relationships, as well as professional status (Hammond and Feinstein, 2005). Especially non-working women felt more self-satisfaction, got a chance to undertake new roles and engage in new activities, realizing that they could successfully respond to tasks other than those they were normally engaged in (Lightfoot and Brady, 2005). Equally significant was the contribution of LLL in the quality of life of older people, helping them to remain active after retirement and enabling them to establish new social relationships (Preston and Hammond, 2002).

In light of the present research findings, existence of a significant percentage of individuals having low educational background, being unemployed or belonging to minorities – minority women face literacy deficiencies – amongst respondents who acknowledged significant benefits, in almost all fields, is indicative of the role LLL can play, as a means to provide new opportunities, mitigate inequalities among individuals, regions or communities, and strengthen social cohesion.

Throughout EU policy papers, there are extensive references to private and social benefits of LLL, whilst investment in LLL has long been an explicit or implicit policy goal within the EU. However, most references are based on hypotheses, lacking substantial evidence to reach sound conclusions. One could argue, for example, that it is not participation in LLL that contributes to improving health levels of the elderly, but that healthy seniors are more likely to participate in LLL. Therefore, further research is required to control variables that might impact data, so as to avoid simplifications.

The present study attempted to draw on the outcomes arising from adult participation in LLL courses, coming up with findings which stressed the necessity for extending the research in the field. They have also indicated the importance of taking targeted action to widen access and participation in LLL, so as to promote inclusion of disadvantaged individuals and social groups and enhance social cohesion.

The present economic situation in Greece has resulted in a deterioration of living conditions for the whole population and especially for the disadvantaged. It is thus, more than ever before, fundamental to provide equal access to LLL for all citizens. It is, moreover, also important to endorse targeted action, as well as to increase incentives and widen opportunities for disadvantaged social groups, so as to develop an integrative framework to approach individuals with learning deficits, confronted with the risk of poverty and social exclusion.

Note

1 The questionnaire used in this study can be provided by the author upon request.

Bibliography

Balatti, J., Black, S. and Falk, I. (2007). Teaching for social capital outcomes: The case of adult literacy and numeracy courses. *Australian Journal of Adult Learning*, 47(2), 245–263.

Behrman, J., Crawford, D. L. and Stacey, N. (1997). Introduction. In: J. Berhman and N. Stacey (eds), *The Social Benefits of Education*. Ann Arbor, MI: University of Michigan Press.

Berelson, B. (1971). *Content Analysis in Communication Research*. New York: Hafner Publishing.

Clemens, A., Hartley, R. and Macrae, H. (2003). *ACE Outcomes*. Adelaide: NCVER.

Cohen, L. and Manion, L. (1994). *Research Methods in Education* (4th ed). London: Routledge.

Commission of the European Communities. (2001). *Communication of the European Commission: 'Making a European Area of Lifelong Learning a Reality'*. Brussels: Directorate General Education and Culture.

Commission of the European Communities. (2003). *Investing Efficiently in Education and Training: An Imperative for Europe*. Brussels: Directorate General Education and Culture.

Commission of the European Communities. (2004). *Social Inclusion in the New Member States: A Synthesis of the Joint Memoranda on Social Inclusion*. Commission Staff Working Paper. Brussels: Directorate General Education and Culture.

Commission of the European Communities. (2005). *Economics of Education: Study on the Returns to Various Types of Investment in Education and Training*. Brussels: Directorate General Education and Culture.

Commission of the European Communities. (2006a). *Adult Education: It is Never too Late to Learn. Communication from the Commission*. Brussels: COM 614.

Commission of the European Communities. (2006b). *Efficiency and Equity in European Education and Training Systems. Communication from the European Commission to the Council and to the European Parliament*. Brussels: COM 481.

Commission of the European Communities. (2007a). *Key Competences for Lifelong Learning: European Reference Framework*. Brussels: Directorate General Education and Culture.

Commission of the European Communities. (2007b). *Education and Training, The Lifelong Learning Programme: Education and Training Opportunities for All*. Brussels: Directorate General Education and Culture.

Commission of the European Communities. (2009). *Consultation on the Future 'EU 2020' Strategy*. Commission Working Document. Brussels: Directorate General Education and Culture.

Côté, J. and Levine, C. (2002). *Identity Formation, Agency and Culture: A Social Psychological Synthesis*. Mahwah, NJ: Lawrence Erlbaum Associates.

Council of the European Union. (2002). The Copenhagen Declaration: Declaration of the European Ministers of vocational education and training, and the European Commission, convened in Copenhagen on enhanced European cooperation in vocational education and training. Brussels.

Council of the European Union. (2010). *Council Conclusions: A New European Strategy for Jobs and Growth*. Brussels: 17.6.2010.

Cross, P. (1992). *Adults as Learners: Increasing Participation and Facilitating Learning*. San Francisco, CA: Jossey-Bass.

De la Fuente, A. and Ciccone, A. (2002). Human capital in a global and knowledge-based economy. Final Report. Brussels: European Commission.

Dewson, S., Eccles, J., Tackey, N. and Jackson, A. (2000). Measuring soft outcomes and distance travelled. Research Report RR219. Nottingham: DfEE.

Downs, S. (2004). Measuring the immeasurable. *Adults Learning*, 16(2), 17–18.

Dymock, D. and Billett, S. (2008). *Assessing and Acknowledging Learning through Non-Accredited Community Adult Language, Literacy and Numeracy Programs*. Adelaide: NCVER.

Eurostat. (2011). Demography data (last modified December 23). http://epp.eurostat.ec.europa.eu.

Falk, I. and Kilpatrick, S. (2000). What is social capital? A study of rural communities. *Sociologia Ruralis*, 40(1), 87–110.

Falk, I., Golding, B. and Balatti, J. (2000). *Building Communities: ACE, Lifelong Learning and Social Capital*. Melbourne, Australia: Adult, Community and Further Education Board.

Hair, J., Anderson, R., Tatham, R. and Black, W. (1995). *Multivariate Data Analysis with Readings*. New Jersey: Prentice-Hall.

Hammond, C. and Feinstein, L. (2005). The effects of adult learning on self-efficacy. *London Review of Education*, 3(3), 265–287.

Lance, K. C. and Bates, D. (1998). *Colorado GED Study: How Colorado Graduates Benefit from Passing the GED Tests*. Denver: Office of Adult Education.

Lightfoot, K. and Brady, E. M. (2005). Transformations through teaching and learning. *Journal of Transformative Education*, 3(3), 221–235.

Miles, M. B. and Huberman, A. M. (1994). *Qualitative Data Analysis: An Expanded Sourcebook.* Thousand Oaks, CA: Sage.

Nunnally, J. C. (1978). *Psychometric Theory.* New York, NY: McGraw Hill.

Official Journal of the European Union. (2006). Modernising education and training: A vital contribution to prosperity and social cohesion in Europe. Joint Interim Report of the Council and of the Commission on Progress under the 'Education & Training 2010' Work Programme. Brussels: C 79/01.

Papastamatis, A. and Panitsidou, E. (2009). The aspect of 'accessibility' in the light of European lifelong learning strategies. Adult education centres: A case study. *International Journal of Lifelong Education,* 28(4), 335–351.

Pitkänen, P., Verma, G. and Kalekin-Fishman, D. (2002). *Education and Immigration: Settlement Policies and Current Practices.* London: Routledge Falmer.

Preston, J. and Feinstein, L. (2004). Adult education and attitude change: Wider benefits of learning, Research Report No 11. London: Institute of Education.

Preston, J. and Green, A. (2003). The macro-social benefits of education, training and skills in comparative perspective: Wider benefits of learning, Research Report No 9. London: Institute of Education.

Preston, J. and Hammond, C. (2002). The wider benefits of further education: Practitioner views: Wider benefits of learning, Research Report No 1. London: WBL and Institute of Education.

Putnam, R. E. (2000). *Bowling Alone: The Collapse and Revival of American Community.* New York City: Simon and Schuster.

Schuller, T., Preston, J., Hammond, C., Brassett-Grundy, A. and Bynner, J. (2004). *The Benefits of Learning: The Impact of Education on Health, Family Life and Social Capital.* London: Routledge Falmer.

Strauss, A. and Corbin, J. (1990). *Basics of Qualitative Research. Grounded Theory Procedures and Techniques.* Newbury Park, CA: Sage.

Swain, J. (2006). Changes to adult learners' identities through learning numeracy. *Write On,* 23(4), 1–6.

Toothaker, L. (1993). *Multiple Comparison Procedures.* Newbury Park: Sage.

Verma, G. and Mallick, K. (1999). *Researching Education.* London: Falmer Press.

Ward, J. and Edwards, J. (2002). *Learning Journeys: Learners' Voices. Learners' Views on Progress and Achievement in Literacy and Numeracy.* London: Learning and Skills Development Agency.

8
EDUCATIONAL POLICIES AND TEACHERS' PROFESSIONAL DEVELOPMENT

Disability issues

Panagiotis Giavrimis, Stella Giossi and Adamantios Papastamatis

Introduction

Teachers are responsible for building learning communities, creating a knowledge society and developing capacities useful for coping with the challenges of the twenty-first century such as innovation, flexibility and commitment to change (Hargreaves and Lo, 2000). For this reason, their professional development is of great value, not only for themselves but also for having a positive impact on their students' learning (Bailey and Erthal, 2006; Papastamatis, 2010).

Research on effective schools has cited that improvement of student learning through systematic assessment progress (Taylor et al., 2000), strong leadership (Waters et al., 2004), fruitful staff collaboration, outreach to parents and ongoing professional development are the main factors that demonstrate effectiveness. Thus, research on effective schools accords with research on school improvement and teacher professional development (Taylor et al., 2005).

There is sufficient evidence to suggest that the professional development of teachers should follow recent trends and changes within the school and within the community. Also, teachers should be aware of the social and cultural contexts of teaching and learning in order to increase learning opportunities for all (Banks et al., 2001). Hence, a focus on diversity emerges as a vital priority. Indeed, diversity is a characteristic of human nature; it has long been signalled in terms of colour and ethnicity. But the scope of definitions of diversity in contemporary social and cultural reality is constantly being expanded. Recent trends in educational policies and in practice as well as in research define diversity to include what in the past was termed 'disability'.

Professional development related to diversity is especially important for teachers who seek to minimise the gap between individuals with disabilities and those considered 'normal'. They share an aim to provide equal opportunities to all in order to make teaching more responsive to students' needs. Usually, most professional development activities related to diversity are addressed by government institutions and policies. These policies indicate that governments not only consider the difficulties that these individuals face, but through the prevailing value system relevant to disabilities they also determine their position in society.

Unfortunately, individuals with disabilities are often characterised as inferior and stigmatised. These individuals are quite often described with a 'stigma'. Stafford and Scott (1986, as cited in Link and Phelan, 2001, p. 366) considered 'stigma' 'a characteristic that is contrary to a norm of a social unit', whereas Jones et al. (1984, as cited in Major and O'Brien, 2005, p. 395) refer to a 'mark' which is linked with the undesirable features of a person. Goffman (2001) emphasises the connection between stigma and stereotypes, while Link and Phelan (2001) added the issues of discrimination, negative stereotyping and exclusion.

The current educational policy and the practices adopted by teachers in the educational system are related to the models described in international and Greek literature. Two prevailing models of approach to disability have influenced research in this field as well as the current Greek, European and world practices that are applied for confronting individuals with disabilities and their functionality in the social structure.

This chapter has attempted to show that in order to deal with disability issues in the educational context, teachers as well as the whole school staff need to contribute to the process of socio-political incorporation of individuals with disabilities. Teachers, who have a dominant position, may develop stereotyped perceptions that influence the behaviour of individuals with disabilities and contribute to their social exclusion. As a result, the educational practices that teachers adopt play a crucial role in undermining the support given to them.

Educational models and studies on disability

Various models, some of which seem to influence one another, attempt to enhance the improvement of the teaching-learning process and explain the behaviour of participants, especially that of individuals with disabilities. Thus, it would seem important to fully describe and analyse their characteristics.

Olkin and Pledger (2003, p. 297), for example, tried to categorise studies based on different models of disability and found four categories with different ideological bases. In the first category, individuals with disabilities are viewed as consumers with an emphasis on self-determination that can lead to their social, educational, political and economic inclusion. In the second, their power, involvement and rights were emphasised through the social model. In the third, disability is regarded as a human condition, and in the fourth, individuals with disabilities are considered to have a 'stigma' and thus, they are cut off from the world.

Indeed, the majority of disability studies are grounded in the social model. But since many of the past educational laws and policies adopted by many European countries, including Greece, were based on the medical model, it is pertinent to briefly describe this model. The medical or 'individualistic' model accepts the naturalistic approach of the human body and within this model the body is conceived as a purely biological entity (Goffman, 2001, pp. 26–27). Following Merton's (1968) terminology, the disability could be described as an example of lawlessness, and as a contradiction to the main social structure; therefore, it should be challenged, so as to become more functional and adaptable to any particular social structure.

This approach was the basis for previous Greek legislative interventions, where individuals with disabilities are defined as 'individuals that deviate from normal people, as they show abnormalities' and 'it is difficult for them, to establish themselves professionally and achieve self-reliant social integration' (Law 1143/1981, article 80, paragraph 1), and 'to be incorporated in productive processes and to be interchangeably accepted by the social community' (Law 1566/1985, article 32). Today, due to the social movement of people with disabilities as well as due to the criticism of the medical model, which blames individuals for their disabilities and overlooks all the external factors that are related to the social environment, the term 'individuals with special needs' has been abolished in Greece.

Many theorists realise that disability cannot be examined without taking into consideration the social environment in which the individual acts. The interaction of the individual with his/her environment (social and natural) has been and continues to be important and closely related to the symbolic conceptualisations of individuals, both those with and those without evident disabilities. Given this, the social model tries to shift the blame from individuals and their imperfections to social variables. But the main reason that the social model has gained domination over other models is that it attempts to shield individuals with disabilities from social exclusion.

Educational policies

Labour Force and Adult Education Surveys indicate that adults' participation in formal education is significantly lower than their participation in non-formal education and training (Eurydice, 2011). This is obviously exacerbated in the case of individuals with disabilities. It holds at all levels of formal education due to various social factors such as persistent stereotypes, prejudices and insufficient knowledge, as well as to structural problems of education such as rules, laws and inadequate infrastructure. Policies implemented quite often ignore or even pass over the right of disabled individuals to have access to educational resources, and this amounts to social and educational exclusion.

In Greece, there is a contradictory history of disability and of how ancient communities behaved towards individuals with disabilities. According to one tradition, there was an abyss near Sparta, called Kaiadas, where Spartans threw criminals and disabled children. Even today, the word 'Kaiadas' can be used as a symbol of social exclusion. Unfortunately, nobody can claim that modern Kaiadas has been eliminated as social exclusion still exists. This is due to Greek legislation that has never developed a holistic approach and has instead confronted the contemporary demand for inclusion passively. Significant improvement is found in the constitution of Law 3699/2008 referring to special education through which the obligatory character of educational studies on disability was established. This reflects the transmission of the responsibility for the socialisation of individuals with disabilities to the social community.

In educational practice, dispositions of the above mentioned laws and subsequent corrective interventions have not been completely fulfilled owing to problems of infrastructure and possibly to the insufficient education of school teachers on disability issues.

Given the issues mentioned earlier, individuals with disabilities still encounter many obstacles in the educational process. Equally important is the reproduction of their social position as individuals with disabilities with an emphasis on social inequalities and hence, social exclusion. Another serious problem which is noted in the relevant literature is the socio-economic position of their family. When the family of students with disabilities support their education financially, they enjoy better educational help due to the reduction of the total cost of their education. Research studies of individuals with disabilities show that the above-mentioned phenomena lead to their exclusion from the labour market as well (Chima, 2005; Magoulios and Trichopoulou, 2012). If, after all, people with disabilities do enter the labour market, they are often placed in low salary jobs that are irrelevant to their interests and skills (National Confederation of People with Disabilities studies – ESAEA, 2005; Sidiropoulou-Dimakakou, Giavrimis and Klouvatou, 2002).

Contemporary Greek and national educational policies pinpoint the acceptance of diversity and the provision of equal educational opportunities for all. They highlight the new curricula which enhance cultural and linguistic identity in the context of a multicultural and diversity-sensitive society. In addition, they emphasise raising an awareness of human rights, world peace and human dignity. These policies not only shape a new framework of educational function and processes, but also transform the teachers' role.

From the above discussion, it is apparent that education plays a fundamental role in the development of the identity of individuals with disabilities, on the societal interpretation of disability issues, and also, on the socialisation of these individuals in a social community. Effective intervention in these issues cannot be accomplished without the professional development of teachers and their knowledge and understanding of such issues.

Professional development of teachers and disability issues

In this rapidly changing environment there is a need for school teachers to deal with their professional development as knowledge easily becomes obsolete and the basic education of teachers is inadequate to cover the educational needs of teachers during the whole of their professional life.

Furthermore, some previous studies show that teachers are likely to have rather negative attitudes towards students with disabilities and their inclusion in a typical school community. This is dependent on factors such as the seriousness of the disability, and the Socio-economic Status (SES) of the disabled (Cook, 2004; Kenny et al., 2000; Milson, 2006). Other studies indicate that primary education teachers who have experience of inclusion are more reluctant to teach students with disabilities (Avramidis and Norwich, 2002). Yet many other studies show that teachers' attitudes towards students with disabilities are closely related to their professional development (Duran, 2009; Milson, 2006; Seltzer, 2011).

In Greece there is a lack of research concerning teachers of secondary education in contrast to the quantity of research on teachers in primary education, and their professional development regarding special education. Thus, it is important for educators to focus on these issues. In many cases secondary school teachers, again in contrast to primary school teachers, have not had any preparatory studies either in general education or in special education. The idea underlying this practice is that secondary school teachers identify with their studies and have the attitude that they teach subjects and not children. This is confirmed by the fact that the prerequisite for their appointment is their specialisation in a particular subject instead of in studies of pedagogy, or of pedagogy for those with disabilities. On the other hand, the limited provision of specialisation courses on disability and special education issues, appropriate for the professional development of secondary school teachers, raises questions about whether they have the appropriate attitude and are prepared to face the difficulties of ensuring the inclusion of individuals with disabilities.

Rationale of the study

The aim of this study was to identify whether secondary school teachers were prepared to realise the importance of inclusive education and the imperative need for giving priority to students with disabilities. For this reason, we investigated, analysed and interpreted their attitudes towards students with disabilities and their inclusion, as well as their experience and knowledge of special education needs. More precisely, we tried to answer questions such as whether secondary school teachers were well informed about the problems students with disabilities face, whether they have had adequate initial education as well as professional development on issues of disability and inclusion and whether they have been offered any specific learning opportunities by their educational system through its relevant policy.

The research instrument and the process

The population of this study was made up of upper secondary school (Lyceum) teachers in Greece. Four of the thirteen Greek geographical areas were selected to be included in this research under the following criteria: one urban region where 4,000 secondary school teachers were employed; and at least one from an island or border area. Therefore, the regions of Attica, Thessaly, Peloponnese and the North Aegean were chosen. The total number of secondary schools in these regions was

646, and the number of teachers was 11,475, 10% of them were finally included in our sample. A stratified sample of 1,147 teachers was requested to respond to the questionnaire of the present research. Fifteen percent of the secondary teachers in our sample did not agree to participate in the research. Thus, the sample consisted of 904 Greek teachers, 474 (52.4%) of whom were male and 430 (47.6%) female. With regard to age, 100 were under 30 (11.1%), 300 were 31–40 (33.2%), 364 were 41–50 (40.3%) and 140 individuals were 51–60 (15.5%).

For the purpose of this research a questionnaire was designed and validated. The questionnaire's internal consistency reliability was found to be 0.77.

The questionnaire dealt with: the education and training of secondary school teachers; teachers' attitudes towards students with disabilities; their opinion of the inclusion of students with disabilities; and how teachers in secondary schools perceive the special traits of students with disabilities. Demographic details such as gender, age, field of expertise and the educational or professional status of the sample group were also requested. The questionnaire was based on a four-point as well as a five-point scale of Likert type related to the research questions. A letter of confidentiality was included. With the permission of school principals who seemed interested in taking into consideration the results of the present study for their future planning and implementation of educational programmes, the questionnaires were distributed by volunteers who had previously received appropriate training and guidance.

The findings

Data were categorised in three thematic areas. The first was related to the training and professional development of teachers on issues of disability. More specifically, the first area included the relationship between the education of teachers referring to individuals with disabilities and their initial education. This category also included the teachers' readiness for teaching individuals with disabilities, the provision of specialised courses and teachers' own participation in any specialised courses. The second thematic area was related to the inclusion of individuals with disabilities in conventional secondary schools. The third thematic area was related to the policies appropriate to the inclusion of individuals with disabilities and the achievement of social cohesion.

Professional development of secondary education teachers concerning individuals with disabilities is crucial to promoting the inclusion of these individuals. Whether this specific training is related to basic (initial) education, readiness for teaching these individuals and opportunities and participation in specialised training programmes constitute the main focus of the first analysed thematic area. Results showed that 796 (88.2%) out of 904 teachers of secondary education had not studied any specific subject within their basic education. Concerning the content of basic education, more than 82% believed that the content of their initial education had had a very low, almost non-existent level of correspondence for coping with the needs of individuals with disabilities. 53.8% of the secondary education teachers believed that the Ministry of Education, Lifelong Learning and Religious Affairs (MELLRA) did not offer opportunities for training on the social inclusion of individuals with disabilities. Moreover, 77.4% of the secondary education teachers had not participated in any training programme concerning individuals with disabilities during the last five-year period.

Concerning the second thematic area, it is clear from the results that the inclusion of individuals with disabilities in conventional secondary schools is connected with the difficulties that these individuals face, the information given to teachers about their inclusion and the appropriateness of the curriculum towards furthering inclusion. Eighty percent (80%) of the teachers believed that an insufficient number of teachers with adequate preparation were to be blamed for the difficulties faced by individuals with disabilities in the educational system, whereas 10% did not consider professional inadequacy of teachers as an important factor. Furthermore, only 8% of the teachers were well informed about the inclusion of those individuals while the 54% were not well informed and 37.8% were informed at an average level. Besides that, the majority of secondary education teachers (88.8%) considered the Greek educational system and its curriculum inadequate or almost inadequate for the inclusion of individuals with disabilities.

The third thematic area stresses the importance of educational policies apart from the appropriate information, the professional development of secondary education teachers on disability issues and the relevant curriculum within the educational system. On the one hand, almost 65% of the teachers in our research agreed with the incorporation of the policy of inclusion of individuals with disabilities in conventional schools. On the other hand, only about 30% of them were likely to agree to accept an individual with disabilities into their class.

In brief, secondary school teachers had not studied any subject concerning disability issues during their initial education and, even more, they had not been aware of the needs of students with disabilities. Half of them blamed MELLRA for not providing opportunities for training on inclusion and disability issues. In addition, the majority of the respondents had not participated in any of this kind of training programme during the last five-year period, whereas more than half of them were not well informed about disability and more than one-third were informed at an average level. Furthermore, most of them considered the Greek educational system and its curriculum inadequate mainly for the inclusion of students with disabilities.

Discussion and concluding remarks

Indeed, individuals with disabilities constitute a vulnerable group that expect special education and a chance to face their difficulties satisfactorily. Teachers play a crucial role in making this possible and hence, teacher education, training and development have a strong impact on inclusion and on their perceptions of themselves as well as on societal attitudes towards them.

Analysing the data collected, it emerges that teachers in secondary education have insufficient knowledge of the issues that concern students with disabilities and of the possibilities of their inclusion. They also have ambiguous and differentiated attitudes towards students with disabilities. Their bias is against the participation of these students in class activities, and the relevant professional development is non-existent or inadequate. The findings of this particular research, considering the educational system and its curriculum inadequate for inclusion are in alignment with the results of other research studies, concerning primary education teachers (Reversi et al., 2007; Soulis, 2002; Wishart and Manning, 1996; Zoniou-Sideris, 2000), where inadequacy of the educational system was highlighted. Other studies stressed the inability of teachers to face the students' inclusion in school and society in an effective way (Kypriotakis, 2000; Ward and Le-Dean, 1996).

From this study, in contrast with the above-mentioned studies, it emerged that inadequate professional development and an inadequate educational system are not the only factors that influence the inclusion of individuals with disabilities. The majority of the teachers in secondary education have not studied any specific relevant subject during their initial education and believed that its content only slightly came up to dealing with the needs of the specific vulnerable group. Also, their non-participation in any training programme concerning individuals with disabilities during the last five-year period (77.4%) was due to an absence of opportunities offered by the MELLRA (53.8%).

It is also important to mention that besides their positive attitude towards the inclusion policy of individuals with disabilities (65%), unfortunately, only about 30% of the secondary education teachers were likely to accept an individual with disabilities in their class. This can be explained through their inadequate initial education which has left them unable and unprepared for teaching inclusive classes. Moreover, they lack the awareness of the current pedagogic approach according to which all of us have disabilities of one kind or another. This ignorance has been a barrier to their professional development as well as to the development of effective inclusion policies.

From all the findings mentioned above, we conclude that the development and pedagogic training of secondary education teachers in their university studies is a necessity. Such education will make teachers sensitive to issues in special education, social inclusion and confronting difficulties which individuals with disabilities are expected to face. The development of a solidarity culture within the school will enhance collaboration and make both teachers and individuals more sensitive to diversity. On the other hand, it is teachers' responsibility to find ways towards a deep understanding of how their students with disabilities approach the learning process and what the circumstances of their living within family and community are (Papastamatis, 2010).

In addition, the implementation of a policy of inclusion depends on suitable infrastructure, on the professional development of teachers towards the inclusion of individuals with disabilities and on the sensitivity of all regarding both respect for and acceptance of diversity. This is supposed to be based on the origins of the social model, where diversity is not a disability but a human characteristic that supports the social, emotional and cognitive development of the individual.

But professional development should have some characteristics in order to be effective. Guskey (2003) suggested that effective professional development enhances teachers' content and pedagogic knowledge; it is based on best available research evidence; it is ongoing and job-embedded; it provides opportunities for a theoretical understanding; it models high-quality instruction; it focuses on individual and organisational improvement; it is driven by an image of effective teaching and learning; it promotes continuous inquiry and reflection; and it helps accommodate diversity and promote equity. Therefore, for students with disabilities, teachers' professional development should emphasise many of these characteristics in order to be effective.

Suggestions for an inclusive approach

To achieve social inclusion, professional development activities, including mentoring, coaching, participation in international research studies, attendance at conferences and workshops and the establishment of a network of experts with different kinds of expertise related to students with disabilities are regarded as the most appropriate options.

On the other hand, appropriate measures should be taken concerning the educational system of each region and its supportive mechanisms. It is evident that one of the most important problems is the non-establishment of a course of study related to special education in academic programmes not even as an elective, as is done with topics such as pedagogy and psychology and as is done in faculties for the education of primary school teachers. Therefore, teachers of secondary schools have to follow a postgraduate course or participate in certified specialised year-long seminars.

Supportive mechanisms and services should be created in order to help teachers of any region enhance their professional development and their specialisation in students with disabilities. Furthermore, well-organised supportive activities for the families of these students can help their holistic inclusion. These mechanisms can facilitate teachers' ability to analyse conditions of students with disabilities and make the right decisions for the achievement of social coherence, critical thinking and mental health of all who participate in the educational system. The centralised professional development that prevails in the Greek educational system should gradually give way to school-based professional development. It is essential to strip away unnecessary bureaucracy in order for professionals, including teachers, to become capable of innovating and to ensure that the system will acquire the capacity and commitment to give every individual a viable chance to succeed. This is in accordance with the statement that 'every child, whether in a mainstream or special setting, deserves a world-class education' and 'everyone who works with disabled children and children with special educational needs (SEN) should have high expectations of them and the skills to help them to learn' (Department for Education, Green Paper, 2011, pp. 8–9). Therefore, teachers' awareness of the needs and problems of disabled students and those who have SEN combined with the appropriate training and skills would make them capable of deriving significant improvements in the quality of their lives and in education.

Finally, the inclusive approach should offer autonomy and independence to teachers in order to teach creatively with innovation and respect for the diversity and uniqueness of each student. In this context, the educational system should be flexible and free from centralisation which can push forward the importance of continuing education and professional development of teachers in order to provoke their interest in creating new techniques and methods of facing individuals with disabilities and supporting their inclusion in class and society.

Following the belief that 'we have all from birth to death experienced, at one time or another, being ill, dependent, abnormal and disabled' (Nocella II, 2006, p. 81), disability pedagogy, or better diversity-focus pedagogy, emerges as a comprehensive approach. This pedagogy is against the socially constructed categories of 'abled and disabled' or 'normal and abnormal' since everyone is different with unique abilities (Fulcher, 1999), and individuality (Bowers, 2001). It is also against competition and shaping individuals for the workforce; instead it suggests that schools can become a place of voluntary interest for those who wish to learn and not an industry for producing the future workforce (Giroux, 2001). Disability pedagogy in connection with critical pedagogy is recommended to teachers in order that effective inclusion can be achieved. Furthermore, the classroom structure and curriculum organisation can play a crucial role on all students' participation in activities and accomplishment of assignments that they could not do on their own. In addition, students' peers can help students with special education needs to understand and clarify important issues of the project while they can also give and encourage feedback. To this path, teachers can leave behind their traditional role and inherit the role of a mentor or a coach. It is evident that an approach that emphasises concrete, meaningful experiences and cooperative learning seems to be successful in the case of inclusive education (Wade, 2011). Therefore, it is teachers' responsibility to create cooperative groups working on student-led projects or complex activities and problems that can encourage motivation, active learning and higher order thinking among students. Teachers' awareness of the continuous change of pedagogical approaches and their complete and updated professional development would mean the end to labelling and segregation in inclusive education.

Bibliography

Avramidis, E. and Norwich, B. (2002). Teachers' attitudes towards integration/inclusion: A review of the literature. *European Journal of Special Needs Education*, 17(2), 129–147.

Bailey, G. and Erthal, M. (2006). *Professional Development for Education*. Retrieved 28 October 2011, from http://.nabte.org/Conference07/Research_Sessions/Bailey&%20Erthal_Artcompl.pdf.

Banks, J. A., Cookson, P., Gay, G., Irvine, J. J., Nieto, S., Schofield, J. W. et al. (2001). *Diversity Within Unity: Essential Principles for Teaching and Learning in a Multi-Cultural Society*. Seattle, WA: Center for Multicultural Education, University of Washington.

Bowers, C. A. (2001). *Education for Eco-Justice and Community*. Athens, GA: University of Georgia Press.
Chima, F. O. (2005). Persons with disabilities and employment. *Journal of Social Work in Disability & Rehabilitation*, 4(3), 39–60.
Cook, B. (2004). Inclusive teachers' attitudes toward their student with disabilities: A replication and extension. *The Elementary School Journal*, 104(4), 307–320.
Department for Education. (2011). Support and Aspiration: A New Approach to Special Educational Needs and Disability. A Consultation. Green Paper. UK: The Stationery Office Limited. Retrieved 10 May 2012, from https://www.education.gov.uk/publications/eOrderingDownload/Green-Paper-SEN.pdf.
Duran, J. (2009). *Barriers to Labour Market for People with Disabilities*. Ikei, Spain. Retrieved 30 October 2011, from http://eurofound.europa.eu/ewco/2008/11/ES0811039I.htm.
Eurydice. (2011). *Adults in Formal Education: Policies and Practice in Europe*. Brussels: Education, Audio Visual and Culture Executive Agency. Retrieved 10 May 2012 from http://eacea.ec.europa.eu/education/eurydice/documents/thematic_reports/128EN.pdf.
Fulcher, G. (1999). *Disability Policies? A Comparative Approach to Education Policy*. Sheffield: Philip Armstrong Publications.
Giroux, H. A. (2001). *Theory and Resistance in Education: Towards a Pedagogy of the Opposition*. Westport, CT: Bergin & Garvey.
Goffman, E. (2001). *Stigma: Notes for the Management of the Worn Identity* [translated in Greek]. Athens: Alexandreia.
Guskey, T. (2003). Analysing lists of the characteristics of effective professional development to promote visionary leadership. *NASSP Bulletin*, 87, 4–20.
Hargreaves, A. and Lo, L. (2000). Professionalism in teaching. The paradoxical profession: Teaching at the turn of the century. *Prospects*, XXX(2), 1–14.
Kenny, M., McNeela, E., Shevlin, M. and Daly, T. (2000). *Hidden Voices: Young People with Disabilities Speak about Their Second Level Schooling*. Cork: Bradshaw Books.
Kypriotakis, A. (ed). (2000). *Special Education* [in Greek]. Rethimno: Pedagogical Department of Primary Education, University of Crete.
L1143/1981, G. G. (1981). About special education, special professional training, employment, social care of handicapped individuals and other provisions. *Greek Government Gazette*, 80/31.03.1981.
L1566/1985, G. G. (1985). Structure and function of primary and secondary education and other provisions. *Greek Government Gazette*, 167/30.09.85.
L3699/2008, G. G. (2008). Special education and education with disabilities or with special educational needs and other provisions. *Greek Government Gazette*, 199/2.10.2008.
Link, B. G., and Phelan, J. C. (2001). Conceptualizing stigma. *Annual Review Psychology*, 27, 363–385.
Magoulios, G. N. and Trichopoulou, A. (2012). Employment status for people with disabilities in Greece. *South-Eastern Journal of Economics*, 1, 25–40.
Major, B. and O'Brien, L. T. (2005). The social psychology of stigma. *Annual Review Psychology*, 56, 393–421.
Merton, R. (1968). *Social Theory and Social Structure*. New York: Free Press.
Milson, A. (2006). Creating positive school experiences for students with disabilities. *Professional School Counselling Journal*, 10(1), 66–72.
National Confederation of People with Disabilities (ESAEA). (2005). *Research*. Proklisis EQUAL. Retrieved 5 April 2012, from http://www.esaea.gr/index.php?module=documents&JAS_DocumentManager_op=viewDocument&JAS_Document_id=106.
Nocella II, A. J. (2006). Emergence of disability pedagogy. *Journal for Critical Education Policy Studies*, 6(2), 77–91.

Olkin, R. and Pledger, C. (2003). Can disability studies and psychology join hands? *American Psychologist*, 58(4), 296–304.

Papastamatis, A. (2010). *Adult Education for Socially Vulnerable Teams* [in Greek]. Athens: I. Sideris.

Reversi, S., Langher, V., Crisafulli, V. and Ferri, R. (2007). The quality of disabled students' school integration. *School Psychology International*, 28(4), 403–418.

Seltzer, M. (2011). The roundabout of special education leadership. *International Journal of Humanities and Social Science*, 1(15), 120–139.

Sidiropoulou-Dimakou, D., Giavrimis, P. and Klouvatou, B. (2002). Professional status and self-esteem of visually impaired individuals. *Nea Paideia*, 103, 110–125.

Soulis, S. (2002). *Inclusion Pedagogy* [in Greek]. Athens: Typothito.

Taylor, B. M., Pearson, P. D., Clark, K. and Warpole, S. (2000). Effective schools and accomplished teachers: Lessons about primary grade reading instruction in low-income schools. *Elementary School Journal*, 101(2), 121–165.

Taylor, B. M., Pearson, P. D., Peterson, D. S. and Rodriguez, M. C. (2005). The CIERA School Change Framework: An evidence-based approach to professional development and school reading improvement. *Reading Research Quarterly*, 40(1), 40–69.

Wade, S. E. (ed). (2011). *Inclusive Education: A Casebook and Readings for Prospective and Practising Teachers*. New York: Routledge.

Ward, J. and Le-Dean, L. (1996). Student teachers' attitudes towards special education provision. *Educational Psychology*, 16(2), 207–218.

Waters, T., Marzano, R. and McNulty, B. (2004). Leadership that sparks learning. *Educational Leadership*, 61(7), 48–52.

Wishart, J. and Manning, G. (1996). Trainee teachers' attitudes to inclusive education for children with Down's syndrome. *Journal of Intellectual Disability Research*, 40(1), 46–65.

Zoniou-Sideris, A. (ed). (2000). *Inclusion: Utopia or Reality? Educational and Political Axes of Disabled Student's Inclusion* [in Greek]. Athens: Ellinika Grammat.

9
GENDER PARITY
Inclusion in Bangladesh education

Samir Ranjan Nath

Context

The aspirations of the people of Bangladesh to develop the nation as *Sonar Bangla* (the Golden Bengal) grew throughout the struggle for Independence. The basics of this are building a nation which is free from all kinds of exploitation and to ensure equity at all levels of society. People's aspiration was articulated through various plan documents including the national constitution. The expansion of education during the past 44 years of Bangladesh's life has been huge. During this period, it has made impressive progress in various aspects of education including gender parity. This chapter examines how education policies in Bangladesh have enhanced girls' and women's participation at various levels and for all aspects of education during the first 44 years. Women-friendly policies, affirmative action and targeted development goals were identified as key to present development. Some policy gaps and the challenges that Bangladesh is facing in its fifth decade were also identified. A number of plausible solutions are suggested to foster women's role in education.

Introduction

The year 2015 marks the 44th anniversary of the independence of Bangladesh – a South Asian country mostly surrounded by India and a relatively small area bordered by Myanmar. Historically, Bangladesh was part of British-India for 190 years (1757–1947). In 1947, India and Pakistan emerged as two independent countries on the basis of a two-nation theory. Bangladesh joined with Pakistan as the Muslim majority province of East Bengal. Pakistan had two parts, viz., East and West – with a distance of over 1,770 kilometres of Indian Territory in between. Economic maltreatment which led to disparity in infrastructure development, budgetary allocation and social sector development including education were the factors creating ground for separation of the two wings of Pakistan. After 24 years of union with the West, the Eastern part broke away from Pakistan in 1971 following a year-long civil war called *Muktijuddha* (struggle for freedom). Disparity in education between the two parts of Pakistan is well recorded (Asadullah, 2010). The number of primary schools during the united period declined by 2.5 percentage points in East Pakistan against a 4.6 times increase in West Pakistan. The increase of secondary schools was 2.2 times in the West against 1.6 times in the East.

During the struggle for Independence, the people of Bangladesh dreamed of a nation called *Sonar Bangla* (the Golden Bengal) which would be free from all kinds of exploitation and ensure basic necessities for citizens. After the birth of the nation, high-level policy makers thought in terms of a radical transformation of society to realise this dream. Some of them drew on socialist ideas of a planned economy (Unterhalter, Ross and Alam, 2003). Although the aspiration was articulated in the constitution as well as in the first five-year plan document, its realisation was hampered due to famine and political turmoil in the mid-1970s and two successive military governments afterwards. Socialist ideas were abandoned throughout the period.

The expansion of education during the first 44 years of Bangladesh has been huge. This was necessary because of the country's large population. Bangladesh had about 70 million people before Independence and the population has grown to over 150 million during the past 44 years. Table 9.1 presents the number of educational institutions, students and teachers in various types of education during 1970–2014. In Bangladesh, the number of educational institutions increased from 37,072 to 145,901, students from 7.3 to over 37.6 million and teachers from 197,916 to more than a million.

TABLE 9.1 Increase in the number of institutions, students and teachers in Bangladesh, 1970–2014

Education type	Number of institutions		Number of students		Number of teachers	
	1970	2014	1970	2014	1970	2014
Primary	29,082	108,537	5,250,819	19,552,979	117,275	482,884
Secondary	5,794	19,684	1,352,700	9,160,365	52,051	232,994
College	394	3,985	300,047	3,506,383	7,507	105,054
Madrasa	1,518	9,341	283,380	3,815,280	16,015	142,749
University	5	112	26,390	853,712	1,434	24,027
Tech and Voc	109	3,766	22,156	645,985	1,703	27,073
Professional	170	476	41,529	122,165	1,931	8,185
All	37,072	145,901	7,277,021	37,656,869	197,916	1,022,966

Source: www.banbeis.govt.org (n.d.) and BANBEIS (2011)

There is an African proverb that says, 'If we educate a boy we educate a person, if we educate a girl we educate a family and a whole nation.' The Convention on the Rights of the Child (CRC) 1989 is the first written document which considered education as the right of every child (irrespective of gender) and obliged national governments to provide formal schooling for all children (United Nations, 1989). Issues such as equal opportunities and the development of children's personality of talents were also mentioned in the document. Although CRC emphasized many issues related to overall development of children with full potentiality, a number of articles were specifically dedicated to education. Following this, the Jomtien declaration of 1990 and the world declaration of 2000 called on national governments and international communities to work together to achieve education for all (WCEFA, 1990; UNESCO, 2000). Although elimination of all types of disparities were aimed at, the enhancement of girls' education was one of the major tasks in these initiatives. Special emphasis was to dissolve gender disparities in education. Two of the eight Millennium Development Goals (MDGs) were on education (United Nations, 2000). These emphasized universal access and completion of primary education and gender equity at all levels of education, including empowerment of women. Bangladesh has actively participated in the above international initiatives and is committed to the goals of Education for All (EFA) and the MDGs. The 1972 constitution of Bangladesh recognized education as a fundamental responsibility of the State to all its citizens including females (Government of Bangladesh, 1998).

The aim of this chapter is to see how education policies in Bangladesh enhanced girls' and women's participation at various levels of education as articulated in the third MDG. It also identifies the policy gaps and challenges that Bangladesh is facing in its fifth decade and suggests some plausible solutions. Finally, some recommendations are made to foster women's role in education.

No primary data were collected. Secondary sources such as Education Watch reports of the Campaign for Popular Education (CAMPE), survey and study reports of the Bangladesh Bureau of Educational Information and Statistics (BANBEIS), Multiple Indicator Cluster Survey reports of the Bangladesh Bureau of Statistics (BBS) and UNICEF, and studies conducted by the Directorate of Primary Education, UNICEF, other national and international agencies and individuals were used in preparing the chapter.

Gender in education policies

The Constitution, education commission reports, five-year plans, education policy documents and annual development plans are the sources for tracing the evolution of gender-sensitiveness of education policies in Bangladesh. A Constitution was adopted within a year of the birth of the nation which directed an approach of equal rights for both women and men in all spheres of the State and of public life (Article 28.2). It further iterated not to discriminate in admission to any educational institution on the grounds of gender.

The Planning Commission and the first education commission in independent Bangladesh simultaneously realized the need of expansion of education at all levels (Planning Commission, 1973; Ministry of Education, 1974). During the first two decades, more emphasis was given to primary education and then to secondary education. Other education also got attention, but not like school education. The need for the expansion of tertiary education was realized in the third decade. The fourth decade saw attention paid to all levels of education. The importance of the education of females had been realized from the very beginning. The aim was primarily to discover the potentialities of women so that they could contribute to society's development. Secondly, if the level of education of females could be increased, they would be suitable candidates for teaching in schools. Giving preference to women as primary and secondary school teachers was considered as a policy (Planning Commission, 1973, 1978, 1983, 1985, 1990, 1998).

Time bound targets were fixed to increase enrolment at various levels. Separate targets were considered for males and females with a policy to accelerate girls' education. The Planning Commission (1973) estimated that in 1973, about 28.5% of all students in Bangladesh were females (33% at primary, 16% at secondary and 8% at tertiary). The targets were to increase these figures respectively to 37, 21 and 14% during the first plan period (1973–78). Although the targets could not always be achieved, increased targets were fixed in successive five-year plans. Overall, the country did not shift from the policy of enhancing girls' share in education.

Separate schools, colleges and polytechnic institutes for girls were established and at the same time women were encouraged to enrol in co-educational institutions. Females were also encouraged to study science; the study of science was introduced in girls' schools and colleges and giving preference in university admission to women candidates with similar qualifications. In addition to merit-based scholarships for high-performing students, an equal number of general scholarships for the students of both genders were introduced.

Fee-free compulsory primary education for all children was introduced throughout the country in 1990 (Government of Bangladesh, 1990). Some years later, food grains were distributed to the poorer 40% of students in rural schools, which was later replaced by conditional stipend. To continue to receive a stipend, eligible students had to fulfil the minimum requirement of attendance in classes and performance in in-school examinations. School uniforms were distributed among primary students in rural areas. BRAC, a non-government organization (NGO), introduced non-formal primary schools for poor children in 1985 which became a huge programme in the 1990s and 2000s (Lovell and Fatema, 1989; Smillie, 2009). Education under this programme is totally free and 70% of the students are girls. Most of the teachers in these schools are women. Some other NGOs also initiated similar programmes. BRAC alone provided pre-primary education to 6.1 million students and primary education to 5.4 million students.

Tuition for all girls in rural secondary schools was waived up to class VIII during the fourth plan period (1990–95) and this was subsequently extended to class XII. A conditional stipend programme was also introduced for all girls in rural secondary schools. In addition to the conditions for primary students, secondary school girls had to refrain from marriage in order to continue to receive the stipend. Provision of free textbooks to all primary school students started in 2008, and this was extended to secondary students (up to class X) beginning in 2009.

Recruitment of females as teachers in primary and secondary schools was a clear policy direction throughout the Bangladesh period. Realizing the positive correlation between the employment of female teachers and girls' enrolment and attendance, recruitment of married female teachers who did not live far from the school was suggested in the first five-year plan (Planning Commission, 1973). Whereas the plan was to increase primary and secondary school women teachers by 5% during the first plan period, the actual increase was 289%. One of the aims was to affect a gradual shift of primary schools from male-dominated teaching to female-dominated teaching. The relaxation of educational qualifications for women candidates was also suggested. Male–female ratio among primary school teachers was targeted to be 2:3.

Although the minimum educational qualification for teaching in primary schools was Higher Secondary Certificate (HSC), it was relaxed to Secondary School Certificate (SSC) for women. However, no such policy was made for secondary teacher recruitment. Additional teacher training institutes for primary and teacher training colleges for secondary level were established. A few of them were exclusively for women. Half of the seats in the co-educational primary teacher training institutions were reserved for women. Residential facilities were increased in these institutes and colleges for women trainees. Additional book allowances and stipends were awarded to women trainees in primary school training institutes.

Compared to school education (primary and secondary) gender-sensitive policies were far less significant at the tertiary level. Gender-sensitive policies in school education were also limited to students' participation and teacher recruitment and training. Other areas like management of educational institutions, education administration, etc. were not brought under gender-related policy consideration.

Proportion of girl and women students

The proportion of female students increased over time at all levels of education, however, at various rates (Table 9.2). In terms of student size, primary and secondary sub-systems are the two most significant provisions and major policy interventions were made for these two sub-systems. Gender parity in participation has been achieved in these two sub-systems where secondary education was ahead of primary. The girls' share has increased 34.8 percentage points in secondary education against 18.9 in primary education. This is because primary education was already ahead of secondary education before Independence and thus it had a smaller gap to bridge. The highest improvement was observed in madrasa education (38 percentage points), but college education had a growth rate similar to secondary education, i.e., 35 percentage points. Before Independence, these two sub-systems had the lowest proportion of female participation. In 2010, madrasa education also achieved gender parity, leaving college and professional education

TABLE 9.2 Percentage of female students at various levels of education in Bangladesh, 1970–2014

Education type	Year					
	1970	1980	1990	2000	2010	2014
Primary	31.8	36.6	44.7	48.7	50.5	50.7
Secondary	18.4	26.1	33.6	52.6	53.3	53.2
College	9.6	19.3	24.6	39.8	44.9	47.6
Madrasa	4.3	4.9	7.7	39.4	50.1	51.8
University	16.8	19.1	20.6	24.8	28.3	30.2
Tech and Voc	–	4.3	5.4	24.5	22.9	28.3
Professional	–	27.1	29.0	35.2	37.8	39.0
Total	**27.3**	**32.7**	**39.5**	**48.1**	**49.9**	**50.2**
Gender parity index	0.376	0.486	0.653	0.926	0.996	1.001

Source: Author's calculation from BANBEIS data (www.banbeis.govt.org, n.d.; BANBEIS, 2011)

behind. All improvements in madrasa education were implemented in the 1990s and onwards when this provision was considered one of the vehicles to reaching EFA goals. The performance of technical and vocational education and university education were much lower than the others with approximately only 30% or less of the students in these types of institutions being women.

A closer look into the data showed that major improvement in girls' participation at primary level occurred from the mid-1980s to the mid-1990s. On the other hand, it was the 1990s when significant progress was made in secondary, college, madrasa and university education. A logical sequence among them is evident.

Considering all types of education together, the female share in the total student population was 27.3% before the Independence of Bangladesh. By 2014 it increased up to 50.2% with a gender parity index of 1.001.

Proportion of women teachers

The proportion of females among teaching staff in each of the sub-systems of education were much lower before Independence than amongst students, with all categories below 8% (Table 9.3).

Although the female share increased in all sub-systems, none could achieve gender parity by 2010. As primary education received the highest policy support regarding recruitment of female teachers, major improvement was observed in this sub-system. Female teachers' share in primary education reached 57.8% by 2014. Overall improvement was 55.6 percentage points – more than one percentage point per year. The least improvement was noticed in the madrasas. There were no female teachers in madrasa education before Independence. Their share exceeded 10% after more than four decades of Bangladesh coming into existence. Secondary schools and universities

TABLE 9.3 Percentage of female teachers at various levels of education in Bangladesh, 1970–2014

Education type	Year					
	1970	1980	1990	2000	2010	2014
Primary	2.2	6.2	20.9	33.8	49.2	57.8
Secondary	7.2	10.1	9.7	15.1	23.1	25.3
College	7.7	7.7	13.5	21.1	21.3	23.0
Madrasa	0.0	0.1	0.8	3.5	10.1	11.9
University	5.6	8.6	12.7	15.4	22.6	25.2
Tech and Voc	–	2.8	3.8	20.0	20.5	20.1
Professional	–	16.2	21.1	26.1	21.6	18.6
Total	**3.6**	**6.9**	**13.2**	**22.4**	**31.5**	**38.3**
Gender parity index	0.037	0.074	0.152	0.289	0.460	0.622

Source: Author's calculation from BANBEIS data (www.banbeis.govt.org, n.d.; BANBEIS, 2011)

reached a quarter by 2014; however, the other education types were below this. Women's share in the total teaching staff was only 3.6% before Independence, which increased to 38.3% in 2014 with a gender parity index of 0.622.

Educational attainment and literacy

The expansion of school education, especially primary and basic, has a direct impact on the increase in ever schooled population as well as in the literacy rate in the country. In 1974, 22.8% of the population aged seven years and above had at least one year of schooling; the rate gradually increased in every decade and reached 73.4% in 2013. The literacy rate for the same population was 26.8% in 1974, which increased to 52.7% in 2013. Therefore, the rate of increase in the ever schooled population was much higher than that in the literacy rate.

The proportion of women who attended school was 13.8% in 1974, which increased to 71.5% in 2013 (Table 9.4). However, their literacy rate only increased from 16.4% in 1974 to 51% in 2013. Males were ahead of females for both indicators throughout the period; however, the gap reduced over time. The gender gap in the ever schooled population was 17.2 percentage points in 1974, which slightly increased to 18.9 in 1981, and then gradually decreased to 3.7 percentage points in 2013. Again, the gap in literacy rate gradually reduced from 20.2 percentage points in 1974 to 3.4 percentage points in 2013. Major improvement in both the indicators occurred in the 1990s.

Internal efficiency indicators

Let us take a look at some other issues important for any education provision and see the place of women in those. In the absence of time series data, findings from

TABLE 9.4 Gender difference in education and literacy rates (7+ years) in Bangladesh, 1974–2013

	Ever Schooled (%)			Literacy Rate (%)		
Year	Males	Females	Difference (% points)	Males	Females	Difference (% points)
1974	31.0	13.8	17.2	36.6	16.4	20.2
1981	44.9	26.0	18.9	33.8	17.5	16.3
1991	52.1	37.3	14.8	38.9	25.5	13.4
2001	65.9	56.5	9.4	49.6	40.6	9.0
2008	71.2	66.4	4.8	50.4	46.5	3.9
2013	75.2	71.5	3.7	54.4	51.0	3.4

Source: Author's calculation from BBS (2003) and Education Watch household survey (2013)

recent studies were used. They specify age specific enrolment rate, attendance in classes, survival rate at various levels and completion of the education cycle. Latest data on age specific net enrolment rate shows that starting from 65% at age six years, it gradually increased to 95% at age nine years and then gradually decreased to 17% at age 20 years (CAMPE, 2009). No gender difference was observed up to the age of eight, girls aged 9–16 were ahead of the boys. There was no difference between boys and girls at age 17 and the boys surpassed the girls afterwards. *Education Watch* studies show that students' attendance in classes increased over time at both primary and secondary levels where the girls were ahead of the boys (CAMPE, 1999, 2005, 2009). As with enrolment and attendance rates, girls were ahead of boys in survival in schools up to class VIII; however, they lagged behind boys afterwards. Thus the survival and completion rates at primary level and beyond were higher for girls than for boys but an opposite trend was found in later years of secondary education (DPE, 2008; CAMPE, 2009; BANBEIS, 2006, 2009, 2011, 2015).

The process of dropping out of school is a complex issue (CAMPE, 2005, 2006, 2009; Rtm International, 2009). Multiple reasons are responsible for this. Due to poverty and the gradual increase of the private cost of education, parents face difficulty bearing the cost of education. The same reason pushes students to work for their families instead of attending school. After some years of study, some students, especially first generation learners, lose interest in education due to lack of guidance and encouragement at home and in school; in addition, there is poor provision for classroom teaching-learning. The early marriage of the girls is another reason for drop out from higher classes of secondary schools (ICDDRB, 2007). Sometimes girls drop out of school in order to take care of younger siblings and help mothers with household chores.

A contrary scenario was observed in the learning achievement of students at primary and secondary levels. As a reflection of survival rates at various classes, the number of girls participating in the primary completion examination was higher than that of the boys and there was a reverse scenario in the secondary school certificate examination. However, the pass rates in both examinations were higher for boys than for girls.

Independently of these, the Directorate of Primary Education (DPE) took tests of the students of class III and V and *Education Watch* took learning achievement tests for primary and secondary students (DPE, 2009; CAMPE, 2001, 2008, 2009). The results of all these studies show that girls lagged behind boys. A study conducted 10 years previously found that teachers, education officials and families had lower expectations for girls than for boys (Shahjamal, 2000). If girls did not do their studies no one worried about it, but the case was just the opposite for boys. Thus, more care was taken of boys' education in school and at home. This ultimately helped boys learn more and do better in learning achievement tests than girls.

Deprivation is also caused by the spread of private tutors. Studies of primary and secondary education have repeatedly shown that the incidence of private tuition has increased over time and it has become an integral part of school education in Bangladesh (CAMPE, 2005, 2006, 2008, 2009; Nath, 2008). A large share of private expenditure for education is spent on private tutoring (CAMPE, 2002, 2007; BBS, 2007, 2011). The studies also show that parents are more likely to provide private tutors for sons than for daughters. The important point is that support from private tutors plays a positive role in learning achievement (Nath, 2012). Consolidation of information on the spread of private tutoring, the costs and the link between tutoring and learning achievement shows that there is a significant gender difference. Findings clearly indicate that girls are even more deprived from the existing provision of additional private tutoring.

No information on survival, completion and drop out of college students was available. However, the number of examinees in the Higher Secondary School Certificate (HSC) examination and pass rate are available from 1990 onwards. The proportion of women examinees increased slowly over time: 26.5% in 1990, 38.3% in 2000, 47.9% in 2010 and 49.3% in 2014 (BANBEIS, 2011, 2015). A similar increasing trend is also evident in the case of Secondary School Certificate (SSC) examination (Table 9.5). Comparing this with the proportion of female students in colleges confirms that survival and dropout rates at this level of education tend to

TABLE 9.5 Percentage of female candidates in secondary and higher secondary school certificate examinations in Bangladesh, 1990–2014

Year	Examination	
	Secondary School Certificate	*Higher Secondary School Certificate*
1990	33.6	26.5
1995	39.4	34.3
2000	43.9	38.3
2005	46.3	42.6
2010	49.7	47.9
2014	50.7	49.3

Source: BANBEIS (2011, 2015)

be equal between males and females. The pass rates were sometimes higher for females and sometimes equal for both.

The government's policy regarding the use of private tutoring is not clear enough. Regulation does not allow teachers of secondary schools and colleges to practise private tutoring; however, there is very little compliance with this rule. On the other hand, no such regulation exists for primary school teachers. It seems that the authorities refrain from interfering intentionally. However, this is not a matter about which it is fair to keep silent; private tutoring creates blatant inequality in academic fields. There should be a clear policy on whether private tutoring should be welcomed or not. If welcomed, to what extent. The other important issue is the question of how we can use the provision of private tutoring in a humanitarian way, such as in a pro-poor mode, from which poor students and first generation learners can benefit. State subsidies for private tutoring may be an option.

Management and administration

Women also lagged behind men in advancing to the position of head teacher and being a member of a school managing committee (SMC). Only a fifth of the heads of primary and less than 5% of secondary educational institutions were women (CAMPE, 2006, 2009). Women's share in primary school SMCs increased over time – 19.2% in 1998 to 25.9% in 2008 (CAMPE, 1999, 2009). On the other hand, they made up only 3.4% of SMC members in secondary schools (CAMPE, 2006). The madrasas lagged behind other institutions in both indicators – only 2% of the heads and 3% of the SMC members of these institutions were female. Scanning minutes of meetings of school managing committees gives a sense of there being no discussion relating to issues and problems specific to girls or the female teachers (CAMPE, 1999, 2009; BANBEIS, 2009).

It is not possible to say anything about women as heads of colleges and their governing boards due to a scarcity of information. The vice-chancellor, pro-vice-chancellor and treasurer are three key positions in university administration. Syndicate and senate in public universities and governing board in private universities are top management bodies. Through scanning of websites of universities it was observed that only two private and one public university had female vice-chancellors. The senates, syndicates and governing boards had less than 10% female members.

The Ministry of Primary and Mass Education (MoPME) and the Ministry of Education (MoE) are responsible for implementing all types of education in Bangladesh. Gender composition of officials and staff of the ministries are thus important. A recent study shows that the proportion of female officials and staff in these two ministries is about 25% (Khatun, 2010).

Challenges of the fifth decade

Policies and actions to increase women's participation at primary level as students and teachers have resulted in an increased proportion in educational institutions.

Affirmative action to increase girls' participation at secondary level has also given a positive result. At the same time no such action was taken to increase the number of female head teachers in schools or increase the number of women members on school managing committees. Both are important to realize the goal of creating a girl-friendly school environment. Providing a role model is also important for female students. If girls see that females actually lead educational institutions and actively participate in its management, they would certainly be encouraged to study more seriously. This is true for all levels of education. Time-bound targeted policy to encourage females should be in place – not only for students but also for teachers, heads of institutions, and members and chairs of management/governing bodies.

Encouraging women to participate in lead positions of education will not give satisfactory results if the quality of education for girls and women in institutions of primary, secondary and tertiary education cannot be ensured. Curriculum, classroom pedagogy and other related issues are important components to quality education. Review of curriculum is a continuous process which should be done at least once a decade. However, it is an irregular activity in Bangladesh. The review and revision of school curricula should include gender analysis of learning objectives, textbooks, classroom teaching and assessment. There should be no issues in the curriculum and no content in the textbooks which undermine female roles in society. On the contrary, it is important to highlight prominent female role models through curriculum and textbooks. The ultimate idea is to promote a sense of equity through all types of curricular and co-curricular activities.

Training is another area which requires policy intervention. It is important that all individuals working in the field of education be gender-sensitive. Properly planned training can be an instrument to achieve gender parity. The provision of teacher training is mostly based on pedagogy and teaching-learning techniques. A gender component should be included in it. Training for head teachers should also bear gender content. At present there is no training for SMC members. This should be started soon and along with management issues, gender-related content should be included. Primary Training Institutes, Teacher Training Colleges, National Academy for Primary Education (NAPE) and the National Academy for Educational Management (NAEM) should be adequately equipped so that they can act as hubs of equitable norms and practices.

Sometimes girls suffer from feelings of insecurity. Boisterous boys disturb them on their way to school. At school, they are also subject to insults by male students and teachers. This no doubt indicates a broader social problem and points to causes rooted in social values and socio-economic conditions. Education has something to do with this. Girls' schooling is disrupted and serious problems arise in the lives of victims. Action from various angles may be required to address such social issues. The formation of a school-level committee to confront such incidents along with a citizens' charter may be considered. Female parents, community leaders and student representatives of both genders should be included in these committees. This can be a starting point. In the future, such committees can work to eliminate all forms of gender discrimination at school level. Redeeming boys from association with offending groups and using education as an instrument to prevent violent behaviour are two important issues. Education has a vital role to play in such circumstances.

Emphasis should be placed on training of all levels of people associated with school (teachers, SMC members and education officials at various levels) so that schools as a whole can be made gender-sensitive. We should not forget that primary education builds the foundation. If children can be made gender-sensitive through primary education, it can be an asset throughout their lives and for the future of the nation.

Along with taking steps to make educational institutions gender-sensitive, initiative should be taken to provide a gender audit of educational institutions. Such an initiative would help trace progress in gender relations at school level. This can be done annually or biannually depending on resource mobilization. BANBEIS can implement such monitoring with support from ministries concerned with education. Results of a gender audit can be useful for the government in order for it to take the necessary steps to ensure gender parity at all levels and for all aspects of education.

Conclusions

After it gained independence in 1971, Bangladesh started out with a dilapidated economy inherited from the 'two-economy' policy of the then Pakistan. The overall infrastructure of the country was damaged further due to the war. This affected the education sector quite generally. Thus, the first task of the new nation was to reconstruct the existing educational institutions and then to move on to increase enrolment and subsequently raise the quality of education. Emphasis on gender equality in education was put forward from the very beginning.

It took Bangladesh education at least two decades to overcome war damages and start moving forward. Owing to various steps taken by the State and other institutions, much improvement has taken place at all levels of education. On the whole, Bangladesh education policies gave more importance to primary education and only afterwards to secondary education. Other education frameworks were also given importance but not as much as these. As a result, a major expansion occurred in primary and secondary education, far broader than that of the others.

Females lagged behind males at all levels and aspects of education at the time of Independence. Due to the introduction of explicit policies and affirmative action to enhance female participation in education, the situation has changed a great deal during the past 44 years of Bangladesh's existence. Gender parity has been achieved in students' enrolment in primary and secondary schools and in the madrasas. There is a lot more to be done at tertiary level and in developing specific aspects of education, among them, teaching staff, heading the institutions and management and administration. Women-friendly policies and targeted development plans may help Bangladesh to achieve gender equity at all levels and in all aspects of education. A gender-sensitive educational environment is thus a challenge for Bangladesh in its fifth decade.

Bibliography

Asadullah, M. N. (2010). Educational disparity in East and West Pakistan, 1947–1971: Was East Pakistan discriminated against? *The Bangladesh Development Studies*, XXXIII, 1–46.
BANBEIS. (2006). Bangladesh educational statistics 2006. Dhaka: Bangladesh Bureau of Educational Information and Statistics.
BANBEIS. (2009). National Education Survey (Post Primary): 2008 Statistical Report. Dhaka: Bangladesh Bureau of Educational Information and Statistics.
BANBEIS. (2011). Bangladesh education statistics 2010. Dhaka: Bangladesh Bureau of Educational Information and Statistics.
BANBEIS. (2015). Bangladesh education statistics 2014. Dhaka: Bangladesh Bureau of Educational Information and Statistics.
BANBEIS. (n.d.). Trends analysis. Dhaka: Bangladesh Bureau of Educational Information and Statistics. Available online: www.banbeis.govt.bd [accessed on 14 October 2015].
BBS. (2003). Population census 2001 national report (provisional). Dhaka: Bangladesh Bureau of Statistics.
BBS. (2007). Household income and expenditure survey report 2005. Dhaka: Bangladesh Bureau of Statistics.
BBS. (2011). Report of the household income and expenditure survey, 2010. Dhaka: Bangladesh Bureau of Statistics.
CAMPE. (1999). *Hope not Complacency: State of Primary Education in Bangladesh*. Dhaka: Campaign for Popular Education and University Press Limited.
CAMPE. (2001). *Question with Quality: State of Primary Education in Bangladesh*. Dhaka: Campaign for Popular Education.
CAMPE. (2002). *Renewed Hope, Daunting Challenges: State of Primary Education in Bangladesh*. Dhaka: Campaign for Popular Education.
CAMPE. (2005). *Quality with Equity: The Primary Education Agenda*. Dhaka: Campaign for Popular Education.
CAMPE. (2006). *The State of Secondary Education: Progress and Challenges*. Dhaka: Campaign for Popular Education.
CAMPE. (2007). *Financing Primary and Secondary Education in Bangladesh*. Dhaka: Campaign for Popular Education.
CAMPE. (2008). *The State of Secondary Education: Quality and Equity Challenges*. Dhaka: Campaign for Popular Education.
CAMPE. (2009). *State of Primary Education in Bangladesh: Progress Made, Challenges Remained*. Dhaka: Campaign for Popular Education.
DPE. (2008). School Survey Report 2007 of Second Primary Education Development Programme. Dhaka: Directorate of Primary Education.
DPE. (2009). National Assessment of Pupils of Grades 3 and 5, 2008, Executive Summary. Dhaka: Directorate of Primary Education.
Education Watch. (2013). Education Watch household survey database 2013. Dhaka: Campaign for Popular Education. Dataset created in 2013.
Government of Bangladesh. (1990). The Education (Compulsory) Act, 1990 [in Bangla]. *Bangladesh Gazette*, 5, Additional issue, 13 February1990. Dhaka: Government of Bangladesh.
Government of Bangladesh. (1998). *The Constitution of the People's Republic of Bangladesh*. Dhaka: Ministry of Law Justice and Parliamentary Affairs, Government of Bangladesh.
ICDDRB. (2007). Consequence of early marriage on female schooling in rural Bangladesh. *Health and Science Bulletin*, 5(4), 13–18.
Khatun, F. (2010). *Women's roles in government services*. Paper presented in a seminar organized by the Bangladesh Mohila Parishad, Dhaka; August 2010.

Lovell, C. and Fatema, K. (1989). *Assignment Children: The BRAC Non-formal Primary Education Programme in Bangladesh*. New York: UNICEF.

Ministry of Education. (1974). Education Commission Report 1974. Dhaka: Ministry of Education, Government of Bangladesh.

Nath, S. R. (2008). Private supplementary tutoring among primary students in Bangladesh. *Educational Studies*, 34(1), 55–72.

Nath, S. R. (2012). Factors influencing primary students' learning achievement in Bangladesh. *Research in Education*, 88, 50–63.

Planning Commission. (1973). *The First Five-Year Plan 1973–78*. Dhaka: Planning Commission, Government of the People's Republic of Bangladesh.

Planning Commission. (1978). *The Two Year Plan 1978–80*. Dhaka: Planning Commission, Government of the People's Republic of Bangladesh.

Planning Commission. (1983). *The Second Five-Year Plan 1980–85*. Dhaka: Planning Commission, Ministry of Finance and Planning, Government of the People's Republic of Bangladesh.

Planning Commission. (1985). *The Third Five-Year Plan 1985–90*. Dhaka: Planning Commission, Ministry of Planning, Government of the People's Republic of Bangladesh.

Planning Commission. (1990). *The Fourth Five-Year Plan 1990–95*. Dhaka: Planning Commission, Ministry of Planning, Government of the People's Republic of Bangladesh.

Planning Commission. (1998). *The Fifth Five-Year Plan 1997–2002*. Dhaka: Planning Commission, Ministry of Planning, Government of the People's Republic of Bangladesh.

RtmInternational. (2009). *Participatory Evaluation: Causes of Primary School Dropout*. Dhaka: DPE, UNICEF and Rtm International.

Shahjamal, M. M. (2000). Gender difference in mathematics education: A case of BRAC schools. An unpublished dissertation submitted for the degree Master of Education to the Institute of Education and Research, University of Dhaka.

Smillie, I. (2009). *Freedom from Want: The Remarkable Success Story of BRAC, the Global Grassroots Organization that's Winning the Fight Against Poverty*. Dhaka: University Press Limited.

UNESCO. (2000). *The Dakar Framework of Action*. Paris: UNESCO.

United Nations. (1989). *Convention on the Rights of the Child*. New York: Office of the United Nations High Commissioner for Human Rights, United Nations.

United Nations. (2000). *United Nations Millennium Development Goals*. New York: United Nations.

Unterhalter, E., Ross, J. and Alam, M. (2003). A fragile dialogue? Research and primary education policy formation in Bangladesh, 1971–2001. *Compare*, 33(1), 85–99.

WCEFA. (1990). *World Conference on Education for All: Meeting Learning Needs*. Jomtien, Paris: UNESCO.

PART III
Challenges and possible responses to inclusive education

10

CHALLENGES FOR EDUCATION AND INCLUSIVENESS IN INDIA

Mohd Akhtar Siddiqui

Context

India, with a population of 1.21 billion people, is the second largest country in the world after China. After gaining independence from colonial rule in 1947, it became the largest democracy in the world. The country is endowed with a mosaic of diverse cultures, religions and languages. It is slowly emerging as an important economic power in the region. Education has always been accorded an honoured place in Indian society. Throughout the nation's struggle for independence, great leaders of the Indian freedom movement always stressed education's unique significance for national development (National Council of Educational Research and Training [NCERT], 1966, xv).

Status of educational development

India's education system has been steadily developing since independence. The pace of development has increased during the last three decades, thanks to the Education Policy of 1986 which resolved to substantially improve access to education at all levels and to make it more relevant and inclusive in its reach. While the succeeding Five Year Plans provided enhanced support to help implement resolutions of the education policy, simultaneously, a favourable climate across the country was also created to encourage greater private participation in improving access especially to professional and technical education. As a result, during this period enhanced institutional facilities have commendably improved access to education at all levels for all social groups in society. One may claim that the democratic principles of equality of opportunity and social justice in education now stand better implemented.

As is evident from the educational statistics (Ministry of Human Resource Development [MHRD], 2013), in 2010–11, 135.3 million children were enrolled in primary schools and the GER (Gross Enrolment Ratio) for primary classes (standard I-V) was 116.0%, whereas 62.0 million children have been brought to the fold of upper primary schools (standard VI-VIII) with a GER of 85.5% (MHRD, 2013). In secondary schools there are as many as 51.1 million students and the GER has gone up to 52.1% (ibid.). Expansion in higher education has also resulted in an improved GER of 19.4% with 27.5 million enrolments. Having almost achieved the goal of universal elementary education particularly due to the support extended through the flagship programme of SSA (Sarva Shiksha Abhiyan) floated by the central government and the enforcement of the Right of Children for Free and Compulsory Education (RCFCE) Act (2009), plans are afoot to universalize secondary education by 2020 and also to enhance enrolment in higher education to at least 25% of the cohort by 2015. To ensure that education will become more relevant and that students passing out of educational institutions will possess skills that the knowledge economy is looking for in young people, school curricula have been overhauled. In the new National Curriculum Framework (NCF, 2005), central support has also been made available for greater integration of ICT in education through the National Policy of ICT in Education announced in 2010 and greater autonomy has been granted to higher education institutions to innovate and improve their programme offerings in both quantitative and qualitative terms.

Challenges

Despite this bright picture of education in India, still there are several challenges to be addressed for better access to quality education that will enable young people to meet the demands of this fast-changing, competitive democratic society. Some of these challenges include the following:

- Access to school education and school participation in recent years has significantly improved. Enrolment in primary schools is almost universal and at upper primary level it is said to be 'just around the corner'. However, the quality of education as seen in the learning performance of children has not been satisfactory by any reckoning – not only by global standards but also by desirable domestic levels of learning. The NGO Pratham's latest nationwide survey report – ASER (Annual Status of Education Report, 2011) for rural districts has once again shown that learning levels of primary school children in reading and basic arithmetic are poor. Over half of the standard 5th children cannot read 2nd standard language texts, and one-third of children of this standard cannot do simple numerical subtraction that children of the 2nd standard are expected to do. The status of learning as shown in ASER for this year is consistent with reports from the previous six years despite improved provision of inputs such as infrastructure, teaching and learning materials and teacher recruitment and development in elementary schools. Another recent study, *Inside Primary Schools* (Bhattacharjea, Wadhwa and Banerji, 2011), revealed that children do learn during the year, but much more slowly than what a particular textbook of their level demands.

- It seems that the heavily funded SSA programme has not been able to make any visible dent in the quality of education obtained in our elementary schools. The learning deficiency created at elementary level only aggravates and accumulates further as the learner moves up to secondary and higher levels of education. Concern for the quality of education becomes all the more serious when we look at it in the global perspective. The prevalence of transnational mobility demands that more competitive learning outcomes be acquired by young people. The poor quality of basic education neither helps enhance the productivity of the common worker to improve national economic development, which otherwise it should, nor does it make a sound foundation for secondary and higher education. Thus it adversely affects quality of education at later levels as well.
- Another important dimension of the quality issue is the enormous gap in quality that persists among different states. For example, if Tamil Nadu, Kerala and Himachal Pradesh are at the upper end of the quality continuum, states such as Bihar, Uttar Pradesh, Rajasthan and Assam are at the other extreme of this continuum (De et al., 2011).
- While both supply side and demand side factors are responsible for the poor quality of education in some states, the more dismal reason is lack of teaching input or low levels of teaching activity for many children which may be attributed to a range of factors. There is a need for more teachers to be appointed; there is a need for teachers to be willing to work in more remote schools and in those with poor connectivity; there is a need for teachers to be present in the school for the duration of the school-day, and for those who are present in school to be teaching. At the same time there is very little support from the Department of Education for mentoring these teachers in carrying out their work, especially with children whose parents lack a formal education. State inertia in the field of education in some states is yet another reason for the poor quality of education there. There is a lack of political concern about the urgency to improve the quality of teaching and to ensure better teacher accountability (PROBE, 2011).
- Pritchett (2011) feels that the Right to Education Act introduced in India enshrines an anti-learning agenda. Following an input-led approach, it focuses exclusively on schooling. The definition of quality it enshrines has no deep intrinsic connection to learning performance. According to him, the RTE is the wrong instrument at the wrong time and it will be a means for inhibiting movement towards an effective learning agenda. In quality discourse, our primary concern should be learning for which the relationship between the learner and the teacher is critical. However, the inputs, the processes of education, the learning environment and the outputs that surround and foster learning are important as well. High-quality educational processes require well-trained teachers who are able to use learner-centred teaching and learning methods and life skill approaches (Ross and Genevois, 2006).

- The National Curriculum Framework (NCF, 2005) emphasizes learner-centred methods, locates itself in the constitutional values and promotes the use of critical pedagogy in classrooms to improve student learning, but it has remained silent on disparities and inequalities that exist in our schools. The Framework is also much publicized but little disseminated among school teachers. The NCF (2005) does not address the inequalities existing in the school system; furthermore, it lacks reasoned arguments for the position taken on a wide range of issues such as whether to have examinations or not, using mother tongue as a medium of instruction and the place of English in primary schools, etc. Thus, it is unlikely to be useful to people on the ground (PROBE, 2011; Raina, 2005). There is a need for NCERT to have a fresh look at the school curriculum and textbooks and ensure that these are more realistically modulated to the levels and contexts of children so that these instruments can really help leverage the quality of school education.
- Owing to near complete withdrawal of the government from the responsibility for teacher preparation (which is not witnessed in such a large measure in any other part of the world) there has been a mushrooming of substandard self-financed teacher education institutions and commercialization of teacher education across India. Today, more than 90% of teacher education institutions in India are in the private self-financed sector (National Council for Teacher Education [NCTE], 2012). Moreover, affiliating universities and examining boards have shown a lack of interest in regular monitoring of the processes of teaching and learning in these institutions. At almost every stage the quality of teacher preparation has been seriously compromised during the last two decades and this has had an obvious trickle-down effect on the quality of school education.
- The quality of in-service teacher education provided to all elementary school teachers every year under SSA, barring some places, also leaves much to be desired. On the school grounds these inadequately trained and routinely retrained teachers are hardly subjected to any serious accountability measures. In these circumstances, the task of improving the quality of teaching and learning in schools looks utopian. Some urgent steps that should be taken to enhance the quality of school education include: a drastic change in the structure and curriculum of teacher education; more extensive 'handholding' and investment in such education by the government; and holding teachers responsible for their own continuous professional development. Teachers should also be held accountable for student learning achievement, and this should systematically be linked to their service conditions.
- The expansion of universal elementary education has raised aspirations and demand for secondary education which is of both a preparatory and terminal nature. Secondary education has not received the attention it deserves from educational planners and administrators. It is for this reason that it remains the weakest link in the entire education system. Currently, besides developing the conceptual base for advanced academic education in different disciplines,

secondary schools are expected to equip graduates with vocational competence to an acceptable standard in identified areas of work so that they can readily be engaged in the employment market. But the existing diversification in secondary education has not yielded satisfactory results so far. Hardly one-tenth of young people enrolled in secondary schools opt for the vocational stream, and even they find it hard to get suitable employment owing to the poor quality of the skill training and a mismatch between the profile of vocational qualifications they obtain and the one needed in the job market. The vocational education programme has not really taken off well. Its inherent weaknesses of poor or no linkage with higher education; limited or no scope of career development for vocational graduates; the general perception that vocational education is an inferior and rather less respectful alternative; and a lackadaisical attitude of the educational administrators towards this stream of education have so far remained inconclusively addressed. Thus the quality of secondary education in neither of the two streams is satisfactory, especially in government-funded schools. Here again, teacher inputs are found to be weak and there is an absence of any serious accountability mechanism for teachers and head teachers. Interestingly, even the new resolve of the government to universalize secondary education by 2020 lacks clarity of object and focus on skill development. A more elaborate secondary education policy addressing the issues of curriculum, skill training and vocational qualification certification, teacher development for both streams of secondary education, better regulation of and support for secondary education, and bridging of gaps in access and quality among regional and social groups needs to be put in place and rigorously implemented. The Rashtriya Madhayamik Shiksha Abhiyan (RMSA) of the central government and the scheme of PPP (Public Private Partnership) for the setting up of 2,500 model secondary schools are again input-focused attempts to improve the state of secondary education and thus may not help enhance its quality substantially.

- The situation of higher education is rather more complex. It is true that enrolment in higher education is steadily rising. In 2006–07 GER of higher education was 12.39%. It increased to 19.4% in 2010–11. Out of a total enrolment of 27.5 million in 2010–11 in higher education, 79.9% were in graduate, 11.9% in postgraduate, 7.8% in diploma, certificate, etc. and 0.4% in research courses. A large number of students in undergraduate programmes (46.6%) were enrolled in arts and social sciences, 13.8% in science and computers, and 13.5% in commerce. Thus around 75% of the enrolments in undergraduate institutions were in arts, science, commerce, humanities and other courses, and 24% were in professional courses and barely less than 1% in agriculture and related sciences. Among professional courses, enrolment in engineering and technology courses was the highest, i.e., 17.7% of the total enrolments, or more than 73% of the enrolments in professional courses. This uneven distribution of enrolments in higher education calls for a policy change. The share of private higher education institutions has gradually gone up from 42.6% in 2001 to 75% in 2013–14 (MHRD, 2015). This share is much higher in undergraduate degree programmes in professional courses. For example, both the number of institutions and the size of enrolment in undergraduate degree courses in engineering in the private sector have gone up from 76% of the total number of institutions and enrolments in undergraduate degree programmes in engineering in 1999–2000 to 85% in 2003–04 (MHRD, 2009a). This indicates an alarmingly declining trend in government's participation in higher education, particularly in the professional and technical education sector, and a steady rise in the interest of for-profit colleges and universities whose standards are often questionable.

- As pointed out by Altbach (2011), India's higher education sector is in poor shape. It can neither serve the growing demand for access, nor does it have the quality required by a growing economy. That quality assurance remains a challenge for India as the current accreditation arrangement is cumbersome and bureaucratic and has failed to cope with the certification needs of all the institutions. India should learn from the century-old well-established accreditation system in vogue in the USA, though of late this system has also faced problems in coping with a rapidly expanding for-profit education industry and distance education. Altbach suggests that India needs an attractive sub-baccalaureate and vocationally oriented institution on the lines of the community college in America which combines market-oriented two-year associate degree vocational programmes and four-year academic courses. This, indeed, may simultaneously help meet the targets and standards of technical and vocational education as well as growing demand for access to higher education.

- Research in education is another serious challenge. It is not up to the mark either in terms of quality or volume. Investment in research is also far below the required levels. While India spends around US$20 billion Purchasing Power Parity (PPP) on research and development, China, the world's other fast-growing economy, invests US$150 billion PPP in this area. The modest investment in research in India has negative implications for innovation in the economy as well as for the quality of education. Incidentally, even this moderate investment on education is not optimally and objectively utilized for meaningful research. Research should inform and refine the formulation of education policy, curriculum and practice. This is not really happening even when it is found to have contemporary implications. Research conducted in a comparative perspective can help Indian educators and administrators solve many educational problems. It can highlight good educational practices that can be adopted and adapted from other parts of the world. Best practices in the field of education in vogue in other societies must be systematically studied and their suitability to Indian conditions must be tested before their adoption. A dedicated institutional setting for continuing research in comparative education, more liberal research funding, more need-oriented and original research and concerted and continuing effort to translate it into practice are essential steps that need to be taken to meet this challenge.

- The inculcation of values, particularly those enshrined in the Constitution, poses a serious challenge for education. Fundamental duties are being emphasized and included in the curriculum; yet in Indian society, there is increasing incidence of social and economic malpractice, a rise of social tensions, conflicts and human rights violations. This demands that a fresh look be given to the content and the approach to value education and practices followed by teachers and institutional authorities for creating a human relations-based ambience that should help in promoting effective inculcation of values.
- Indian society is full of diversities. It has a rich variety of religions, languages, cultures, regions, castes, tribes, etc. It is a great challenge to ensure that different groups of people get equal opportunity to grow and develop in all spheres of life without any discrimination and deprivation. In the modern democratic society this may successfully be done through the instrumentality of education which is essentially arranged in an inclusive setting. Inclusiveness in education would mean that the entire education system, its policies, curriculum, textbooks, pedagogy, evaluation system and attitude of teachers, educational administrators and other educational workers, etc., is geared to an inclusive approach and consciously removes all barriers to inclusion in education. Thus 'inclusion describes the process by which a school attempts to respond to all pupils as individuals by reconsidering its curricular organization and provision. Through this process, the school builds its capacity to accept all pupils from the local community who wish to attend and, in so doing, reduces the need to exclude pupils' (Sebba and Ainscow, 1996, p. 9). The educational situation and status in developing countries and the one obtained in developed countries are distinctively different, and so the two need two different kinds of approaches to inclusive education. In developing countries this situation is marked by the presence of a good proportion of children who either do not attend school or discontinue education prematurely for varied reasons (Jha, 2007, p. 34). Appreciating this situation, the Salamanca World Conference in 1994 recommended that 'a school should accommodate all children regardless of their physical, intellectual, social, linguistic or other conditions. This should include disabled and gifted, street and working children, children from remote and nomadic populations, children from linguistic, ethnic or cultural minorities and children from other disadvantaged and marginalized areas and groups' (UNESCO, 1994, pp. 11–12). It is in this perspective that the identification of 'children with special educational needs' is seen by some experts as labelling and discriminatory. The segregation of these children from others for their special education would be treated as a barrier to their educational development (Mittler, 2000).
- In India, attempts are being made to follow the broader approach of inclusive education as is recommended for developing countries. The NCF (2005) stresses a child-centred approach in curriculum formation and implementing it in an inclusive environment. Teachers are expected to help children construct knowledge in their own perspectives. The Right of Children for Free and

Compulsory Education Act (2009) is another attempt to provide education of comparable quality to all children by stressing the provision of prescribed inputs including teachers in all schools. At the heart of this legislation lies a guarantee for quality education to all children in the age group 6–14 years. The Act also mentions that every child would be given education, knowledge, skills, etc., appropriate to his/her age. So, for example, a child of 12 years of age from any socio-economic and regional background, as a result of the inclusive approach followed by the teachers, would surely possess knowledge and skills of grade VI. However, this does not seem to be happening in many primary schools in the country as has been proved by Pratham in its annual report (ASER, 2011). As stated earlier, a majority of class V students were able to read only class II texts and could only solve simple second grade arithmetic problems. Although these children are included in schooling, they have not really been included in education and are left out or finally excluded. Pritchett (2011) argues that the Indian school system, which is based on a rapid curriculum, has been geared to producing elite students. The teachers and the school system are under tremendous pressure to get through a curriculum that is moving at too fast a pace. So what happens is that children who fall behind never catch up (note ASER reports). Though children may be having difficulty with basic problems in addition, the mathematics curriculum moves on, on the presumption that addition has been learnt and now division and fractions can be taught. The exclusion will continue until we stop teaching to the curriculum and start teaching to the student according to their capacity. Endorsing this view, Banerji (2011) argues that the faster the curriculum moves, the bigger the gap between expectations and reality. In her view, the big decision is whether we need to move more slowly – to lower our curriculum expectations for children or move much faster in order to equip the school system to deliver the expectations that our policy documents and curriculum promise. The second alternative will never lead to inclusive education as it is geared to an input-led approach and its focus is on schooling rather than on learning. The RTE Act and the SSA both have mainly followed this approach and hence have failed to forge an inclusive education agenda, particularly in government schools.

- Although curricular modulations are basic to inclusive education yet the approach and the attitude of the teacher towards child-centred education and the teachers' own classroom practices of encouraging equitable participation of all groups of learners in the teaching learning process will ensure inclusion in education. This depends both on teachers' professional training and development and on their beliefs and values. In many classrooms teachers have been found to discriminate between children on the basis of their caste or religious background, often making children from particular social groups withdraw from active learning and who then end up with a poor performance.
- The medium of instruction is another source of exclusion in education, especially in those areas where the children belong to language minorities and

teaching-learning is arranged in the medium of the majority. In bordering districts of many states children from the neighbouring state are forced to study in the language of the host state instead of in their mother tongue (Siddiqui, 2007). This affects their learning performance.
- The current examination system, despite all claims of its being continuous, comprehensive, objective and grade-based, is a great challenge to inclusion. In the classroom, the economically deprived, first-generation learners and minority children have to compete with middle-class peers who enjoy extra tuition and coaching at home, as well as parental guidance and an informed home environment. They often remain poor or mediocre achievers, and this further narrows the range of choices available to them for their future educational pursuits. The policy of conducting common terminal and entrance examinations for children coming from diverse kinds of schools (which are placed in a hierarchy) is also exclusionary. It provides an advantage to children coming from schools located higher in the hierarchy and helps them gain entry into more prestigious institutions and programmes of further education. Hierarchies in educational institutions only help reproduce inequality such that individuals who begin with certain advantages are able to maintain or even enhance those advantages. Here, intelligent policies can tilt the balance in favour of individual mobility and away from the reproduction of inequality (Beteille, 2011, xix).
- Even after securing access to education, the inclusion of children, especially those belonging to marginalized and disadvantaged groups, remains a big challenge as several factors operating within and outside the educational institutions continue to force them to drop out or be pushed out of the institution. While factors such as poverty, malnutrition, migration, cultural traditions, etc. force children to drop out of school, factors such as a poor and often hostile environment especially for weak and marginalized children, the attitude of teachers and administrators towards these children, etc. often push them out of schools (Sinha and Reddy, 2011; Govinda, 2011).

Conclusion

Thus there are several challenges for education and inclusiveness in education that need to be addressed through policy initiatives, curricular and examination reform and more importantly through changes in the attitudes of teachers and educational administrators towards children who are disadvantaged.

Bibliography

Altbach, P. G. (2011). Not many lessons for India from US. *The Hindu*, New Delhi, 8 November.

Anuradha, D., Khera, R., Samson, M. and Kumar, A. K. S. (2011). *PROBE Revisited: A Report on Elementary Education in India*. New Delhi: Oxford University Press.

Banerji, R. (2011). How much does she know. *Indian Express*, New Delhi, 15 November.
Beteille, A. (2011). Foreword. In: R. Govinda (ed), *Who Goes to School? Exploring Exclusion in Indian Education*, pp. xvii–xix. New Delhi: Oxford University Press.
Bhattacharjea, S., Wadhwa, S. and Banerji, R. (2011). *Inside Primary Schools*. Mumbai: Pratham Mumbai Initiative.
De, A., Samson, M., Khera, R. and Kumar, A. K. S. (2011). *PROBE Revisited – A Report on Elementary Education in India*. New Delhi: Oxford University Press.
Govinda, R. (2011). Issues and priorities for action and research. In: R. Govinda (ed), *Who Goes to School? Exploring Exclusion in Indian Education*, pp. 404–420. New Delhi: Oxford University Press.
Jha, M. M. (2007). Barriers to student access and success: Is inclusive education an answer? In: G. K. Verma, C. R. Bagley and M. M. Jha (eds), *International Perspectives on Educational Diversity and Inclusion*, pp. 33–43. London: Routledge.
MHRD. (2009a). *Education in India*. New Delhi: Department of Higher Education, Government of India.
MHRD. (2009b). *Right of Children for Free and Compulsory Education Act, 2009*. New Delhi: Department of School Education, MHRD.
MHRD. (2013). *Statistics of School Education, 2010–11*. New Delhi: Government of India.
MHRD. (2015). All India Higher Education Survey, 2013–14. New Delhi: Government of India.
Mittler, P. (2000). *Working Towards Inclusive Education: Social Context*. London: Fulton.
NCERT. (1966). Report of Education Commission 1964–66. New Delhi: NCERT.
NCERT. (2005). *National Curriculum Framework (NCF)*. New Delhi: NCERT.
NCTE. (2012). Justice Verma Commission Report. New Delhi.
Pratham Resource Center. (2011). Annual status of education report (rural) 2010. Mumbai: Pratham.
Pritchett, L. (2011). Interview on education. *The Indian Express*, New Delhi, 8 November.
Raina, V. (2005). Comment: National Curriculum Framework. Seminar, Issue on Forests and Tribals, No. 552, August. In: PROBE (2011). www.India-seminar.com/2005/552/552%20comments.htm.
Ross, K. H. and Genevois, I. J. (2006). *Cross National Studies of the Quality of Education*. Paris: IIPA, UNESCO.
Sebba, J. and Ainscow, M. (1996). International development in inclusive schooling: Mapping and issues. *Cambridge Journal of Education*, 26, 5–18.
Siddiqui, M. A. (2007). Inclusive education for working children and street children in India. In: G. K. Verma *et al.* (eds), *International Perspectives on Educational Diversity and Inclusion*, pp. 162–180. London: Routledge.
Sinha, S. and Reddy, A. N. (2011). School drop-outs or push-outs? Overcoming barriers for the right to education. In: R. Govinda (ed), *Who Goes to School? Exploring Exclusion in Indian Education*, pp. 166–204. New Delhi: Oxford University Press.
UNESCO. (1994). *The Salamanca Statement on Special Needs Education*. Paris: UNESCO.

11

BILINGUAL IMMIGRANT STUDENTS AND INCLUSIVE LEARNING

Issues and challenges

Eleni Griva

Introduction

Inclusion and language development

Diversity of student population is becoming reality within the educational context in most societies. Recognition and acceptance of differences and similarities as well as whole-school approaches to learning are often employed in an inclusive setting where teaching emphasises the connection between social, cultural and linguistic aspects of students' experiences and understanding. It is widely accepted that in such a context teachers should assume responsibility to stimulate a classroom environment where students develop language and cognitive skills along with their cooperative skills and recognition of perspectives rather than their own (Griva et al., 2011a).

It is also advocated that throughout schooling, equality of access to learning should be promoted, irrespective of students' cultural, linguistic background and abilities. For this purpose, inclusive practices are often adopted aimed at enhancing learning of less competent students and providing the same opportunities for holistic learning and participation in all aspects of school life. There is also some evidence to suggest that through the adoption of appropriate approaches to learning, responsible behaviour in the classroom and adequate development of language skills, the following outcomes can be potentially achieved: improvement of interpersonal and intercultural relationships, understanding of individual differences, bias and stereotypes (Santora, 2006) which contribute to the immigrant students' inclusion in the school. However, Greek teachers often express their anxiety and uncertainty about teaching bilingual immigrant students due to a lack of proper and relevant training on issues related to bilingualism within a pluralist context (Griva et al., 2011b).

A number of issues are associated with bilingual students' language development and educational attainment, such as students' personal characteristics, ethnic and linguistic origin, socio-economic factors, parents' education and basic skills, and parental involvement (Lindholm-Leary, 2001). However, despite the fact that school plays a vital role in literacy development, other influences that are likely to affect children's everyday life in and out of school cannot be underestimated. It should also be noted that since effective education responds to the learning needs of individual children and the needs of their families, collaboration between school and family is essential to achieving education for all.

Parental involvement also plays a central role in children's successful literacy attainment (Marsh, 2006). It has been suggested that children whose parents are actively involved in their development are more likely to succeed in school (Desforges and Abouchaar, 2003). In addition, the attitudes of immigrant parents towards the majority language also tend to affect the speed and quality of children's second language (L2) acquisition (Griva and Stamou, 2014; Li, 1999). It is widely believed that immigrant parents' supportive attitudes towards both languages and their active involvement in their children's linguistic progress can result in children's acquisition of language skills.

Issues and strategies in writing skills

While writing is considered to be an important part of literacy development, it is regarded as a complicated process which imposes some constraints on bilingual students. Children who do not learn to read and write and communicate effectively in primary school are more likely to leave school early, be unemployed or find themselves in low-skilled jobs, and are most likely to end up in poverty (Barnados, 2009). Students who encounter literacy difficulties are more likely to experience educational failure, and therefore they leave school without qualifications (Eivers et al., 2004). Not having the skills and qualifications to participate in today's knowledge-based society, the individual faces a low-level quality of life (Kennedy et al., 2009). Those individuals do not enjoy certain outcomes that determine human well-being, such as psychological, economic, physical and social well-being (Maxwell and Teplova, 2007).

Given the fact that first language (L1) writing process depends on mastering a number of processes and sub-skills, such as generating and drafting ideas, producing content, revising and editing text (Griva et al., 2009; Reid, 1992), L2 writing involves all of these processes mixed up with L1 competence issues, which overwhelm the writing process, especially in the case of poor writers (Bereiter and Scardamalia, 1987).

Some research suggests that bilingual students' L2 literacy depends on the literacy developed in L1 (Cummins, 2001; Baker, 2002). These students develop metalinguistic awareness and use a wider range of language learning strategies compared to monolingual ones (Cenoz and Valencia, 1994; Griva et al., 2011a).

Furthermore, some studies have also shown that skilled writers tend to view planning and composing as a continual process which includes developing an initial set of goals or plans to guide the writing process (e.g. Goddard and Sendi, 2008). In contrast, poor writers seldom set writing goals, monitor their final product as regards the writing goal and rarely revise a text (ibid., 2008). They believe themselves to have weaknesses in the following areas of language (Victori, 1995): a) size of vocabulary; b) correctness of language; c) unconscious processing of language; d) language creation; e) mastery of the functions of language.

Given the above described context, the present study was aimed at:

- mapping the range of cognitive/meta-cognitive writing strategies employed when bilingual students write a task in Greek (L2);
- identifying the possible differences between more and less competent bilingual students in their use of cognitive and meta-cognitive strategies;
- identifying the potential difficulties encountered by bilingual students while composing a text in Greek;
- recording immigrant parents' views on their children's literacy development;
- recording immigrant parents' attitudes in relation to their involvement in their children's education.

The research

The reason for conducting this study stemmed from the growing number of second-language students in Greek primary schools, justified by the fact that Greece has been receiving immigrants for the last several decades. As might be expected, immigrant students, especially those who enter the Greek educational system at a later age, face unequal opportunities in their studies, as their educational and cultural capital and mother tongue (L1) tend to be ignored by the Greek system of education (Paleologou and Evangelou, 2003; Griva and Panitsidou, 2013). The Greek primary education system tends to adopt the process of assimilation where immigrant children are expected to learn the Greek language once they enter school, while they receive no instruction in their home language. They are expected to acquire a functional command of the Greek language achieving the level of first language-users.

The sample, chosen for this research, consisted of a total of 32 bilingual students, aged between 10 and 12 (M=11.4 years old, SD=0.45), from Albanian, Russian, Armenian and Georgian families who had moved to Greece as immigrants. Sixteen students were born in Greece or had moved to Greece before the age of 5, and 16 students had entered the Greek school at a later age. All of them can be described under the category of early bilingualism.

The participants were selected from 13 classrooms in 7 Greek primary schools from a total of 58 bilingual students according to: a) to their higher (standard score: 13 or above) or lower writing ability (standard score: 7 or less) based on the scores of a group-administered screening writing test, and b) their language competence based on the classroom teachers' judgements. Both 'good' and 'poor' writers can read and write in L1. All of them (100%) stated that they almost always speak their L1 at home and 65.6% of the participants said that they also speak Greek at home in some cases.

In addition, 32 immigrant parents of the children who participated in the study (27 women and 5 men) aged from 32–45 years were interviewed. They were of four different ethnic and linguistic origins (Albania, Armenia, Georgia and Russia) and their permanence in Greece ranged from 2 to 15 years.

Procedures adopted

a   A Greek standardised writing test (Porpodas, Diakogiorgi, Dimakou and Karantzi, 2004) was used to identify the writing strengths and weaknesses of the students.
b   Verbal report data were collected from students through think-aloud sessions. During each data-collection session, the researcher worked with each student on a one-to-one basis. Every student was requested to produce a piece of writing in Greek, between 200 and 250 words. While writing the text, the students were also asked to think aloud all the techniques and procedures they used, as well as the difficulties they encountered.
c   After the think-aloud sessions, retrospective interviews were conducted with each student in order to gain further insight into their usual approach to writing and the strategies they employed.
d   Semi-structured interviews were conducted with children's parents. The interviews comprised 23 open-ended questions, which were grouped under the following basic sections: a) parents' views on children's development and use of L2, b) parents' views on children's development and use of L1, c) parents' perspectives on children's school attainment, d) parental cooperation with school (directors, teaching staff) and involvement in children's education.

The findings

Students' writing difficulties and strategies

Qualitative analysis of the verbal data (Miles and Huberman, 1994) from the writing task in Greek resulted in a number of categories and subcategories, which were grouped into five basic thematic strands: a) pre-writing processes and strategies, b) while-writing processes and strategies, c) meta-cognitive strategies, d) social skills, e) writing difficulties.

The majority of the good writers reported that they relied on external resources for generating content and they thought about organising the content of the task in Greek (L2). They showed a preference for drawing on prior knowledge to make sense of the topic they were writing about and to generate ideas. Moreover, they suggested that they generated new ideas as their composing process went on. Some participants even stated that they generated alternative ideas at paragraph/sentence boundaries, which were constantly evaluated, checked against the context and often re-structured. In contrast, the poor writers did not devise an initial plan when writing as they preferred to 'write sentence by sentence'. Their writing process was sometimes accompanied by comments such as 'I don't know what else to write', or 'let's see if something else comes up'.

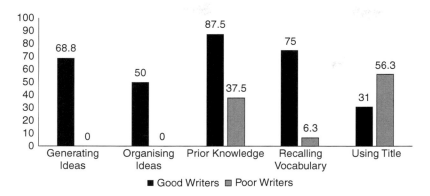

FIGURE 11.1 Pre-writing processes

The cross-tabulation indicated statistically significant differences between the two sub-groups in the following processes and strategies (Figure 11.1):

a   Generating ideas ($X^2=18.462$, df=2, p=0.000), since 68.8% of the good writers used this strategy efficiently, on the other hand none of the poor writers was found to use it in an effective way.
b   Organising ideas ($X^2=27.246$, df=2, p=0.000); 100% of the poor writers used it inefficiently, but only 6.3% of the good writers underused it and 50% of them employed it in an efficient manner.
c   Activating background knowledge ($X^2=8.533$, df=2, p<0.005). 87.5% of the good writers followed it but 37.5% of the poor ones showed a preference for this strategy.
d   Recalling vocabulary ($X^2=15.676$, df=2, p<0.001). This strategy was used more by poor writers (75%) compared to more competent writers (6.3%).

While-writing processes and strategies

While composing the text, most of the students followed certain sub-processes and employed a number of cognitive strategies, such as drafting, redrafting, composing without drafting/redrafting, rereading what they have written, writing sentence by sentence, translating, using resources.

The comparison between the two groups indicated statistically significant differences between poor and good writers in relation to two sub-processes while composing a piece of writing (Figure 11.2):

a   Drafting and redrafting ($X^2=12.857$, df=2, p<0.005) was employed mostly by good writers either efficiently (26.7%) or partially (33.3%). However, 100% of the poor writers were not engaged in drafting and redrafting during text construction.
b   Composing sentence by sentence ($X^2=9.309$, df=2, p<0.005) was followed by the great majority of the less competent writers (93.8%) in contrast to more competent writers (43.8%).

162 Eleni Griva

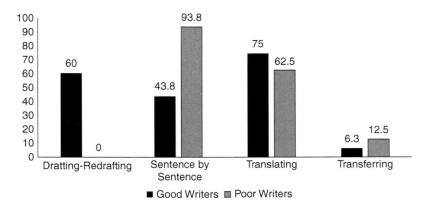

FIGURE 11.2 While-writing cognitive strategies

It is interesting to note that while the students were composing the text, they employed some *compensation strategies* in order to overcome their limitations in writing, such as adjusting the message, switching to L1, using a synonym/circumlocution, getting help and avoiding communication partially. In some cases, poor writers avoided using some expressions or they abandoned writing midway, because they were not able to use a wide range of vocabulary and grammatical items. On the other hand, when the good writers could not come up with the right or desirable expression, they were able to adjust the message by making the ideas simpler or less precise and by using a synonym.

The cross-tabulation indicated statistically significant differences between the two sub-groups in the following compensation strategies (Figure 11.3). The good writers were more willing to be engaged in 'adjusting the message' ($X^2=9.890$, df=2, p<0.05) and to 'use a synonym' ($X^2=11.768$, df=2, p<0.005) (56.3% and 56.3% respectively) in order to overcome some knowledge limitations. However, only 6.3% of the poor writers used 'adjusting the message' and 0% could use a

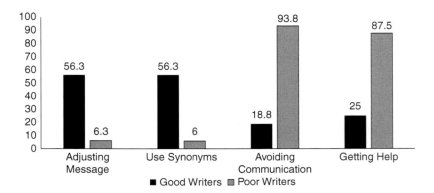

FIGURE 11.3 While-writing compensation strategies

synonym or a circumlocution effectively. On the other hand, the latter showed greater preference (93.8%) for 'avoiding communication' (X^2=18.286, df=2, p=0.000) and for 'getting help' (X^2=12.698, df=2, p=0.000) compared to more competent writers (18.8% and 25% respectively).

Meta-cognitive strategies

It is worth mentioning that the majority of the participants showed a positive attitude towards evaluating their own writing and got involved in the processes of identifying difficulties and problems, and self-correcting. They reviewed and commented on their drafts, focusing on the style, content, spelling and punctuation.

Cross-tabulation revealed statistically significant differences between poor and good writers in the range of meta-cognitive strategies (Figure 11.4). In relation to 'planning for the writing task' (X^2=7.385, df=2, p<0.05), although 37.6% of the good writers indicated that they plan for their writing before starting to compose, none of poor writers were found to do so. Similarly, the poor writers showed no 'selective attention' (X^2=21.895, df=2, p=0.000), while a great part of the good writers (81.3%) paid attention to certain language elements while composing. In addition, 'reviewing' (X^2=13.714, df=2, p<0.005) was a more favourite strategy for good writers (87.5%) than poor ones (25%).

Regarding 'self-evaluation', the more competent learners evaluated themselves more highly than the less competent ones (X^2=19.444, df=2, p=0.000). More precisely, 68.8% of the good writers ranked themselves as 'very good' and 25% as 'good enough'. In contrast, 68.8% of the poor writers ranked themselves as 'weak' and 31.3% as 'good'. In addition, in the retrospective interviews, they declared that they had to improve some aspects of their writing. Concerning 'organising ideas' (X^2 =0.821, df=2, p>0.05), 25% of the good writers expressed their desire to improve this skill; whereas, only 12.5% of the poor writers focused on developing this process.

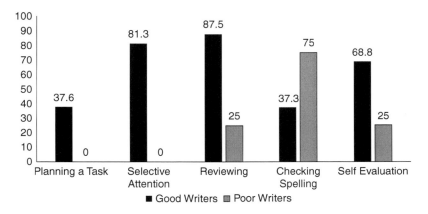

FIGURE 11.4 While-writing meta-cognitive strategies

TABLE 11.1 Differences between poor and good writers in cognitive, compensation and meta-cognitive strategies in Greek

Strategies	Greek (L2)	
	Poor Writers	Good Writers
Cognitive strategies	0.2766 (Std 0.1838)	0.4766 (Std 0.37)
Compensation strategies	0.6500 (Std 0.1243)	0.5000 (Std 0.1633)
Metacognitive strategies	0.1125 (Std 0.1628)	0.6250 (Std 0.2049)

On the other hand, poor writers referred to more local processes dealing with: a) 'spelling words' (X^2=8.127, df=2, p<0.005), since a vast majority of them (81.3%) would like to be better at spelling compared to good writers (31.3%); and b) 'accuracy' (X^2=5.236, df=2, p<0.05), with half of the poor writers (50%) expressing their desire to be better at 'accuracy', and only 12.5% of the more competent students focused on this skill.

The one-way ANOVA test indicated that there were statistically significant differences between the two subgroups in using both cognitive (F (30)= 4.821, p<0.05) and meta-cognitive strategies (F (30)= 7.846, p<0.001) when performing the task in Greek (L2) (Table 11.1).

Writing difficulties

Most students, irrespective of their language level, stated that they encountered certain difficulties while writing the task. However, the less skilled writers had problems with gaining control of the 'basics' of writing (spelling, vocabulary and grammar) while the poor writers' major concern was to recall and use the appropriate vocabulary and the correct spelling (Figure 11.5).

Specifically, a statistically significant difference was identified in relation to encountering difficulties at the vocabulary level (X^2=12.374, df=2, p<0.005); the

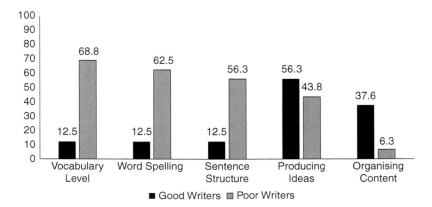

FIGURE 11.5 Writing difficulties

less competent learners encountered greater difficulties in recalling and using the appropriate words (68.8%) than the more effective learners (12.5%). In addition, statistical differences were indicated ($X^2=8.583$, df=2, p<0.05) between poor writers, who had greater problems with 'word spelling' (62.5%) than the more competent ones (12.5%). Moreover, for struggling writers, writing correct and effective sentences was a significant problem ($X^2=7.770$, df=2, p<0.05). More precisely, they encountered difficulties in structuring a sentence to a greater degree (56.3%) than the good ones (12.5%) did.

The immigrant parents' views and opinions

Rich insights into the parents' viewpoints were obtained through the interviews with parents whose comments and suggestions complemented the data provided by the students. The verbal data, after being coded qualitatively using the techniques by Miles and Huberman (1994), resulted in 35 codes, which were grouped into seven categories classified into two basic themes:

a   *Parents' views on children's language development*, including the following categories: development and use of L2, development and use of L1, reasons for hindering L1 development, suggestions for enhancing L1 development.
b   *Parents' perspectives on children's school attainment*, including the following categories: academic performance (attainment) of bilingual children, parental involvement in children's education, difficulties in parental/school co-operation.

Parents' views on children's language development

During the first part of the interview attempts were made to identify the parents' views as to their children's development and use of L2, which seemed to be of a major concern to all of them. They were of the opinion that their children can best develop the Greek language 'through formal tuition' and acknowledged the need to 'shift to L2 given its status as the dominant native language'. Immigrants who had been living in Greece for a limited period of time, two to four years, heavily prioritised the development of L2 and also supported its 'usage within the family environment' at the expense of L1, along with 'out of school reading in Greek' to promote its mastery probably as a means of integration in the host country of their settlement. This was not the case, however, with parents who had lived in Greece for a longer period of time and tended to value the development of both L1 and L2.

It should be pointed out that despite the fact that the need for proper development of L2 was strongly supported by most parents so as to ensure that it could be used comprehensively by their children, their 'wish of maintaining L1' was equally an issue of major significance. To them L1 mastery was mainly 'a tool for maintaining the students' cultural capital'. As to the development of L1, they seemed to favour L1 acquisition to take place 'within the family environment' by encouraging 'out of school reading in L1' while they highlighted the fact that their children do have 'poorly developed or even undeveloped writing skills in L1'.

In an attempt to find the reasons for such a scenario, which is most likely responsible for hindering L1 development, they put forward the argument that the development of L1 either functions as 'an obstacle to school attainment (achievement)' or 'as an obstacle to L2 acquisition', while they underlined the fact that L1 development is perceived as 'an obstacle to school and social inclusion'. It ought to be noted that a limited number of the interviewees supported the view that their children should be given every chance to develop reading and writing skills only in L2 and not in L1, most possibly influenced by the need to assimilate in Greek society.

When asked to make suggestions for enhancing L1 development, the interviewees provided useful insights. First of all, a significant percentage of the parents opted for 'mastery of L1 through formal schooling' while 'private institutions run by the country of origin' were also considered. They also called for promoting students' familiarity with their mother tongue and culture 'through intercultural activities which take place within the school environment' and is aimed at the 'activation of the non-native students' cultural capital'. Moreover, many of them seemed to be in agreement as to the significance of 'the development of both the productive and the receptive skills not only in L1 but also in L2'. In effect, training in relation to reading, writing, speaking and listening skills in Greek and the students' mother tongue were highly valued by a considerable percentage of the parents.

Parents' views on children's school attainment

Academic performance of bilingual children

The academic performance of their children was a major issue for most of the parents, as 'the students' competence in L2 was viewed in relation to school achievement'; it was believed that the higher the L2 competence of the students, the better would be the achievement in school subjects. On the same line, 'underachievement in L2' was related to poor academic performance, namely lower achievement in most of the school subjects. However, it was emphasised that 'bilingual students' attainment in sciences' was considerably high irrespective of their level of L2 competence. It was also striking that for a vast majority of the parents their role was influential concerning their children's progress as 'school attainment is related to parental involvement'.

Parental involvement in children's education

Concerning parental involvement in children's education, most of the interviewees showed their 'willingness to engage in school activities' and stressed the 'significance of their own L2 development for providing assistance to their children' in line with their wish to get involved in their children's 'reading and writing activities in L1 and L2'. They admitted, however, that their involvement tended to be limited.

Similarly, 'parental counselling for school subjects' as well as 'counselling for dealing with out of school activities' were highly regarded. Some of them also considered themselves unable to assume an active role in terms of their 'involvement in out of school activities' due to practical constraints such as the language barrier, lack of familiarity with the Greek school system, differences in cultural capital and level of education.

Difficulties in parental/school co-operation

As all of the parents were immigrants to Greece, they inevitably had to face a number of difficulties in fulfilling their parental role in relation to their children's school responsibilities. They confessed that their major problems came about as the result of their 'difficulties in involvement due to language barriers' and their 'insecurity in relation to their level in L2' especially for those with a limited period of stay in Greece. 'Lack of education' was also indicated as a major factor which made it difficult for them to get involved in their children's everyday school tasks and 'cope with their children's needs' especially 'in upper grade activities'. Moreover, other factors related to the life of immigrants such as 'practical constraints', 'heavy work schedule' and 'difficulties in co-operation with schools due to lack of understanding of school operations' were also put forward.

Conclusions

The present research revealed some useful insights with regards to writing skills of bilingual immigrant students included in mainstream classes. The findings suggest the adoption of intervention strategies, such as additional support especially for poor writers, through a language strategy training programme, that can then be put into place at this early stage for improving their writing skills. The poor writers' results showed that they had a limited knowledge of the writing task and they adopted lower-level processes and strategies (Goddard and Sendi, 2008; Griva et al., 2009; Zimmerman and Risemberg, 1997). They did not display a wide range of organisational strategies and they did not revise or rethink ideas; however, they had adequate awareness of their own writing problems at the word level and they used certain compensation strategies to overcome these problems.

In contrast, the good bilingual writers, who fell into the category of early bilingualism, held a much broader and complex view of their own writing process and showed more strategic knowledge, since they were more flexible in using both cognitive and meta-cognitive strategies and employed a wider range of more 'elaborated' strategies, such as 'drafting/redrafting', 'activating background knowledge', 'adjusting the message', 'using synonyms', 'organising content' and 'reviewing' (Stein, 2000).

Parents' opinions clearly showed that although some parents cared about their children's education, they demonstrated a low level of involvement in it. An explanation of this paradox may be the barriers encountered by immigrant parents.

This is particularly the case of parents who have been living in Greece for less than five years, and have to face issues such as the language barrier (inability to understand Greek), unfamiliarity with the school system, and differences in cultural capital and lack of education (Griva and Samou, 2014). It is worth mentioning that some of the parents believe that their children should develop reading and writing skills only in L2 and not in L1. It was also noted that the low level of support and encouragement provided by the school and the difficulties in communicating effectively in Greek made them feel uncomfortable when visiting their children's schools, and consequently this discouraged them from getting actively involved. Fewer of the immigrant parents, especially those who have been living in Greece for more than ten years, valued both their home and school involvement. For this, they try to offer their children help with tasks at home and they believe that they should get more involved in a range of reading and writing activities with their children both in L1 and L2.

Implications for inclusive education

It is hoped that the findings of this study make a small contribution to the promotion of inclusive practices for immigrant children. The findings also provide signposts for teachers to help develop children's literacy skills and strengthen their full inclusion in school life. Although the study was carried out in one country, i.e., Greece, the results echo the school situation of immigrants in many countries.

The Greek Educational system should examine the implementation of more effective literacy practices. Many writers believe that inclusive practices should be implemented, which support immigrant children's development, and their adjustment to a new school and social reality (Suarez-Orozco and Suarez-Orozco, 2001). School should a) expand opportunities for bilingual students to become autonomous readers and writers; b) provide a strategy training programme that helps bilingual students become strategic readers and writers; and c) provide parents with opportunities to participate more actively in school activities and to get involved more actively in their children's language development. In this way, school can constitute a place, where 'citizenship education' should be encouraged and home-school communication and collaboration should be fully facilitated in order for a supportive home learning environment to be established.

It is widely accepted that children with limited proficiency in the language of schooling are certain to experience increased difficulty in coping both academically and socially. Therefore, it is important to identify these difficulties at the initial stages in order to understand what intervention, support and remedial approaches are needed (Bialystok, 2008). Every effort should be made to develop teaching courses which aim to promote the bilingual students' linguistic and cognitive development, encourage their growth of meta-cognitive and social skills and promote their social inclusion so as to create citizens of a literary society and educate students for 'global citizenship' (Tanner, 2007). In this way, Greece can be seen as an inclusive society.

Bibliography

Baker, L. (2002). Meta-cognition in comprehension instruction. In: C. Block and M. Pressley (eds), *Comprehension Instruction: Research-Based Best Practices*. New York, NY: The Guilford Press.

Barnados (2009). *Written Out, Written Off: Failure to Invest in Education Deprives Children of Their Potential*. Dublin: Barnardos.

Bereiter, C. and Scardamalia, M. (1987). *The Psychology of Written Composition*. Hillsdale, NJ: L. Erlbaum.

Bialystok, E. (2008). Second-language acquisition and bilingualism at an early age and the impact on early cognitive development. In: R. E. Tremblay, R. G. Barr and R. DeV Peters (eds), *Encyclopaedia on Early Childhood Development*. Available at: http://www.child-encyclopedia.com/documents/BialystokANGxp_rev.pdf.

Cenoz, J. and Valencia, F. (1994). Additive tri-lingualism: Evidence from the Basque Country. *Applied Psycholinguistics*, 15, 195–207.

Cummins, J. (2001). Instructional conditions for trilingual development. *International Journal of Bilingual Education and Bilingualism*, 4(1), 61–75.

Desforges, C. and Abouchaar, A. (2003). *The Impact of Parental Involvement, Parental Support and Family Education on Pupil Achievement and Adjustment: A Review of Literature*. London: Department for Educational Skills.

Eivers, E., Shiel, G. and Shortt, S. (2004). *Reading Literacy in Disadvantaged Primary Schools*. Dublin: Educational Research Centre.

Goddard, Y. L. and Sendi, C. (2008). Effects of self-monitoring on the narrative and expository writing of four fourth-grade students with learning disabilities. *Reading and Writing Quarterly*, 24(4), 408–433.

Griva, E., Tsakiridou, E. and Nihoritou, I. (2009). Study of FL composing process and writing strategies employed by young learners. In: M. Nikolov (ed), *Early Learning of Modern Foreign Languages* (pp. 132–148). Bristol: Multilingual Matters.

Griva, E., Chostelidou, D. and Tsakiridou, E. (2011a). Assessment of metalinguistic awareness and strategy use of young EFL learners. In: L. Warfelt (ed), *Language Acquisition*. Nova Science Publishers, Inc.

Griva, E., Geladari, A. and Tsakiridou, H. (2011b). Primary school teachers' beliefs and misconceptions about bilingualism and bilingual education in Greek Educational context. Paper presented at the 8th International Symposium of Bilingualism, Oslo, June 2011.

Griva, E. and Panitsidou, E. (2013). Immigration and education: Policy and practices for integration and inclusion in the Greek context. In: J. Yu (ed), *Immigrants: Acculturation, Socio-economic Challenges and Cultural Psychology* (pp. 265–280). Nova Science Publishers, Inc. Available at: https://www.novapublishers.com/catalog/product_info.php?products_id=46148.

Griva, E. and Stamou, A. G. (2014). *Researching Bilingualism in the School Context: Perspectives of Teachers, Students and Immigrant Parents*. Thessaloniki: D. Kyriakidi.

Kennedy, G., Dalgarno, B., Bennett, S., Gray, K., Waycott, J., Judd, T., Bishop, A., Maton, K., Krause, K. L. and Chang, R. (2009). *Educating the Net Generation: A Handbook of Findings for Practice and Policy*. Melbourne: University of Melbourne. Accessed: 15 Oct 2011. Available at: http://www.netgen.unimelb.edu.au/outcomes/handbook.html.

Li, X. (1999). How can language minority parents help their children become bilingual in a familial context? *Bilingual Research Journal*, 23(2&3), 211–224.

Lindholm-Leary, K. (2001). *Dual-Language Education*. Clevedon, England: Multilingual Matters.

Marsh, J. (2006). Involving parents and carers. In: M. Lewis and S. Ellis (eds), *Phonics, Practice, Research, Policy* (pp. 60–70). London: Chapman.

Maxwell, J. and Teplova, T. (2007). *Canada's Hidden Deficit: The Social Costs of Low Literacy Skills*. Ontario.

Miles, M. B. and Huberman, M. (1994). *Qualitative Data Analysis: An Expanded Source Book* (2nd ed). Thousand Oaks, CA: Sage.

Paleologou, N. and Evangelou, O. (2003). *Intercultural Pedagogy: Educational, Teaching and Psychological Approaches*. Athens: Atrapos.

Panitsidou, E., Griva, E. and Papastamatis, A. (2011). Greek education policy and practices related to immigration. Paper presented at the International Conference on Education and Social Integration of Vulnerable groups, University of Macedonia – Thessaloniki, June 2011.

Porpodas, K., Diakogiorgi, Kl., Dimakou, I. and Karantzi, I. (2004). *Testing Writing Difficulties* [in Greek]. Athens: YPEPTH, EPEAEK.

Reid, J. (1992). The writing-reading connection in the ESL composition classroom. *Journal of Intensive English Studies*, 6, 27–50.

Santora, E. D. (2006). Narrating democratic education. *Social Studies Research and Practice*, 1(1), 17–29.

Stein, S. G. (2000). *Equipped for the Future Content Standards*. Washington, DC: National Institute for Literacy.

Suarez-Orozco, C. and Suarez-Orozco, M. (2001). *Children of Immigration*. Cambridge, MA: Harvard University Press.

Tanner, J. (2007). Global citizenship. In: D. Hicks and C. Holden (eds), *Teaching the Global Dimension: Key Principles and Effective Practice* (pp. 150–160). London: Routledge.

Victori, M. (1995). EFL writing knowledge and strategies: An integrative study. Doctoral dissertation, Universitat Autònoma de Barcelona, Bellaterra, Spain.

Zimmerman, B. J. and Risemberg, R. (1997). Becoming a self-regulated writer: A social cognitive perspective. *Contemporary Educational Psychology*, 22, 73–101.

12

DYSLEXIA

A learning disability in the Indian context

Mona Tabassum and Manju Kumari

Introduction

It has been estimated that in India 13–14% of school children have a learning disability. Unfortunately, most schools fail to address their problems. As a result, these children are branded as failures, often neglected and tagged as retarded or abnormal. The concept of learning disability refers to children who can see, hear and do not have any marked intellectual deficit but who show some deviation in behaviour, and often in their psychological make-up, to such an extent that they are unable to adjust at home or to learn by standard methods in school.

Dyslexia is the most prevalent learning disability among children. Those having the problem have significant difficulty with word recognition, reading comprehension and typically written spelling as well. When reading aloud they omit, add or distort the pronunciation of words to an extent unusual for their age. The growing body of scientific research suggests that there is a malfunction in the neurological wiring of those with dyslexia, which makes reading extremely difficult for them. The complexity of a language in orthography or its spelling system has a direct impact on how difficult it is to read that language. In reading, the brain has to pull words apart into their constituent sounds or phonemes. In the case of dyslexia, the brain struggles with phonological processing. The dyslexic also finds it hard to recognise voices.

This chapter argues that despite the fact that it is a known disorder, dyslexia has not reached its optimum awareness level in schools in India. Indeed, it is less commonly observed in India because the standardised tools for testing are not easily available throughout the country. Therefore, the integration of dyslexic children in mainstream schools is an important social and educational issue. These children should be offered programmes with an emphasis on life skills. In addition, parents and teachers need training in order to detect and understand the problem in its initial stages and to manage it properly. They can play an effective role in strengthening self-confidence and lessening the fear of failure in dyslexic children.

The concept of learning disability

In India it is estimated that tens of millions of people have learning difficulties; however, the government pays little attention to their condition and therefore does not allocate funds to deal with the problems. It has often been found that there are some children in the family who have normal intelligence, but face problems when tackling academic activities. They are unable to pay attention to academic work, hence they shy away from it or disturb the class. So, they are branded as stupid, absent-minded or retarded. Most parents lack awareness and do not try to understand the exact problem faced by their children. Stories like those of Sripath Aiyyer and Aditya Bawa, whose mothers found ways to help them overcome their learning problems in a mainstream school, are rare. There is a need to create awareness among Indian people regarding the nature, cause and solution to Special Learning Difficulties. As Dr. Akira Uno (2003), an expert on dyslexia, says, 'We cannot get rid of disability but we can teach people methods to compensate for it.'

The systematic analysis of patterns of reading difficulties commenced with the work of classical neurologists in the late nineteenth century. Neurologists, such as Charcot (1884) and Dejerine (1892), wanted to ascertain if a relationship between disorders of spoken language and the impairment of reading and writing existed. Dyslexia is considered to be a language disorder. Hallahan and Cruickshank (1973) described it as referring to 'those children who could see and hear and do not have a marked intellectual deficit, but who show deviation in behaviour and in psychological development to such an extent that they are unable to adjust at home or to learn by standard methods in school'. The definition issued by the National Joint Committee on Learning Disabilities (1982) is the one which schools and Special Educational Needs Coordinators (SENCOs) in India often use. Learning disability as a general term refers to a heterogeneous group of disorders manifested by significant difficulties in the acquisition and use of listening, speaking, reading, writing, reasoning or mathematical abilities. These disorders are intrinsic to individuals, presumed to be due to a central nervous dysfunction, and may occur across a life span. Problems in self-regulatory behaviours, social perception and social interaction may exist with learning disabilities but do not in themselves constitute a learning disability. Although learning disabilities may occur concomitantly with other handicapping conditions (for example, sensory impairment, mental retardation, serious emotional disturbance) or with extrinsic influences (such as cultural differences, insufficient or inappropriate instruction), they are not the result of those conditions or influences.

Dyslexia is the most prevalent learning disability among children. The term was first coined by Rudolf Berlin of Stuttgart, Germany, in 1887 but it took more than five decades before it became commonly used in the West. In India, it has taken even longer. There are several descriptive definitions of the disability. The World Federation of Neurology (WFD) defines dyslexia as: 'A disorder manifested by difficulty in learning to read despite conventional instructions, adequate intelligence and socio-cultural opportunity.' The National Institute of Neurological Disorder and Stroke (NINDS, 2010) gives the following definition:

> Dyslexia is a brain-based type of learning disability that specifically impairs a person's ability to read at levels significantly lower than expected, despite having normal intelligence. Although the disorder varies from person to person, common characteristics include difficulty with spelling, phonological processing (the manipulation of sound) and/or rapid visual verbal responding. In adults, dyslexia usually occurs after a brain-injury or in the context of dementia. It can also be inherited in some families.

In short, a child with dyslexia has significant difficulty with word recognition, reading, comprehension and typically written spelling as well. When speaking aloud they are likely to omit, add or distort the pronunciation of words to an extent unusual for their age.

Given the various interpretations of the term, it may be said that dyslexia is a learning difficulty that can occur due to a neurological cause or because of intrinsic or extrinsic influences. It is very important, therefore, that symptoms be identified at the initial stage.

Role of the brain in dyslexia

There is a growing body of scientific evidence which tends to suggest that there is a malfunction in the neurological wiring of people with dyslexia that makes reading extremely difficult for them.

In *Overcoming Dyslexia,* Shaywitz (2003), a Yale University neuroscientist, discloses that according to the latest brain scan research it is now possible to really understand 'the steps of how you become a reader and how you become a skilled reader'.

According to the author, reading requires the brain to rejigger its visual and speech processors in such a way that artificial markings, such as letters on a piece of paper, become linked to the sound they represent. It is not simply to hear and understand different words; the brain has to pull them apart into their constituent sound or phonemes. When we see written words, our brain hears the sound and assimilates them. Words are processed as visual units rather than as a series of single letters. Indeed, a whole word recognition stage is incorporated in most contemporary models of the reading process. Dyslexics may have problems with any aspects of the complex process.

Chomsky (1959) believes that the brain has evolved in such a way that it is prepared to learn language, just as other organs have evolved so that they are prepared to perform other functions. Researchers such as Galaburda et al. (1978) have long been aware that the two halves or hemispheres of the brain tend to specialise in different tasks. The left side is particularly adapted to processing language and the right is more attached to analysing spatial cues (Shaywitz, 2003). The specialisation does not stop there. In each hemisphere different regions of the brain break down various tasks even further. So reading a poem, catching a ball or recognising a face requires the complex interaction of a number of different regions. In the 1990s, with the development of techniques called functional magnetic resonance imaging (fMRI), researchers have made it possible to see which parts of the brain are getting the most blood and hence are more active at any given point of time. Shaywitz (2003) found that good readers show a constant pattern of strong activation in the back of the brain with weaker activation in the front during a reading task. In contrast, the brain activation pattern in a dyslexic is the opposite: the front part of the brain becomes over-active with weaker activation in the back during a reading task. Shaywitz (2003) points out, 'it is as if these struggling readers are using the system in the front of the brain to try to compensate for the disruption in the back'.

Many neuroscientists have used fMRI to identify three regions on the left side of the brain that play a key role in reading. These are known as the left inferior-frontal gyrus, the left parieto-temporal area and the left occipito-temporal area. The left inferior-frontal gyrus works as a phoneme producer, the left parieto-temporal area works as the word analyser and the left occipito-temporal area works as an automatic detector. All these areas work simultaneously like sections of an orchestra, but the high speed assembly line breaks down in children with dyslexia.

Still, it is well-known that there are some additional irregularities in the way the brain works (Kimura, 1981). Dyslexics with a reading disorder also find it hard to recognise voices. A voice recognition study has a broader application for brain science. It shows that for split-second recognition, the brain's social-oriented right side works together with speech perception. People affected with dyslexia miss out on that interaction.

Researchers discovered that dyslexic readers under-activate the superior temporal cortex for the integration of letters and speech sounds. This reduced audio-visual integration is associated directly with a more fundamental deficit in auditory processing of speech sounds, which in turn predicts performance on phonological tasks. The results also showed a neuro-functional account of developmental dyslexia, in which phonological processing deficit are linked to reading failure through a deficit in neural integration of letters and speech sound.

Dyslexia affects different parts of children's brains depending on which language they read. Using fMRI technology, researchers compared children who were raised reading English with children who were raised reading Chinese and found that the children reading English used a different part of the brain to those reading Chinese. The surprising findings may help lead to an understanding of (a) neurological cause (s) of dyslexia (Turkeltaub et al., 2005).

Clearly, the structure and function of our brain is very complex, and it is very difficult to ascertain the exact neurological cause of dyslexia.

Role of genetic factors in dyslexia

Genetic research into dyslexia has its roots in the work of Galaburda et al. (1985) and his examination of the post-autopsy brains of people with dyslexia. When he observed anatomical differences in the language centre of a dyslexic brain, he showed microscopic cortical malformations known as actopias were rarely vascular micro-malformations and in some instances these cortical malformations appeared as a micro gyrus. These studies and that of Cohen et al. (1989) suggested abnormal cortical development, which was presumed to occur before or during the sixth month of actual brain development.

Molecular studies have also linked several forms of dyslexia to genetic markers (Grigorenko et al., 1997). Several candidate genes have been identified, including in the two regions first related to dyslexia: RoBo on chromosome 3, DCDC2 and KIAA0319 on chromosome 15. A new candidate for specific language impairment has been identified by a research team directed by Rice at the University of Kansas, in collaboration with Smith, University of Nebraska Medical Centre (Rice, 2009). They reported that a gene on chromosome 6-KIAA0319 was associated with variability in language ability. Genetic factors play a very important role in the occurrence of learning difficulties, especially dyslexia. Effort is being made by scientists to overcome the flawed genetic problems. They are trying to modify genetic disorders with the help of genetic engineering.

Effects of language orthography

Dyslexia is identified in every country. However, its prevalence is not seen equally in all cultural and linguistic groups. The complexity of a language's orthography or writing system can be a significant contributing factor to the difficulties experienced by dyslexic readers (Goswami, 2005). Current psycholinguistic models of dyslexia are largely developed on the basis of alphabetic writing systems such as English (Karnath and Jing, 2002) but some logographic orthographies especially Chinese and Japanese are very significant (Xu and Jing, 2008). In mainland China and in Japan for example, dyslexia rates are estimated at less than 5% compared to 20% in the USA (Spaeth, 2003). The complexity of a language in orthography or a spelling system has a direct impact on learning the language. English has a comparatively deep orthography within the Latin alphabet writing system, with a complex orthographic structure that employs spelling patterns at several levels: principally, letter sound correspondence, syllables and morphemes. Other languages, such as Spanish have alphabetic orthographics that employ only letter sound correspondence, so-called shallow orthographics. It is relatively easy to read a language like Spanish; it is much more difficult to read a language with more orthographics, such as English (Henry, 2005). Comparative studies of German and English have shown that the greater depth of English orthography had a 'marked adverse effect on reading skills' among Dyslexic children (Landerl et al., 1998).

Logographic writing systems, especially Japanese and Chinese characters, have graphemes that are not linked directly to their pronunciation (Chung et al., 2010). A study of eleven Chinese brain-damaged patients with reading disorders showed that reading aloud a non-alphabetic script, like reading alphabetic script, can be accomplished using two distinct routes: one which associates a whole written word with its complete pronunciation, and one which utilises parts of the written word. Each route can be selectively impaired by brain damage, resulting in a different pattern of reading disability, i.e., 'deep' and 'surface' dyslexia. These data are consistent with the independent neural organisation of each routine, and the generality of the two routine models for reading alphabetic and non-alphabetic scripts (Siok et al., 2008; Yin and Butterworth, 1992).

These studies show the effect of language complexity on dyslexia.

Dyslexia in the Indian context

Conducting studies on learning disabilities in India is a Herculean task due to its multicultural and multilingual composition. There are many states and Union territories in India which are divided from each other not just geographically but also culturally and linguistically. Every state in India has its own regional language which is further divided into multiple dialects. The plethora of languages and various dialects spoken in the country presents a scenario where most people are either bilingual or multilingual. Most of the states follow a three language formula. Apart from people speaking Hindi in most states, English as a foreign language is compulsory in most schools. A child is also expected to be fluent in the regional language of their state. In India, therefore, all school children learn their native language, secondly the national language and English. Abdunnasar (1997) conducted a study of language disabilities in the Malayalam language and Chakravarthi (2012) the Kannada language. Abdunnasar found that there were many significant differences between normally achieving children, children with mild language disabilities and children with severe language disabilities. The findings revealed that children with language disabilities had difficulty in responding. Prakash and Sunita (1998) compared 16 dyslexics and 21 normal readers in the Kannada language on various tasks such as rhyme recognition, phoneme oddity detection, phoneme deletion, syllable deletion, syllable reversal, a serial (sequential) recall test, identification of body parts, repeating polysyllabic words, a visual retention test and a test of knowledge of orthographic principles. Sixteen reading disabled children of grade 4 were compared with 16 normal readers of grade 4. Five matched normal readers of grade 2. They found that the dyslexics performed worse on most of the tasks than did either of the other two groups.

In the southern part of India various research studies have been carried out to identify children with dyslexia and writing disabilities (Ramaa, 1985; Ramaa et al., 1993). Other than this, work has been done on Kannada, Malayalam and Hindi. Table 12.1 gives the prevalence of learning disabilities among Indian students noted in these studies.

In India 13–14% of all school children suffer from learning difficulties. Unfortunately, most schools have failed to pay attention to it and consequently children are branded as failures (Malik, 2009). Identification and diagnosis of learning difficulties are extremely challenging. Despite the fact that dyslexia is a known disorder, it has not reached its optimum awareness level in schools in the country. Teachers

TABLE 12.1 Prevalence of children with learning disabilities, Ramaa (2000)

Investigator	Type of learning disability (LD)	Language of students studied	Number of children screened for LD	% Children screened for LD
Ramaa, 1985	Dyslexia	Kannada	550	3
Ramaa, 1991	Dyscalculia (without reading and writing disabilities)	Kannada medium in Karnataka State	359	6
Abdunnasar, 1997	Language disabilities	Malayalam in Kerala State	400	7.25
Bindu, 1996	Dyslexia	Malayalam in Kerala State	330	3
Indu, 1996	Different types of LD	English medium	1,380	3
Geetha, 1997	Dyscalculia	English medium in Tamil Nadu State	1,442	3
Gowramma, 1998	Dyscalculia	Kannada medium in Karnataka State	1,408	6
Umadevi, 1996	Dyslexia	English medium in Karnataka State	612	4

either ignore the disorder or blame it on the child's personality, branding them as lazy and/or aggressive. This leads to behavioural problems. Moreover, these types of problems are not disclosed at an early age. Neither parents nor teachers are trained or sensitised to understanding the problem. Proper training is needed to ensure positive results. There is a need to sensitise and equip health care professionals, parents and teachers to check for these problems as early as possible.

It is estimated that there are approximately 90 million people with varying degrees of learning disabilities in India and an average school class has about five students with one (Sunil et al., 2003). Yet we do not have a clear idea about the incidence and prevalence of learning disabilities in the country as a whole (Karnath, 2001). Even though there has been some research conducted in the field (Ramaa, 2000), at school level learning disabilities still go undetected because of a lack of teacher training. Children with learning disabilities are considered a burden in schools, or labelled as dumb or lazy, and forced to leave the school. In addition, parents are reluctant to have their children tested (Nakra, 1996) because often it only ends in nothing more than the child being labelled. Often due to ignorance, parents refuse to accept that their child has a learning disability. This happens in most schools in India, which are not equipped to deal with the special needs of children with learning disabilities.

Along with all these problems, standardised tools for testing are not easily available in India. There are 15 official languages and they are spoken in over 1,600 dialects, and an estimated 880 languages are in daily use (Online Computer Library Centre [OCLC], 2004). The languages of the testing instruments are not suitable for those Indian students who may not be proficient in English.

The learning disabilities movement in India is recent in origin compared with that of its Western counterparts. The Nalanda Institute report has highlighted that in India during the last two decades or so there has been an increasing awareness and identification of children with learning disabilities. The Rehabilitation Centre of India, Ministry of Human Resource Development, Ministry of Social Justice and Empowerment, and the Government of India, with the help and intervention of the country's strong academic community and specialists, studied the instructional techniques, strategies and conditions that best enable students to learn critical skills especially in the area of reading.

The producer of the film *Taare Zameen Par* has successfully created awareness about dyslexia among Indian parents and educationalists. In recent years, different non-governmental organisations (NGOs) supported mostly by parents are creating awareness, regarding dyslexia. NGOs are taking notice of dyslexia. They are effectively trying to integrate dyslexic children into mainstream education.

- Action Dyslexia Delhi is an organisation that was launched in 1997 by Mrs. Anjuli Bawa, who has experienced the challenges of being a parent of a dyslexic child.
- Maharashtra Dyslexia Association is a non-profit organisation started in 1996 by a group of parents and professionals committed to securing the rights of students with dyslexia to an appropriate education.
- Friends of Dyslexia is a voluntary organisation working for the cause of dyslexia. It is represented by a committed core team from various professional and intellectual walks of life.
- Kids Learning Centre is an organisation which provides instruction in the basics of learning written language, mathematics and organisational skills using innovative, multisensory techniques and strategies.
- Madras Dyslexia Association is a non-profit organisation which takes a pragmatic approach to help dyslexic children.
- SAMDEVA Research and Training Centre Kolkata, the brain child of Surendranath P. Nishanimut, a young entrepreneur turned Special Educational Needs (SEN) enthusiast, rehabilitates children with learning disabilities in India.
- The Tata Interactive Learning Disability Forum 2008 (TLDF), held in Mumbai on November 29, 2008 and Kolkata on December 2, 2008 focuses on the urgent need to address Learning Disability issues. Focusing on the theme of 'Special Deeds for Special Needs', the TLDF 2008 underlined the importance of early remedial action to help learners with Special Needs.

Inclusive education of children with learning difficulties

The inclusion of special learning disabled children in mainstream education is an important social issue, because separating and excluding children from their natural school environment does not always have positive consequences (Colfer et al., 2000).

The UNESCO Salamanca statement (1994) states that:

> Inclusion and participation are essential to human dignity and the exercise of human rights. The fundamental principle of the inclusive school is that all children should be taught together, wherever possible, regardless of any difficulties or differences they may have.

According to Inclusive Education for Disabled Children (IEDC, 1986),

> Inclusion is based on a social model of disability that views disability as a socially created problem and management of the problem requires social action in the form of environmental modification necessary for the full participation of persons with disabilities in every sphere of life.

Inclusive education results in improved social development and academic outcomes for all learners. It leads to the development of social skills and improved social interaction because learners are exposed to a natural environment in which they have to interact with other learners, each one having unique characteristics, interests and abilities. By looking at current approaches to pedagogy in some of the best schools in Delhi with an inclusive educational setting, Ahmad (2010) explores the use of the different techniques and provisions that are in practice and which can be introduced into all schools. The various provisions given by different education boards in India can prove to be a silver lining for these students to learn on a par with their non-disabled peers in inclusive educational settings. Use of assistive devices, assistive technology, resource room support, and acceptance by peers, teachers and society are all innovative ways of helping to promote and sustain inclusion. There are cases where dyslexic children have been exempted from learning the second language. One mother, for example, Mrs. Aiyyer, whose son's first language is Tamil and second Hindi, conducted some research in 1998. She succeeded in showing that he should be exempt from studying Hindi. After this his confidence level and performance at tests increased dramatically.

As noted, in India, teachers are not trained to deal with children with learning disabilities (Edwards, 1994). Many programmes and schemes such as Equal Opportunities, protection of rights, and Full Participation Act 1995 (PWD Act 1995) have been introduced, but they all need appropriate sensitivity and actual implementation. Dyslexic children should be offered a programme with an emphasis on life skills and pro-social skills. They should be given physical, education, sports, arts and craft training. Investigators have stressed the need for managing high anxiety and low self-esteem in children with learning difficulties (Ramaa, 2000). Success heals many wounds and strengthens children's self-image (Edwards, 1994). This area is important to understand because the emotional stability of dyslexic children is a pre-requisite, which underpins teaching and research (Edwards, 1994). Parents and well-prepared teachers can play an important role in improving self-confidence and lessening the fear of failure (Otto, 1997).

This is not to say that dyslexics cannot succeed in life. Despite their disability, they can succeed in the fields of art, science and business. Since their brains are wired differently, they are often skilled problem solvers, arriving at solutions from novel or surprising angles. They talk about being able to see things in 3-D Technical or as a multidimensional chess game. Samir Parikh, a child psychiatrist, sums up the approach advocated here, when he says that dyslexia is not a disease but a lifelong problem and presents challenges that need to be overcome on a daily basis (Malik, 2009). He argues that with proper diagnosis, appropriate education, hard work and support from family, friends, teachers and others, a dyslexic can lead a successful and productive life.

Bibliography

Abdunnasar. (1997). Diagnosis of language disability in primary school children in Malayalam language. M.Ed. dissertation, University of Mysore, India, 118–130.

Ahmad, F. K. (2010). A study on the use of assistive devices for children with learning disability in Delhi's schools. Submitted at the National University of Educational Planning and Administration, New Delhi, 315–382.

Bindu, V. S. (1996). Diagnosis of reading and writing difficulties among children with dyslexia in Malayalam language. Dissertation, University of Mysore, India.

Birla, P. (2001). Kids with learning disabilities still occupy cold place in class. *Newsline, Mumbai*, 3(241–48).

Chakravarthi, S. (2012). Assessing children with language impairments: A study on Kannada, a South Indian language. *Disability, CBR & Inclusive Development*, [S.l.], 23(3), 112–136.

Chapter three: Specific learning difficulties. (2001). www.actionresearch.net/living/rawalpdf/Chapter3.pdf.

Charcot, J. M. (1884). *'Differential Formed' Afasia*. Milan: Vallardi.

Chomsky, N. (1959/1976). On the biological basis of language capabilities. In: R. W. Rieber (ed), *Neuropsychology of Language*. New York: Plenum.

Chung, K. K. H., Ho, C. S.-H., Chan, D. W., Tsang, S.-M. and Lee, S.-H. (2010). Cognitive profiles of Chinese adolescents with dyslexia. *Dyslexia*, 16, 2–23. doi:10.1002/dys.392.

Cohen, M., Campbell, R. and Yaghmai, F. (1989). Neuropathological abnormalities in developmental dysphasia. *Annals of Neurology*, 25(6), 567–570.

Colfer, J., Farrely, M., Limerick, C., Greatly, T. and Smyth, F. (2000). A Place to Learn: Inclusive Education for Children with Learning Disabilities. Discussion Document. Psychological Society of Ireland Learning Disability Group (online) (2002).

Dejerine, J. (1892). Contribution à l'étude anatomique et clinique des différentes variétés de cécité verbale. *Mémoires de la Société de Bioiogie*, 4, 61–90.

Edwards, J. (1994). *The Scars of Dyslexia: Eight Case Studies in Emotional Reaction*. London: Cassell.

Galaburda, A. M., Sherman, G. F., Rosen, G. D., Aboitiz, F., and Geschwind, N., (1985). Developmental dyslexia: Four consecutive patients with cortical anomalies. *Annals of Neurology*, 18(2), 222–233.

Galaburda, A. M., LeMay, M., Kemper, T. L., and Geschwind, N. (1978). Right-left asymmetrics in the brain. *Science*, 199, 852–856.

Geetha, T. (1997). Efficacy of remedial package in augmenting primary school teachers' skills to help dyscalculic children. Unpublished Ph.D. thesis, Avinashilingam Deemed University, India.

Goswami, U. (2005). Orthography, phonology and reading development: A cross-linguistic perspective. In: J. Malatesha, *Handbook of Orthography and Literacy*, 462–464. Lawrence Erlbaum. Available online: http://www.dysabilityindia.org/pwdacts.cfm. 2003.

Gowramma, I. P. (1998) Development of remedial instruction programme for children with dyscalculia in primary school. Ph.D. thesis, University of Mysore, India.

Grigorenko, E. L., Wood, F. B., Meyer, M. S., Hart, L. A., Speed, W. C., Shuster, A., and Pauls, D. L. (1997). Susceptibility loci for distinct components of developmental dyslexia on chromosomes 6 and 15. *American Journal of Human Genetics*, January.

Hallahan, D. and Cruickshank, W. (1973). *Psychoeducational Foundation of Learning Disabilities*. Englewood Cliffs, NJ: Prentice-Hall, Inc.

Henry, M. K. (2005). The history and structure of the English language. In: J. R. Birsh, *Multisensory Teaching of Basic Learning Skills*, 154. Baltimore, MA: Paul H. Brookes.

Inclusive Education for Disabled Children (IEDC). India 1986: Section, 3.1. (Updated in 1992).

Indu, D. (1996). An analysis of the deficiency in the development of basic concepts among children with Learning Disabilities in primary schools. M.Ed. dissertation, University of Mysore, India.

Karnath, P. and Jing, J. (2002). The search for deep dyslexia in syllabic writing system. *Journal of Neurolinguistics*, 15(2), 143–155.

Karnath, P. (2001). *Learning Disabilities in the Indian Context*. The Nalanda Institute. Available online: http://www.nalandainstitute.org/aspfiles/learning.asp. 2004.

Kimura, D. (1981). Neural mechanism in manual signing. *Sign Language Studies*, 33, 291–312.

Landerl, K., Wimmer, H., and Frith, U. (1998). The impact of orthographic consistency on dyslexia: A German English comparison. *Cognition*, 63(3), 315–334.

Malik, S. (2009). Learning difficulties in India. Meri News, 16 August. Available online: http://www.merinews.com/article/learning-disability-in-india/15781618.shtml.

Nakra, O. (1996). *Children and Learning Difficulties*. New Delhi: Allied Publishers.

National Institute of Neurological Disorders and Stroke (NINDS). (2010). Dyslexia Information Page.

National Joint Committee on Learning Disabilities. (1982). Learning disabilities: Issues on definition. *Asha*, 24(11), 945–947.

OCLC. (2004). Languages of India. OCLC online Computer Library centre. Available online: www.ocic.org2005.

Otto, P. (1997). *How to Detect and Manage Dyslexia: A Reference and Resource Manual*. Oxford: Heinemann.

Prakash, P. and Sunita, N. (1998). Reading disability in Kannada. *Psychological Studies*, 43, 99–107.

Ramaa, S. (2000). Two decades of research on learning disabilities in India. *Dyslexia: An International Journal of Research and Practice*, 6(4), 268–283.

Ramaa, S. (1985). Diagnosis and remediation of dyslexia: An attempt. Unpublished doctoral dissertation, University of Mysore, India.

Ramaa, S., Miles, T. R., and Lalithamma, M. S. (1993). Dyslexia: Symbol processing difficulty in the Kannada language. *Reading and Writing*, 5(1), 29.

Rice, M./University of Kansas. (2009). Gene associated with language speech and reading disorders identified. *Science Daily*. Available online: http://www.sciencedaily.com. Retrieved: 28 October 2011.

Shaywitz, S. E. (2003). *Overcoming Dyslexia: A New and Complete Science-Based Program for Reading Problems at Any Level*. New York: Random House.

Siok, W. T., Chen, W. S. Y., Luke, L., and Tan, K. K. (2008). Developmental dyslexia is characterized by the co-existence of visuospatial and phonological disorders in Chinese children. *Proceedings of the National Academy of Sciences of the United States of America*. 105(14), 5561–5566.

Spaeth, A. (2003). Mind at risk: Dyslexia is less common in Asia than the U.S., but it is still a largely unnoticed problem. *Time Asia*, 8 September, 42–43. Available online: www.time.com/timeasia/covers/501030908/Dyslexia_asia.html. Retrieved: 21 September 2009.

Sunil, T. K., Bhautej, N., and John, S. (eds). (2003). *Dealing with Dyslexia*. London and Hong Kong: Lippincott, Williams and Wilkins.

Turkeltaub, P. E., Weisberg, J., Flowers, D. L., Basu, D., and Eden, G. F. (2005). The neurobiological basis of reading: A special case of skill acquisition. In: H. Catts, A. Kahmi (eds.), *The Connections Between Language and Reading Disabilities*, 103–130. Mahwah, NJ: Erlbaum.

Umadevi, M. R. (1996). Effectiveness of a remedial programme on improving reading comprehension skills among dyslexic children. Ph.D. thesis, Kuvempu University.

UNESCO. (1994). World Conference on Special Needs Education: Access and Quality, Salamanca, Spain, 7–10 June 1994.

Uno, A. (2003). The new science of dyslexia. *Times Magazine*, September, 43–44.

Xu, G. F. and Jing, J. (2008). Major achievements in relation to dyslexia in Chinese characters. *Chinese Medical Journal*, 121(17), 1736–1740.

Yin, W. and Butterworth, B. (1992). Deep and surface dyslexia in Chinese. *Advances in Psychology*, 90(C), 349–366.

13

INCLUSIVE LEARNING

The challenge of special needs

Royston Flude

Introduction

Inclusive education is a significant project towards furthering egalitarianism. Laws that support inclusion are aimed at ensuring that all students have access to high-quality education regardless of their level of ability. Inclusive teaching and learning combine into educational practices in which students with special needs are incorporated into mainstream classrooms. Such inclusion seeks to provide all students with opportunities to access high-quality education from professionally trained teachers and aides. Proponents of inclusive education contend that desegregated classrooms lead to higher quality education for all students – both those labelled as having special needs and those who meet the demands of the school system. They believe that segregated classrooms result in inferior educational quality for students relegated to the low-ability classrooms.

Inclusive learning proposes that all students are capable of learning so long as accommodations are made to their specific needs. In the 'full inclusion' setting, the students with special needs are integrated into classes which maintain appropriate supports and services. At the extreme, full inclusion is based on the elimination of segregated special education classes with the integration of all students. Thus, it includes even those that require the most substantial educational and behavioural supports and services to be successful in regular classes. Special education is considered a *service*, not a *place*, and those services are integrated into the daily routines and classroom structure, environment, curriculum and strategies and brought to the student, instead of removing the student from contact with her/his peers presumably in order to meet his or her individual needs.

There have been many examples throughout history of students that have 'struggled' with the education system. 'During his schooling days Gandhi was an average student and passed his matriculation exam from Samaldas College, Gujarat with some difficulty' (Government of Maharashtra, 2015). The Chinese philosopher Lao Tsu described as 'all' being connected (within the Dao) and that it is through this 'connectedness' or inclusion that we may excel in all our activities.

Clearly, inclusive education relies on inclusive teaching. Such teaching requires that teachers recognise, accommodate and meet the learning needs of all their students. It means acknowledging that students have a range of individual learning needs and are members of diverse communities: a student with a disabling medical condition may also have English as an additional language and be a single parent. Inclusive teaching avoids pigeonholing students into specific groups with predictable and fixed approaches to learning.

In summary, inclusive teaching involves the whole school. It:

- matches provision to student needs;
- takes a coherent approach which is anticipatory and proactive;
- has a strategy for delivering equal opportunities and diversity policies;
- incorporates regular reflection, review and refinement of strategies and methods that actively involve disadvantaged students.

United Nations commitment to inclusive education

The need for 'inclusion' is incorporated in the Millennium Development Goals of the United Nations which set objectives of eradicating extreme poverty and hunger; promoting gender equality and empowering women; reducing child mortality and improving maternal health; ensuring environmental sustainability; along with *achieving universal primary education*.

> Inclusive education is based on the right of all learners to a quality education that meets basic learning needs and enriches lives. Focusing particularly on vulnerable and marginalised groups, it seeks to develop the full potential of every individual. The ultimate goal of inclusive quality education is to end all forms of discrimination and foster social cohesion. …. In 2013, 74 million primary age children are excluded from education. Seven out of ten live in sub-Saharan Africa or South and West Asia. Sixty per cent of them are girls living in Arab States and 66% in South and West Asia. A further 112 million adolescents are also out-of-school. The main reasons for exclusion are poverty, gender inequity, disability, child labour, speaking a minority language, belonging to an indigenous people, and living a nomadic or rural lifestyle.
>
> *(UNESCO, 2015)*

'Vulnerable' and 'marginalised' are loose terms encompassing many different individuals and groups deprived of their right to education.

The UNESCO Task Force on Education for the 21st Century considers that education takes place throughout life in many forms. The drafting of the new UN Disability Convention represents an opportunity to build into international human rights law the imperative for governments to develop a single, inclusive system of education which includes disabled persons from the outset. It is a fallacy that separate systems have to be developed before inclusive systems can be put in place. There is nothing inherent in education which necessitates the development of separate education for disabled persons before the development of inclusive education. The rights of children who currently have no education at all, difficult though their situation is, cannot be fulfilled through segregated schooling. It is far more economically efficient to target resources towards a single inclusive education system from the outset than to develop a dual system of separate education for disabled and non-disabled persons and then have to work towards bringing about inclusive education.

The World Economic Forum (WEF, 2014–15) ranked 144 economies considering 111 variables in twelve pillars of competitiveness as part of its Global Competitiveness Index (GCI). The WEF concluded that Human Capital, especially the average skill level of the labour force, directly affects productivity and thus has a significant impact on national economic competitiveness. There is, therefore, a requirement for different educational policies (Johansen and Sahlberg, 2011). To ensure a society based on mutual respect and equality of opportunity, educational inclusion is critical. It is the key to the full development of Human Capital which will enable individuals to develop the productivity level of their societies as well as their individual potential. The barriers to inclusion require consideration so that they may be effectively mitigated.

In 1998, UNESCO concluded that goals of universal education should be represented by four pillars, which can be expressed in the form of the four intelligences:

- *Learning to do* (physical intelligence – PQ)
- *Learning to live together* (emotional intelligence – EQ)
- *Learning to know* (mental intelligence – IQ)
- *Learning to be* (spiritual intelligence – SQ)

Barriers to inclusion

As is well known, all people are driven by natural survival instincts. Typical driving forces for survival include the need for food and drink, warmth, shelter and clothing, love and appreciation, governance systems to provide safety, self-preservation and preservation of the species, and, given all of these, self-actualisation (Maslow, 1970). Educational dysfunction may prevent the realisation of these basic needs and so the many mainstream barriers to inclusive education have to be overcome. Among these are:

- *Natural abilities*: Many children are categorised in schools as less capable or ultra-capable, and therefore they do not function according to expectations.

- *Disability*: The condition of children who have to deal with motor defects, defects of vision or hearing, or with largely invisible challenges such as dyslexia, for example, is exacerbated by exclusion.
- *Caste, status, gender*: In many societies access to education is restricted because children are labelled according to the caste or status of their family origin. Many barriers have to be overcome by girls especially.
- *Poverty*: Children from families with incomes below the poverty line are often excluded from access to schooling.
- *Health*: Often connected with poverty, children who suffer from ill health may have extended periods of absenteeism from schools.
- *Motivation*: Traditions of appropriateness and peer-group forces may limit the individual's 'willingness to learn'.
- *Trauma*: Social and economic deprivation and conflict causes trauma (also Post Traumatic Stress Disorder or PTSD), which may restrict learning capability.
- *Availability*: And from a macro viewpoint, in many areas of the world, access to education is restricted because of perceived limitations on state budgets, or because of geographical inconvenience.

The height and effectiveness of each perceived barrier will depend on the circumstances of each individual and their environment. One aspect of such an environment is that of the individual's self-worth. Low self-worth leads to a cycle of chaotic despair, dysfunction, helplessness and lack of educational engagement. The alternative of learned optimism leads to harmonious, engaged living with the potential of high educational outcomes. Therefore, a critical aspect of inclusion is to maximise the self-worth of challenged individuals so that they can climb the 'staircase of development'.

Positive psychology (Seligman, 1991) has done much to address these issues and has extended its reach from its health roots into education and enterprise. Happiness is an important metric of self-worth. A model of happiness developed by Dr. Sonja Lyubomirsky (2008) and others describes our happiness as deriving from three components.

- *Out point*: This refers to a person's general outlook. There are people who seem always to be happy, and others who seldom laugh or seem joyful.
- *Circumstances*: Positive and negative experiences influence our happiness, but typically over a short time period. Humans are very adaptable and so major boosts or dips in our happiness are generally short lived.
- *Intentional activity*: 'The term "intentional activities" refers to those thoughts and behaviours that require effort. This effort may be apparent only to the actor (for example, making a list of goals for the week) or it may be visible to others (for example, doing a favour for a friend). The literature suggests that intentional activities are the key to making lasting changes in happiness because such activities are more resistant to adaptation (the process by which we get used to something and become unaffected by it). Happiness can be

developed by deliberately engaging in activities that make us happy while varying them enough to ward off adaptation.'

Developing happiness through highly focused high intensity short term (HISD) interventions and following these with low intensity long duration interventions (LILD) may facilitate the recovery of disadvantaged young people, who have undergone traumatic situations, including war, abuse, natural disasters, etc. They can be helped to re-stabilise, overcome traumatic experiences, attain the chance to create new friendships, learn new skills, renew family ties, and finally to return to the world as dynamic responsible and happy citizens. In inner-city areas, where trauma is common, this provides an approach, whilst originally developed for 18–24-year-old youths, which may have a powerful positive impact on young children who have been 'excluded' from the education system (Flude, 2000, 2012).

Every individual must also have a 'dream' or vision of a goal. It is a bit like climbing a staircase, which has a series of steps with the individual's attention focused on the next step and where the staircase is going. Progress happens in a series of steps, with inevitable failures, but a positive attitude of mind creates the ability to change and achieve happiness. Looking at life as a staircase, where failure can be addressed by reclaiming the steps, provided a much better basis for inclusive education.

However, even if children are motivated and happy, they must participate in a complex system that will either help or hinder their sense of inclusion. This system includes at its core the interaction between family, teachers and peers with links to health, education and enterprise providers to achieve positive wealth, citizenship and positive environmental outcomes.

Inclusive learning

In order to be effective, inclusion must be part of a lifelong learning strategy with primary education being a critical period that has a long-lasting influence on outcomes throughout life.

In the development of the child, it is necessary to consider an approach that covers all dimensions of child development: physical/motor, social/emotional, cognitive, communicative/language and learning strategies in the context of family, culture and community.

The models developed by Urie Bronfenbrenner (1977, 1979, 1989) are based on the internalised journey of the child in their 'voyage of discovery'. Bronfenbrenner puts forward the view that there are five components to human behaviour:

- *Cognitive component*: perceives, stores, processes, and retrieves information;
- *Affective component*: can modify perceptions and thoughts before and after they are processed cognitively;
- *Conative component*: directs and manages input and output functioning;
- *Spiritual component*: guides the approach to the unknowns of life, how we define and relate to the sacred; and

- *Behavioural system*: controls the overt action of the organism (output of the individual).

Young people absorb all input both positive and negative. Repetition and reinforcement by authority figures, not necessarily the teacher or parent, creates long-term behaviours, relationship skills, mind sets and beliefs, sometimes mistaken. In the long run, however, learning is accomplished through interaction. As the theoreticians of communication Littlejohn and Foss (2008) describe it, there are ascending levels of engagement.

- Communication is presentational relying on the five senses for its dissemination and engaging primarily Physical Intelligence (PQ).
- A dialogue or relationship that engages Emotional Intelligence (EQ).
- The stimulation of Mental Intelligence (IQ) to create a 'shaft of knowledge' that represents a system or process of understanding.
- The creation of a self-replicating engine of wisdom that can apply conceptual frameworks in new and previously unknown situations as a demonstration of Spiritual Intelligence (SQ).

This description coincides with the analysis by UNESCO. Interactive learning requires the stimulus of multiple intelligences that embrace physical (PQ), emotional (EQ), mental (IQ) and spiritual (SQ) dimensions (Flude, 2012). The tradition of storytelling (PQ) confirms that Information can be presented in exciting ways and transmitted from generation to generation. This is followed by interactive Dialogue (EQ) approach of discussion to develop Knowledge. From this base it is possible to use Synthetics (IQ) to learn the symbols and structure of a discipline to facilitate Understanding.

Teaching strategies shed light on the different mechanisms that facilitate retention. (The cumulative percentages noted were found in research conducted by Flude (2010).) They include:

- *Presentation (Story Telling)*: 10% retention;
- *Dialogues*: using triads to create Action Learning Sets where each child takes on the role of Story Teller, Listener and Observer each taking a turn – 30% retention;
- *Synthetics*: again using triads with the Story Teller, Listener and Observer roles to process the knowledge to develop understanding in the form of Critical Action Teams – 70% retention;
- *Visualisation*: where individuals and groups use creative visualisation to apply knowledge and understanding to create wisdom that may be applied in new situations – 90% retention.

As a culmination, visualisation (SQ) empowers the concept through the individuals' own creative imagination to convert information, knowledge and understanding into personalised wisdom that may be used in new Applications.

The application of these concepts can take many different forms depending on children's levels of development. They can be integrated within the school-day without additional teaching resources and can be applied to all learners, including those with special needs. When, for example, teachers in inner-city Leeds were trained in visualisation, there was a measurable impact on 25,000 children. Longitudinal review indicated that both literacy and numeracy improved by between 40 and 60% (Flude, 2011a). The 'story teller', 'the listener' and 'the observer' roles are rotated in the triads to optimise knowledge transfer, retention and resilience.

Ensuring change

A clearer understanding of the conceptual framework for education may be obtained by introducing a model of change driven by the conception of the hierarchical pyramid of needs (Maslow, 1970; Flude, 1996). These needs or dimensions empower us at a number of levels commencing at the physical world, then emotional defining our feeling responses, then mental controlling our cognitive interactions and then at the highest level spiritual which drives our values and beliefs. These concepts are re-enforced by the work on emotional intelligence (Goleman, 1997) and on spiritual intelligence (Zohar, 2000). Spiritual in this context does not refer to establishment religion. Rather it represents the inner 'spark' of beliefs that makes people different and drives lives through directed 'will', so that we may understand or illuminate the experience of 'being-in-the-world'. The focus of existential philosophy, therefore, is on the 'way of being' of the person and the qualitative texture of their relationship with self ('Eigenwelt'), others ('Mitwelt') and the physical world ('Umwelt') (Laing, 1960, 1961).

These dimensions of change may be regarded as 'engines' that interact with reality and can be better understood by seeing them as a chain. Our values and beliefs (spiritual engine – SQ) drive our thinking (mental engine – IQ), which in turn drives our feelings (emotional engine – EQ) and on to manifest the way we create our reality in our actions (physical engine – PQ).

The education process can be considered as an inner journey of reflection and an outer journey of expression that engages the physical, emotional, mental and spiritual intelligences and is anchored by virtues, values, vision and volition (Will) to deliver self-sustaining educational outcomes. An educability index would provide a basis for assessing the interventions required to assist the student into sustainable, outcome driven education.

To summarise,

- *Essence*: There are unique qualities in each individual that define the way they look at the world. These are virtues, values, personal clarity in envisioning the future and their trust in the institution or system in facilitating them through the education process and the volition or will to achieve.
- *Inhibitors* are the major factors influencing the student by the 'World' or environment in which they live.

- *Inner journeys* are the qualities of the individual represented by actual and potential abilities that may be challenged by physical, emotional, mental or spiritual disadvantage.
- *Outer journeys* are the vehicle through which the student interacts with the educating institution to be motivated, acquire skills, build relationships and achieved defined education outcomes.
- *Facilitating institution's effectiveness*: This is the effectiveness of the facilitating institution and service providers, which may be indexed on past or predicted performance outcomes. When considering outcomes, the most important point is assessing the extent to which the barriers impact on the self-worth or the 'light within' and on each individual's ability to construct a personal vision for the future.

The impact of the education system for the teachers is, of course, key to the success of inclusive education. Excessive administration, poor syllabus control and restrictive practices take their toll on motivation or reduce the 'light within' with the outcomes 'mirrored' onto the students. In the worst case a state of 'learned helplessness' disables performance and may lead to psychological 'meltdown'. A framework that has been found helpful in determining affective interventions and their impact includes five dimensions. These are awareness, vision, responsibility, action and review (AVRAR). In the final analysis, inclusive education requires the integration of many dimensions and levels of interaction to develop a holistic solution that can ensure sustainability.

And from UK experience

Creative special needs teaching has already transformed the lives of hundreds of thousands of children through the use of special grants that take the child from early years through to higher education with, in the UK, the Disabled Student Allowance (DSA) and employment with 'Access to Work'. However, many people drop out between the schemes and nobody knows where they go. There is a need for an improved central tracking system that connects islands of 'good practice' with accurate data to inform sensible conclusions and facilitate each individual on their optimal 'life journey'. The unanswered questions are:

- Could more people be supported at less expense if funding targeted the disability rather than individuals labelled as disabled?
- Would it be more cost effective to give the technology to the whole population and expect those with special needs to use them or just target the individuals?

The implementation of a 'holistic system' would mean that even those with 'invisible disabilities' will get the urge to use the tools without having to disclose their special needs, which could eradicate the negative stigma that exists in our society. The pioneering work by Ron Davis to treat dyslexia using a combination of multisensory learning and internal self-management tools (mind's eye meditation) for accuracy of perception, energy management and dissipation of stress is already providing evidence that alternative approaches can be extremely effective (Davis and Braun, 2010).

The use of assistive technology (AT) may be developed to facilitate lifestyle choice, instead of just being a special needs tool, with the uptake of users soon mushrooming globally. Assistive technology relating to lifelong learning, computers and augmentative communication applies to such areas as: study skills, reading, writing, information gathering, learning, productivity and communication, work station design, hardware adaptations, computer literacy and software. Related devices include large print books, modified computer keyboards for persons with limited hand capabilities and communication boards for those with speaking difficulties. Whilst e-learning provides a very helpful education and training toolbox, it is not a universal panacea with the continued necessity for human interaction and the building of consciousness nets with teachers, parents, grandparents and mentors, where Internet connectivity can be an excellent facilitator.

Assistive technology gives access to all potential dyslexic learners, as well as those having literacy problems through other forms of disability, the chance to participate in the educational curriculum without the need to flag their disability. Mass deployment, as well as making the solution much cheaper, also offers the potential of reducing the cost to schools by replacing teaching assistants who are paid to help learners with reading and writing difficulties. Still, while inclusive education is a goal for all children with learning difficulties, there may be some with severe challenges that require specialist support. It must not be forgotten, of course, that the competence and 'passion for education' of teachers is crucial to learning outcomes for those with special needs (Sahlberg, 2011).

Concluding remarks

Inclusive learning is a complex topic in a complex system of agents that are not always directed to achieving the best solution for the child. The United Nations Convention on the Rights of the Child (1989) seeks to deliver greater clarity, particularly with reference to non-discrimination:

> The Convention applies to all children, whatever their race, religion or abilities; whatever they think or say, whatever type of family they come from. It doesn't matter where children live, what language they speak, what their parents do, whether they are boys or girls, what their culture is, whether they have a disability or whether they are rich or poor. No child should be treated unfairly on any basis.

Inclusive learning as a programme ensures access to all potential learners who have a chance to participate in the educational curriculum without the need to flag their disability. Mass deployment, as well as making the solution much cheaper, also offers the potential of reducing costs to schools through the use of assistive technology and an effective model to reinforce the human capital of all students. Interactive learning requires the stimulus of multiple intelligences that embrace physical (PQ), emotional (EQ), mental (IQ) and spiritual (SQ) dimensions. Story telling (PQ) is a key means for facilitating the transmission and the absorption of data. Similarly, the interactive Look & Say (EQ) approach of discussion and dialogue develops in-depth knowledge. From this base it is possible to use synthetics (IQ) to learn the symbols and structure of a discipline to facilitate understanding. Finally, visualisation (SQ) empowers the concept through the individual's own creative imagination to convert data, knowledge and understanding into personalised wisdom.

Engaging students in self-managed action learning sets and critical action teams also engages parents and grandparents as part of a consciousness net to facilitate societal change. Inclusion should now be part of general policy to optimise human capital. There is great value in learning to work together for all children within diverse groups and capabilities. It helps each child explore both themselves and others to facilitate more a resilient and tolerant society by promoting innovative thinking (driven by diversity and sharing multiple perspectives) as well as a much greater fulfilment of the society's human capital. The Golden Rule of Life is to respect all (Flude, 2013).

Bibliography

Bronfenbrenner, U. (1977). Toward an experimental ecology of human development. *American Psychologist*, 32, 513–530.

Bronfenbrenner, U. (1979). *The Ecology of Hum Dev*. Cambridge, MA: Harvard University Press.

Bronfenbrenner, U. (1989). Ecological systems theory. In: R. Vasta (ed), *Annals of Child Development*, 6, pp. 187–251. Greenwich, CT: JAI.

Davis, R. D. and Braun, E. M. (2010). *Gift of Dyslexia: Why Some of the Brightest People Can't Read and How They Can Learn*. London: Souvenir Press.

Flude, R. A. (1991). *People in Business: The Key to Success*. London: Graham & Trotman.

Flude, R. A. (1996). Facilitating the culture change that is required in resource budgeting. Paper presented at Resource Budgeting in Central Government Conference, AIC Conferences, London, March.

Flude, R. A. (1999). *The Journey into Work*. Manchester: Howdomado.

Flude, R. A. (May 1999). The journey into work – A Bright Future? European Policy Forum, London.

Flude, R. A. (June 1999). The journey into work – The CASEPT Programme. Paper at the Fifth Annual Research Conference of British Association for Counselling & Psychotherapy (BACP), Leeds.

Flude, R. A. (2000). The challenge of the disadvantaged: The inner and outer journeys of inclusion. ISEC 2000 Conference, Manchester.

Flude, R. A. (2005). Corporate governance and social responsibility: A change management perspective. World Council for Corporate Governance; Making Corporate Governance Work Better, London.

Flude, R. A. (2006). Life skills education for youth development. Life Long Learning Conference, Chennai, India.
Flude, R. A. (2010). Developing self sustaining people in times of crisis. World Forum for Spiritual Culture, Astana, Kazakhstan.
Flude, R. A. (2011a). *The Journey into Education: Primary Years*. Manchester: Howdomado.
Flude, R. A. (2011b). Inclusive learning: The challenge of Special Needs. Keynote Address, International Conference on Educational and Social Inclusion, Patna, India.
Flude, R. A. (2012). Maximizing education and social impact with restricted resources in times of crisis. BETT Conference on Education, 2012, London.
Flude, R. A. (2013). *Self-Sustainability: The People Dimension*. Manchester: Howdomado.
Fuller, R. B. (1969). *Operating Manual for Spaceship Earth*. Carbondale, IL: Southern Illinois University Press.
Fuller, R. B. and Applewhite, E. J. (1975). *Synergetics*. New York, NY: Macmillan.
Fuller, R. B. (1981). *Critical Path*, pp. xxxiv–xxxv. New York, NY: St. Martin's Press.
Fuller, R. B. (1981). Introduction. In: *Critical Path*, p. xxv. New York, NY: St. Martin's Press.
Goleman, D. (1997). *Emotional Intelligence*. New York, NY: Bantam Books.
Goleman, D. (2009). *Ecological Intelligence*. New York, NY: Broadway Books.
Johansen, J. and Sahlberg, P. (2011). Educational policies for raising national economic competitiveness: Perceptions, measurements and practice. Annual Meeting of the American Educational Research Association, New Orleans.
Laing, R. D. (1960). *The Divided Self*. Harmondsworth: Penguin.
Laing, R. D. (1961). *Self and Others*. London: Tavistock Publications.
Littlejohn, S. and Foss, K. (2008). *Theories of Human Communication* (9th ed). Belmont: Thomson and Wadsworth.
Lyubomirsky, S. (2008). *How to be Happy* (X, Trans.). Seoul, South Korea: Knowledge Nomad.
Government of Maharashtra. (2015). Mahatma Gandhi biography. https://sjsa.maharashtra.gov.in/en/mahatma-gandhi-biography.
Maslow, A. H. (1970). *Motivation and Personality*. New York: Harper and Row.
Prakash, V. (2010). Broadstreaming, not mainstreaming: An approach towards solutions for inclusive development. Inaugural address at 'Solutions to Inclusive Development' conference, XLRI, Jamshedpur, January 29, 2010.
Sahlberg, P. (2011). *Finnish Lessons: What Can the World Learn from Educational Change in Finland?* New York: Teachers' College Press.
Seligman, M. (1991) *Learned Optimism: How to Change Your Mind and Your Life*. New York: Penguin Books.
United Nations Commission on Human Rights. (1990). *Convention on the Rights of the Child*. New York.
UNESCO. (1998). *Education for the 21st Century: Issues and Prospects*. Paris: UNESCO Publishing.
UNESCO. (2015–2013). UNESCO Statistics. http://data.uis.unesco.org.
Wasdell, D. (1993). *Learning Systems and the Management of Change*. London: Meridian Monograph, Meridian Programme.
World Economic Forum. (2015). The Global Competitiveness Report 2014–2015. World Economic Forum, Geneva. http://www.weforum.org/reports/global-competitiveness-report-2014-2015.
Zohar, D. (2000). *SQ: Connecting with Our Spiritual Intelligence*. London: Bloomsbury Publishing.

14

REACHING THE UNREACHED

Traverse of alternative and innovative schools

K. Gireesan

Context

The centrally sponsored District Primary Education Programme (DPEP) launched in India in 1994 was introduced to universalise primary education and ensure quality education in a mission mode. DPEP initiated a number of systems, processes and structures aimed at the quality improvement of primary education in the country (Ministry of Human Resource Development [MHRD], 1995). After the formal closing of DPEP in 2003 which initiated several activities touching almost all areas of primary education, Sarva Shiksha Abhiyan (SSA) was introduced. SSA was a flagship programme for achievement of universalisation of elementary education for children in the 6–14 years age group in a time-bound manner (MHRD, n.d.). A number of varied and flexible strategies were designed and implemented under this programme to ensure the participation of children of underprivileged and marginalised groups. The launching of Multi-Grade Learning Centres (MGLC) was one such unique initiative made to intervene effectively among the children of marginalised sections of society. Experiences of schools like 'Rishi Valley', 'Sarang' and 'Kanavu' have contributed to the evolution of Multi-Grade Learning Centres. Subsequently, the Multi-Grade Learning Centre (MGLC) was renamed as an Alternative and Innovative School (AIS). To address the issues of non-enrolment and drop out in remote and unserved areas, and provide access to primary education for all children, the strategy of Alternative and Innovative Education was developed (Gireesan, 2011).

Geographical remoteness, social factors, poverty, linguistic factors, lack of sufficient educational facilities, sibling care, gender discrimination, etc. were identified as the major factors that blocked universal elementary education in the remote tribal habitations. There are members of some communities, especially tribal, which are still not aware of the benefits of education. Some of them felt that the formal school curriculum would result in the alienation of their children from their own customs, traditions, language and culture. Children of these communities, especially tribal, experience adjustment problems also and drop-out is a common feature among them. The medium of instruction is at variance with the spoken dialect of these communities. And, most of the teachers do not belong to the community and hail from the 'mainland' and many are not sensitive enough for the very specific issues of these children. No single strategy could address this problem (Gireesan, 2011). In this context, Alternative and Innovative Education was introduced as an alternate strategy to ensure the participation of children of underprivileged and marginalised groups living in geographically remote locations. It provides wide use of self-learning materials which the students learn as per their interest, level and pace of learning, and it is facilitated by the Education Volunteer (SSA-K, n.d.). It encourages use of diverse methods aimed at ensuring active involvement of students in the learning process through small group discussions, debates, role plays, etc. It enlivens participatory learning in the classroom and outside between the teacher and the students, and among the students as well, making it student-centric as well as participatory, aiming at their empowerment.

Introduction

Through a research study, this chapter analyses how Alternative and Innovative Schools (AIS) function in selected districts of the Indian state of Kerala – Palakkad, Idukki and Ernakulam. These districts were selected in consultation with the State Project Office of SSA. This study is relevant and unique in view of inclusive education, as the thrust here is to understand the strategies and approaches carried out in the field during the operationalisation of Alternative and Innovative Education. In addition, it would be pertinent to analyse how far the four pillars of education (learning to know, learning to be, learning to do and learning to live together) as envisaged by the International Commission on Education for the 21st Century (UNESCO, 1996) are manifested during the operationalisation of AIS in the study area.

Primary data was obtained from Education Volunteers/Instructors in the AIS, elected members of Local Government Institutions (LGI)/Panchayati Raj Institutions (PRI), members of Parent Teacher Associations (PTA)/Mother Parent Teacher Associations (MPTA), members of the local community and representatives of teachers' organisations. In addition, SSA officials and selected educationists were also contacted. Secondary data was collected from the documents and reports of the State and District Project Offices of SSA, Education Department of the Government of Kerala, LGIs at different levels and educational institutions.

This chapter also analyses the operationalisation of AIS, with thrust on the strategies and approaches used by the Education Volunteers (EV)/Instructors by incorporating an interactive teaching-learning process to reach out to marginalised sections of society. It examines the support and co-operation received from PRIs and other sections of the local community by mobilising resources for the development of

AIS. It tries to portray how far these institutions could make strides towards 'reaching the unreached' segments of society.

Methodology

The study was carried out in three districts of Kerala – Palakkad, Idukki and Ernakulam. Secondary data was gathered from documents, reports and other materials from the State/District Project Offices of SSA, Education Department of the Government of Kerala, District/Block/Grama Panchayats and all other available sources. The collection of primary data was done by administering the following tools in the Ernakulam, Idukki and Palakkad Districts of Kerala.

a   Interview schedule for Education Volunteer (EV)/Instructor.
b   Schedule for AIS.
c   Interview schedule for community members.
d   Interview schedule for teachers of formal schools (Class V only).
e   Interview schedule for functionaries of teachers' organisations.

The research team consisted of a Chief Investigator, 3 Research Assistants and 15 field investigators for the collection of data from the field. Every member of the research team maintained a tour diary to record their observations and reflections during the field work. This made it possible to correct, substantiate and analyse the scenario obtained from the data through other structured schedules.

The majority of the field investigators were *Preraks* of Continuing Education Centres, functioning in the field for nearly five years. (A Prerak is the facilitator of a Continuing Education Centre/Nodal Continuing Education Centre established as part of the Total Literacy Campaign/Continuing Education programmes.) In addition, research assistants, having experience in undertaking similar field assignments, were used to co-ordinate the data collection. The field investigators and research assistants were given orientation training before the work commenced. As part of the orientation, the significance of following a systematic approach during the data collection was communicated to all members of the team.

A specific pattern and order for the collection of data was adopted towards incorporating various schedules and gathering the relevant information from the respondents in the field. On reaching the Centre, a self-introduction of the investigator was given to the EV/Instructor, followed by a brief overview of the assignment. While the EV conducted the class/session, the investigator(s) observed the teaching-learning process and other aspects using the 'Schedule for AIS'. Necessary instructions were given to the investigator not to record anything during the visits to the Centre, as the body language and reactions of the children and the EV may get affected by such recording. However, the investigators were asked to fill out the schedule immediately on completion of the session. 'Interview with the EV/Instructor' was conducted only after the classroom session. About 4–5 personnel from the PTA/MPTA and members from the locality were contacted to seek certain data as cited in the 'Schedule for Community Members'. On completion of all Centres in the selected area, elected representatives of the PRIs, especially the President, Chairperson of Standing Committee (Welfare) and one or two elected members, were interviewed.

The learners who complete the teaching-learning process in AIS are permitted to join the mainstream schools at Class V. Hence, the assessment of learners transferred from AIS to formal schools was also included, which was made based on the information gathered from the Schedule for EV/Instructor. Some of the teachers of formal schools in the nearby areas were contacted for collection of data using 'Schedule for Teachers of Formal Schools (Class V)'. Representatives of prominent teacher organisations were also contacted to understand their views, comments and suggestions about the programme.

Strategies and approaches

This section highlights the specific strategies and approaches used by the EV in the operationalisation of AIS, with special focus on the interactive and participatory teaching-learning process. This is very significant considering the educational backwardness, poverty, social factors, geographical remoteness, cultural factors, etc. of those learners from marginalised regions, when compared to other places. As many of them were first-generation learners and their parents could not provide any guidance and support to them in their studies, it is noted that the traditional 'chalk and talk method' will not be effective at all.

An overview of certain dimensions like classroom environment, classroom processes and practices, evaluation strategies by the EVs, the practice of seeking community opinion regarding the functioning of Centres and measures to ensure convergence in the activities have been made here. These strategies and approaches were considered very significant, as they are crucial in 'reaching the unreached', in view of their educational backwardness, cultural moorings and other social aspects which influence the teaching-learning process. A brief on the major dimensions is given below.

- *Classroom environment*: Dressing pattern of EV, facial expressions of EV, intimacy/caring for the learners, neatness of classroom area and classroom management.
- *Classroom processes and practices*: Pattern of seating, method of grouping, approach of introducing a topic in the class, nature of activities adopted to introduce the topic, type of questions asked and use of chalkboard while teaching.
- *Evaluation strategies by the EVs*: Mode of assessment of learner's performance, nature of giving home assignment and mode of evaluation of home assignment.
- *Seeking community opinion regarding the functioning of Centres*: Regularity of EV, sincerity of EV, regularity in the functioning of AIS and progress of children studying in AIS.

- *Convergence of activities*: Mobilising funds, resources, contributions and assistance from different departments/institutions/agencies/individuals for the smooth functioning of Centres.

Indicators for quality dimensions and options

As some of those cited above are quality dimensions, extreme care was made to avoid the element of subjectivity by developing certain indicators, while considering them during the operationalisation of programmes and for bringing objectivity to the responses.

- *Dressing pattern of EV*: Use of costly dress materials, jewellery and footwear. (Options: Simple, Average and High)
- *Facial expressions of EV*: During the normal course of teaching, while replying to the queries from learners and while raising queries to the learners. (Options: Non-pleasing, Average and Pleasing)
- *Intimacy/caring for learners*: Understanding about the personal issues of learners, enquiring about their family details and enquiring about their after-school activities. (Options: Low, Medium and High)
- *Neatness of classroom area*: Proper positioning of pictures/illustrations in the classrooms, non-presence of paper bits and pieces in the classrooms and general cleanliness of the classroom and surroundings. (Options: Below Average, Average and Above Average)
- *Classroom management*: Arrangement of teaching-learning materials in the classroom, arrangement of benches, chairs, desks, etc. in the class (Options: Below Average, Average and Above Average)
- *Regularity of EV*: Presence in the Centre every day and making alternative arrangements in case of sickness/absence. (Options: Poor, Average, Good)
- *Sincerity of EV*: Discuss the progress of children with their parents, involvement of community members in various activities and initiative for arranging programmes at the AIS. (Options: Poor, Average, Good)
- *Regularity in the functioning of Centres*: Opening of the Centre on time every day, involvement of School Support Group (SSG) in the day-to-day activities of the Centre and the timely conduct of PTA/MPTA meetings. (Options: Poor, Average, Good)
- *Progress of children studying in Centres*: Progress of learners in academic activities and involvement of learners in co-scholastic activities. (Options: Below Average, Average, Above Average)

Profile of education volunteers

Four-fifths of the EVs (80%) were female and more than three-fourths of the EVs (78.2%) were in the age group of 21–35 years. More than half of them (52.7%) had the qualification of pre-degree/higher secondary or above. This indicates that the programme was able to attract educated young women to function as EVs.

Discussion and analysis

This section includes the outcomes/responses from the field regarding the classroom environment, classroom processes and practices, evaluation strategies adopted by the EVs, seeking community opinion regarding the functioning of Centres, and measures to ensure convergence in the activities.

Classroom environment

The dressing pattern of EV, his/her facial expressions during the class, intimacy/caring for the learners, neatness of classroom area and classroom management have been analysed here. It is noted that the dressing style of the teacher has an influence on the learners from marginalised regions. As most of the learners come from very poor socio-economic backgrounds, it is likely that they tend to develop a feeling of alienation if they that find the dressing pattern of the EV is 'High'. And the chances of developing a 'too distant approach' and feelings of alienation by the learners is all the more possible, when the EV comes from a distant place, which will be coupled with their dressing pattern. The need for adopting simplicity in dressing by the teacher has been highlighted here, which may encourage the learners to interact with them in a more familiar environment. It was noted from the responses that a large segment of EVs (49.1%) follow a 'Simple' pattern, followed by 'Average' (40%), in terms of dressing.

Pleasing facial expressions and positive body language of the teacher are also acknowledged as the factors influencing classroom environment. This is an important aspect considering that many of them are 'first-generation learners' and the positive exposition of the teacher is very significant to encourage them to take part effectively in the sessions. It is observed during the field visits that the majority of the EVs (63.6%) do have 'Pleasing' facial expressions, be it during the normal course of teaching, while raising queries with the learners or replying to various queries from the learners, which will encourage the learners to interact freely and clear their doubts with the teacher.

Irrespective of the geographical setting, the aspect of intimacy/caring for the learners by the teacher plays an important role in their upbringing. Efforts made to understand the family background and other details of learners, understanding their personal issues, documenting their progress at regular intervals and enquiries about their after-school activities have been cited here. The uniqueness of expressing intimacy/care by the teacher towards the learners needs no emphasis, and is even more important as the primary teacher may be the most influential person outside their home/locality, who can play a major role in their upbringing. Regarding the intimacy/caring for learners, the majority of the EVs (63.6%) have expressed 'Medium' standards. This may be due to the reason that a good number of EVs come from places away from the Centre (beyond 3 km) and may not be fully aware of the after-school activities of the learners. However, just more than a quarter of the EVs (27.3%) have expressed 'High' standards.

Regarding the neatness of classrooms and neighbouring areas, it is noted that just less than half of the Centres (49.1%) keep 'Above Average' standards. Classroom management, indicated by arrangement of seating facilities and availability and use of teaching-learning materials, could be graded as 'Above Average' in a large segment (47.3%) of the Centres.

Classroom processes and practices

Various classroom processes and practices like pattern of seating, method of grouping, approach of introducing a topic in the class, nature of activities adopted to introduce the topic, type of questions asked, raising questions by the learners and use of chalkboard during teaching are included here.

The pattern of seating in the classrooms is an important element in the teaching-learning environment. It is noted that even those who are generally shy or introvert in regular classroom sessions, actively take part in the group discussions. Hence, it is noted that such group-wise seating of the learners plays a positive influence among them by developing team work, mutual understanding, spirit of tolerance, leadership qualities, etc. This will also enable the learners from the marginalised sections to get along with the students from diverse backgrounds, when they join formal schools. It is noted that the pattern of seating followed in most of the Centres is either in groups or in small groups. During the field visits, it was noted that a 'group wise' seating pattern was adopted in the majority of the Centres (56.4%), followed by small groups (29.1%).

Regarding the method of grouping the learners in the classrooms, different patterns have been adopted in the Centres like Grade-wise, Learning level-wise or Subject-wise. Learning level-wise grouping has an advantage over the other methods as the slow learners get additional care and attention, when compared to others. However, it was observed that Grade-wise learning was preferred by the majority of the EVs (53%).

During the teaching-learning process, it is noted that how you introduce a topic is more important than what you introduce, depending on its acceptability and difficulty levels. In this context, the approach of introducing a topic in the AIS is even more important, as it generates interest among the learners, the majority of them being 'first-time learners' from their family. It was observed that direct, indirect and mixed patterns have been adopted by the EVs in introducing a topic in the classroom. Among these approaches, a mixed pattern of combining direct and interactive ways of introducing the topic was adopted by the single largest segment (38.18%). Regarding the nature of activities adopted to introduce a topic, a large section of EVs (47.3%) preferred 'Group' activities followed by 'Small group' activities (40%) and only a small segment used 'Individual oriented' activities.

During the classroom practices, the EV used to put forward different types of questions to the learners, a large segment of them (40%) generated by them. It was significant to note that questions based on life experiences (10.9%) and questions generating innovativeness/creativity (3.6%) also found their place during the sessions. And, 'Mixed' type of questions, a combination of all these types, has been noted among a significant section of EVs (32.7%). With regard to raising questions by the learners, no gender difference was cited in most of the classes observed (80%). However, during the field visits, it was noted that in some of the Centres (7.3%), the questions were raised by boys only.

It was generally observed that unless the teacher encourages the learners to raise questions, many of them may not be inclined to interact during the sessions. It was observed that the questions prepared by the EVs themselves based on life experiences and questions capable of generating creativity/innovativeness among them, could play an important role in enhancing their understanding, analytical skills, critical thinking and creative thinking. This is viewed as an important strategy in equipping the learners from educationally backward and geographically remote areas to develop their self-confidence. In addition, by putting forward questions based on their life situations, they will be able to make a self-assessment of the situation more realistically.

Use of chalkboard during the teaching-learning process was carefully examined as it played an important role in shedding the inhibitions of the learners and helps them to enhance their confidence level during classroom practices. As most of the learners are exposed to such formal methods of teaching for the first time, involving the use of a chalkboard is an effective strategy for enhancing their understanding, confidence and self-esteem during the teaching-learning process. It was interesting to note that in majority of the classes (54.6%) observed during the field visits, both EV and the learners used the chalkboard during classroom practices.

Evaluation strategies adopted by the EVs

Evaluation strategies adopted by the EVs to enhance the learner's performance and to get feedback about their academic progress include continuous assessment of a learner's performance, provision of home assignments given by the EV to learners and evaluation of home assignments.

The mode of assessment of learners during classroom situations is an important element in evaluating their level of understanding. And, continuous assessment is an important tool to measure their progress in learning, based on which appropriate changes in the teaching strategies may be incorporated by the teacher. Asking questions about the topics covered during the earlier sessions, asking them to reflect upon the issues discussed, initiating a quiz among the learners, etc. were some of the practices adopted for oral assessment of the learners. Carrying out planned and/or surprise written examinations also were used by the EVs to make an assessment of the progress of the learners. During the field visits, it was noted that most of the EVs (95%) used both oral and written methods for assessing learners' performance.

Provision of home assignment is another practice incorporated by the EV to develop the retentivity of the learners and enhance their understanding of topics. It is noted that the nature of the home assignment given by the EV to the learners plays an important role in making them think logically, systematically and critically, in addition to improving their writing and presentation skills. It was noted that assignments made by the EVs tops the list (32.73%), which itself highlights the seriousness of this practice. It is noted that such a practice manifests the autonomy and freedom enjoyed by the EV during the process of evaluation and will also enhance the capacity of the learners and the teacher. A quick appraisal through the type of assignments offered to the learners during the field visits has only consolidated this premise. It was noted that a combination of book-based and EV-made assignments (18.18%) and mixed type assignments (14.55%) also found their place. It is interesting to observe that assignments relating to environment and family issues were also included.

The mode of evaluation of home assignments also could be used for building the capacity of the learners. 'Peer evaluation' was adopted in some Centres (9.09%) in Palakkad and Idukki. 'Peer evaluation' by the learners has an element of empowerment for the learners themselves, as they are being exposed to the nuances of evaluation under the direction of the EV, in the formative stages of learning itself.

Seeking community opinion regarding the functioning of Centres

Opinions expressed by the community members about the functioning of AIS bear an ample testimony to their effectiveness and efficiency. In this context, the opinions of the community members like the elected members of PRIs, functionaries of PTA/MPTA and members of the local community living near the AIS were analysed. They expressed their opinions on the overall functioning of AIS and its contributions, with emphasis on the regularity and sincerity of the EV, regularity in functioning of Centres and their views on progress noted among learners.

Regularity of EV was taken up for an assessment considering their regular reporting at the Centre and making alternative arrangements for handling/engaging the class in case of any professional/personal engagements. To the questions put forward to the community members about the regularity of the EV, most of them (97.92%) responded as 'Good'. Only a small segment from the community (2.08%) expressed their displeasure about the irregular approach of the EVs. It was noted that on certain occasions, the EVs had to proceed to the SSA office for meetings at short notice and no alternative arrangement could be made.

Conduct of discussions made by the EV with the parents of learners about their progress, efforts made by them to organise various programmes aimed at the overall development of learners and the initiatives made to involve members of the community in the different activities of the Centres were considered to make an assessment about the sincerity of EVs. It was noted that nearly three-quarters of the responses (74.48%) were rated as 'Good', followed by 'Average' (25%). There was a negative response from one of the community members in Idukki District about the sincerity of the EV. This was verified using 'triangulation method' and it was noted that there was no valid base for this opinion. It was realised that personal enmity of that respondent with the EV was the prime reason for expressing a negative opinion.

Regular operations of the Centre were analysed here considering aspects like opening of the Centre every day at specified times, constitution of the School Support Group (SSG), involvement of the SSG in Centre activities and regular conduct of PTA/MPTA meetings. Regarding the specific queries put forward to community members about the operations of the Centre, the responses were 'Good' in almost all except one, which again turned out to be based on some personal reasons.

Progress of children studying in the Centres was assessed based on the opinions expressed by community members, regarding the involvement of learners in academic and co-scholastic activities. More than four-fifths of community members (87.5%) opined that the progress of learners could be rated as 'Above Average'. And, most of the community members acknowledged the positive influence of the programme among learners coming to the AIS.

Measures to ensure convergence in the activities

Resources from different departments, institutions, agencies and individuals can be converged during the operationalisation of any programme, which allows creation of a synergy during the scheme implementation. It was noted that specific efforts were made during the operationalisation to bring in convergence in their activities. Specific efforts were made to ensure convergence in terms of human and material resources, mobilising finance and developing support systems by enlisting Community Based Organisations, educational institutions, financial institutions and government departments. It was noted that a number of PRIs earmarked and utilised adequate funds for SSA activities, which definitely manifests the credibility, sustainability and responsiveness of the local administration. In general, the community is encouraged to make a contribution of resources in cash, kind or services for the development of infrastructure and other facilities during the operationalisation of the Centres. However, it was observed that the majority of the resource/support/assistance/ facilities provided to the Centre were only a temporary assistance/stop gap arrangement to overcome an emergency situation. For example, the supply of rice and condiments to some of the Centres were made only to address a crisis situation owing to the delay in supply of mid-day meals to the learners. Convergence of resources/support/assistance/facilities to the Centres by different agencies resulted in rejuvenating the programmes in the State. More significantly, it also manifests the ownership by the community in the operationalisation of the programme, which will go a long way to ensuring sustainable results.

Shortcomings noted during operationalisation

Certain glaring shortcomings noted during operationalisation of the Alternative and Innovative Schools are indicated below.

a Infrastructure facilities:

- Unsafe physical conditions.
- Absence of sanitation facilities.
- Lack of adequate play materials for the children.

b Supply of food materials:

- Delay in supply of food materials.
- No proper provision for the supply of food materials to Centres in remote places.

c Teaching-Learning process:

- Complete set of Self Learning Materials (SLM) cards were not available in some places.
- Revision/updating of learning materials was not done.
- Lack of sufficient training for EVs.
- No proper training on grading of the students to EVs.
- No alternative arrangements for handling the children when EV is not available.

d Community participation:

- Lack of active involvement of parents/community members.
- Lack of ownership and support from Local Government Institutions.

Suggestions and recommendations

Certain programme-specific suggestions and policy-level recommendations are put forward here.

a Programme-specific suggestions and recommendations:

- Emergency repair of buildings where AIS is functioning.
- Regular supply of food materials to the Centres be ensured by linking with the Public Distribution System.
- Updating, improvement and revision of SLM Cards to be made at regular intervals.
- Organise camps, cultural and sports festivals jointly for students of AIS with students of formal schools.
- Regular meetings of PTA/MPTA be conducted in all Centres.
- Organise sensitisation sessions and advocacy at local level towards generating a feeling of ownership among elected members of PRIs and other community members.
- SSG for each AIS needs to be constituted and made functional.
- Process documentation needs to be taken up and EVs be equipped for carrying out the same.

- Conduct a study on the achievement level of students transferred from AIS to mainstream schools in scholastic and co-scholastic areas.
- Conduct a micro-level study regarding the adjustment issues of students transferred from AIS to mainstream schools.

b Policy-level recommendations:

- AIS need to be included as a part of the teacher-training curriculum.
- Necessary advocacy with the State Government and the Local Government Institutions be carried out towards earmarking a reasonable share from the plan fund of PRIs towards primary education.
- Special sanction may be provided to PRIs by the State Government towards constructing multi-purpose buildings which can house different activities including AIS.
- Carrying out external monitoring of the initiatives and interventions at regular intervals to assess the impact.

Conclusion

It was noted that various strategies and approaches adopted during the operationalisation of Alternative Innovative Schools are important in the functioning of every educational institution, but they are more significant as these institutions are located in geographically remote and educationally backward regions of the State and many of the learners were 'first generation learners' from their family. Simplicity of the Education Volunteer in the use of dress materials, jewellery and footwear was important while analysing the classroom environment. 'Pleasing' facial expressions and body language of the EV during classroom situations created significant influence among the learners by encouraging them to sharpen their questioning skills and to encourage them to interact more freely and effectively with the teacher. Group-wise seating of the learners was another approach capable of encouraging team work, mutual respect, co-operation, spirit of tolerance, in addition to enhancing their leadership qualities. The majority of the EVs used both oral and written methods for assessing the learner's performance. Providing home assignments based on different life situations, helped the learners to internalise the topics more easily and analyse them effectively, and enhance their creativity and critical abilities, in addition to problem-solving skills. Enabling the learners to use chalkboard during the teaching-learning process played a key role in enhancing their self-confidence and self-esteem. 'Peer evaluation' practised by some EVs has an element of empowerment, as the learners are exposed to the nuances of evaluation in the early stage of learning itself. It was noted that EVs secured support from members of SSG, PTA/MPTA and made necessary efforts for convergence and support in their activities, which helped significantly.

Analysis of AIS indicate that critical thinking and problem solving (*learning to know*); self-confidence and self-esteem (*learning to be*); hands-on experience (*learning *to do*); and, inter-personal relations, co-operation and empathy (*learning to live together*) have been more evident in their functioning. It is noted that the approaches and strategies manifested by the EVs have significantly influenced the operationalisation of these Centres in the area of study.

Co-ordination and co-operation of different agencies is essential for the smooth functioning of AIS. In this context, ensuring the wholehearted involvement and participation of community members is an important aspect. There is a need to have a close rapport, continuous advocacy and confidence building with the PRIs and other community members, so as to generate a sense of ownership in them, along with ensuring the financial viability and sustainability of the schemes. Since the representatives of the PRIs are leaders of the local community, they not only reflect community attitudes but also serve as individuals capable of prompting community involvement. PRIs can take a lead role in ensuring convergence of various departments, agencies, institutions and every other stakeholder of the programme. It is visualised that PRIs, ably guided by SSA officials and strongly supported by the community, can act as catalytic forces to affect a substantial improvement in the quality of primary education in the tribal and coastal regions of the State.

An intervention like this is even more important in the context of the Right to Education (RTE) Act, which is an important move to enable 'Universalising Primary Education' among the underprivileged and marginalised sections of society. It is still an unfinished dream of the 'Father of the Nation', Mahatma Ghandi, founding members of the Indian Constitution and successive governments of the country. It is visualised that policy makers, academicians, administrators and social activists would benefit from an exercise like this. It is expected that the strategies and approaches cited here could contribute immensely to the strengthening of such innovative measures within the state, country and even in other parts of the world.

Bibliography

Gireesan, K. (2011). Reaching the unreached: Life skills approach in alternative and innovative schools of Kerala. In: A.R. Nair and S. Ranjan (eds), *Impact of Life Skills Education: Evidences from the Field*. Sriperumbudur: Rajiv Gandhi National Institute of Youth Development.

Ministry of Human Resource Development. (1995). *District Primary Education Programme Guidelines*. New Delhi: Publications Division.

Ministry of Human Resource Development. (n.d.). Department of School Education and Literacy, Sarva Shiksha Abhiyan. Retrieved: 2 February 2011 from http://www.ssa.nic.in.

Sarva Shiksha Abhiyan-Kerala. (n.d.). Alternative and Innovative Education. Retrieved 2 February 2011 from www.ssamis.com/web/html.

UNESCO. (1996). Report to the UNESCO of the International Commission on Education for the 21st Century. Paris: UNESCO.

AFTERWORD

Devorah Kalekin-Fishman

Many groups of students are barred from inclusion in schools. Because of unconscious biases or because of inadequate preparation, educators may foster the exclusion of the very people who need special care and attention. Among the difficulties educators face are the challenges of how to deal with: bilingualism, dyslexia, physical disability such as deafness and diverse types of psychological predicaments. Educational exclusion may, moreover, resonate with the social and economic rejection that minority groups or immigrants encounter in adulthood. All the chapters in this book look at how to promote educational and social inclusion among the groups that frequently endure discrimination. Apart from analyses of the difficulties, each chapter also provides hints, comments and instructions to parents and teachers/ educationists for overcoming prejudiced behaviours. The cases documented are impelled by urgent concerns for the future of the students and for the structure of the adult world. When all is said and done, the concern with educational inclusion comes into play because of the fear that through exclusion, schools are contributing to the reproduction of alienated social positions and to a passive acceptance of alienating social structures. These were described extensively by Marx when he analysed the effects of capitalist industrialism on social change (Bourdieu and Passeron, 1977; Kalekin-Fishman and Langman, 2015; Langman and Kalekin-Fishman, 2006).

According to Marx (1977 [1844]), relations of production under capitalism are inexorably exploitative. For one thing, owners of the means of industrial production determine objectives, methods of production and marketing strategies. In recompensing workers for their labour, capitalists are concerned only to ensure workers' self-maintenance, a steady supply of factory hands. But workers' contribution to production goes far beyond their immediate personal needs. Working with auxiliary machines, labourers create profit for the capitalist owners.[1] Marx's description refers, of course, to industry as it developed in the nineteenth century. But his conclusions are still relevant. Theoreticians and researchers have repeatedly shown that although they still prevail in traditional industries today, the types of relations cultivated under capitalism are not limited to the industrial workplace. Exploitative relations are the norm for relations between dominant and subordinate groups in every social framework: political institutions, business firms, service organizations, families, group life in general and in educational institutions. What is designated as the profit of dominant groups may change in different social contexts, but the consequences in the lives of subordinates and subalterns are similarly far-reaching (Hochschild, 1983; Leidner, 2003). Summing up the implications that have been drawn from the Marxist analysis of labour by critical sociologists, David (2006: 71) formulates the pervasive effects as 'disembodiment, exploitation, ideology, and anomie'. That is to say, that under the structural conditions of alienation people are distanced from spontaneous identification with their bodies; they are insensitive to exploitation; they embrace ideas and opinions that support the status quo, and do not realise that these arrangements are not innate. As a result, people contribute to their own subordination and have problems in understanding how to behave in a wide range of situations. Because of their pervasiveness, the conditions David describes are taken for granted as human nature.

In a classic literature review, Seeman (1959) found that there are often practical social psychological consequences of alienation which can be described as:

- *Powerlessness* – the feeling that one is unable to act to overcome discrimination;
- *Meaninglessness* – the feeling that one is unable to foretell the outcome of actions – neither of one's own, nor of one's partners;
- *Normlessness* – anomie, the feeling that one cannot know what behaviours are expected of one, what norms are valid in any given situation;
- *Social isolation* – the feeling that one is cut off from one's social milieu;
- *Self-estrangement* – the feeling that one is not familiar with one's true nature and true aspirations.

In 1996, Kalekin-Fishman raised the possibility that alienation was likely to have two contradictory effects in regard to norms of behaviour. The one delineated by Seeman is the Durkheimian form of anomie (*normlessness*). But it is possible to understand that structural alienation may lead to *normfulness*, i.e., extreme conformity inspired by a feeling that one should not deviate from accepted codes of behaviour, or from accepted ways of thinking, however they are interpreted.

Seeman insisted that the proposed terms were not meant to be interpreted as a syndrome of social psychological alienation; they were simply a summary of ideas that had appeared before his time. Still, researchers have examined these dimensions in more enterprising ways. By contrast with the critical Marxian view that alienation is so all-encompassing that people are rarely aware of their alienated circumstances or of the alienating conditions, respondents are likely to be alert to the dimensions of feeling that Seeman defined. Many studies have examined the extent to which people are aware of dimensions of alienation and how their awareness correlates with attitudes toward democracy, racism, nationalism and with their political activities. These researches have established that there are often connections among the different dimensions.

As the outcome of structural limitations, these feelings toward oneself and toward one's surroundings appear to each individual as the natural and therefore inevitable framework of human life. Given that these reactions to conditions of alienation are pervasive in adult society, they can be seen to be part of what children absorb as taken for granted at an early age. A most likely outcome is for children, as for adults, to accuse oneself of failure to live up to the legitimate expectations of the social environment. For those enrolled in schools, derogation of one's abilities may cause feelings of powerlessness, meaninglessness, social isolation and even self-estrangement, and thus may affect the capacity for learning in many different ways. Research presented in this volume highlights some of the problems that emerge because of socially constructed 'weaknesses' as well as how education can help overcome these drawbacks. In reviewing the chapters of this book, we can see that the pedagogical means suggested are, knowingly or not, directed toward 'curing' aspects of the social psychological alienation that Seeman identified.

The alienated perceptions portrayed in Marx and in subsequent literature combine into the defamed state of *false consciousness*. This is a general term that designates people's disbelief in change or in their capability of bringing about change toward improving their lives. Whether or not they agree with the Marxian analysis, the educator-researchers do agree with what is implied by the moral category of *false consciousness*: namely, that every person has the potential to exercise power, to understand the surround and the implications of his/her behaviour, to discern the adequacy of norms, to be partner to social processes and to achieve self-actualisation. For researchers whose themes turn around education, the realisation of human potential is a highly realistic goal, which, knowingly or not, arranges children's lives so that they may escape the throes of alienation. More modestly, educationists deal with practical ways to operationalise social and educational inclusion, by organising learning in ways that can help students of any age to achieve emancipation from alienation.

With consummate zeal, the contributors to the chapters in this book describe ways in which social and educational inclusion can be advanced. On the basis of the ambitions and good will of people involved in education – teachers, supervisors and principals – there are, as we have seen, programmes and projects that intend no less than to promote the de-alienation of large populations through schooling, while overcoming the limitations of false consciousness.

In this volume, researchers present a wide sweep of suggestions for overcoming alienation through education. As a general introduction to the following chapters, Verma provides a detailed portrayal of how the actions that underline social and educational exclusion induce, better, reproduce alienation in (minority) schoolchildren and have lasting effects on the quality of their lives. The call for social and educational inclusion is a call for revising discriminatory norms, and for accepting that minorities of every stripe must have equal rights. After Verma's general introduction, each of the chapters can be seen to be proposing ways to avoid one or another social psychological consequence of alienation. I will point out a reading of articles as implicit resistance to one or another of the aspects of alienation.

Kalekin-Fishman proposes that the capacity for overcoming hardships can be fostered if children are encouraged to deal with problems that trouble them from early childhood and throughout their schooling. By defining issues in their own lives, discussing possible solutions and working together to find those that are most effective, they are acquiring concrete capacities to negotiate troubles, and avoiding *powerlessness*. From Bangladesh, Nath explains the context for understanding how *powerlessness* among women is being prevented by the legislation that regulates the promotion of women's education. This, however, only became possible when a conducive political context emerged with the overturn of the military regime in the country. Clearly the discrimination suffered by women until now has not simply 'gone away', but requires careful tending. In the chapter by Griva on bilingualism and its challenges among immigrant children, the suggestions for treating the complexities of dealing with two often very different languages point to ways of overcoming the hazard of *powerlessness* in negotiations with the regime of the country to which they have come. Similarly, cautious strategies can help them avoid *meaninglessness* in the sense of not being able to use either language in a way that provides them with a clear grasp of the realities in which they are operating. But this is not a problem unique to immigrant children. Relating to children's experiences in contending with a standard curriculum, Prakash goes into detail about how what he calls 'broadstreaming' can make a difference in children's self-assessments of their cognitive powers, and thus enable them to avoid the experience of *meaninglessness*.

Looking at the gigantic challenges of education in India, Sinha and Lakshmi point to the drawbacks of diversity, and how the encounters and mis-encounters among people of different classes and different religions are likely to foster an aspiration to distance, thus to advance exclusion and perpetuate *social isolation*. Grant and Zwier insist that only if parents and teachers and the community as a whole relate to children with the respect they deserve as unique and complete human beings, will it be possible to further social and educational inclusion for all, and this will prevent *social isolation*. A specific school population in danger of *social isolation* is the large group of children whose learning difficulty is defined as dyslexia. Tabassum and Kumari show that if dyslexics fail to experience early diagnosis and intensive individualised teaching, they, too, will be doomed to *social isolation*, even beyond their careers as school children. Moreover, the growing conviction of their incompetence is likely to cause them *self-estrangement*, a feeling of negligible self-worth. In his chapter on broadstreaming, Prakash proposes a practical pedagogical approach that is likely to help children avoid *self-estrangement* once they are enabled to take part in Creative Learning.

Similar problems beset students with disabilities. Giavrimis, Giossi and Papastamatis show that in Greece teachers can be educated to understand the difficulties of pupils who are 'different', to encourage them in their unique talents, and to save them from *social isolation* and from s*elf-estrangement*.

Flude also sees solutions; he sees the digital age as one in which there are resources that create opportunities for the educational and social inclusion of pupils who present a wide range of learning disabilities. He suggests that in schools, people can be saved from the negative effects of educational exclusion – *social isolation* and *self-estrangement* – if technological innovations are used systematically and in ways that are adapted to individual needs. Many of the possibilities are realised in new kinds of schools. While special programmes are in place in state schools, Alternative and Innovative schooling is part of a widening educational movement. As Gireesan shows, it is highly possible that these schools that undertake to help minority children, immigrant children and children with disabilities make the most of learning situations, are bringing a holistic message to education that can promise a comprehensive reprieve from the *powerlessness, meaninglessness, normlessness, social isolation* and *self-estrangement* that children absorb from the adult world because they are often reinforced by the strait-laced programmes of conventional schooling.

Relating to educational developments in New Zealand, Crothers' historical overview of educational policy in that state demonstrates the dialectical complexity of overcoming alienation. Vicissitudes in educational policy in New Zealand have been on the side of preserving the status quo of minority discrimination, inducing *social isolation* (from the 'white' ruling classes) and *powerlessness*. Current policy has taken a thoroughly liberal tack. However, as Crothers points out, the impact of policy is often countered by teachers' biases; and children are left in a state of *normlessness* that the contradictions of guidance in schools do nothing to modify. Panitsidou relates to similar hazards of long-range failures in learning when she describes how the Lifelong Learning policies introduced by the European Union can help to overcome *normlessness*, confusion about what actions to take, in adults who are limited in their skills, or whose skills are no longer relevant in the labour market of the twenty-first century.

In a comprehensive survey, Siddiqui reviews the obstacles to promoting inclusive education in India, but shows that legislation and serious attempts to apply progressive policies are making a difference slowly but surely by confronting different aspects of alienation.

Concluding remarks

In one of his newspaper articles, Marx complained that the compulsory schooling that proliferated in the nineteenth century would condemn students to a tolerance for exploitation and an acceptance of subordination in childhood. Hopefully, the insistent efforts to further educational and social inclusion through projects and programmes designed to pinpoint learning difficulties of widely different kinds will be seen as an effective drive to counter his pessimistic prophecies. Schools can be mobilised to work meaningfully for de-alienation, and the careful tracking of programmes done by researchers is serving to further the potential for free creative learning. Such educational struggles cannot pretend to accomplish the gigantic task of restructuring relations of production or their rude consequences for thinking and feeling. But the changes that schools can make in the capacities of people to act, to understand, and to see through the limitations of the status quo give promise of initiating steps toward helping students as they mature, to overcome at least some aspects of the discrimination that is likely to condemn them to the passive acceptance of social exclusion.

Note

1 Of course, some of the surplus is reinvested in the firm. Detailing the means by which capitalism makes constant progress was in fact Marx's life work.

Bibliography

Bourdieu, P. and Passeron, J. C. (1977). *Reproduction in Education, Society and Culture* (trans. R. Nice). London: Sage.

David, M. (2006). Embodiment and communication: Alienation, genetics, and computing. What does it mean to be human? In: L. Langman and D. Kalekin-Fishman (eds), *The Evolution of Alienation: Trauma, Promise and the Millennium*, pp. 69–88. Lanham, MD: Rowman and Littlefield.

Hochschild, A. R. (1983). *The Managed Heart: Commercialization of Human Feeling*. Berkeley, CA: University of California Press.

Kalekin-Fishman, D. (1996). Tracing the growth of alienation: Enculturation, socialization, and schooling in a democracy. In: F. Geyer (ed), *Alienation, Ethnicity, and Postmodernism*, pp. 95–106. Westport, CT: Greenwood Press.

Kalekin-Fishman, D. and Langman, L. (2015). Alienation: The critique that refuses to disappear. *Current Sociology*, 63(6), 916–933.

Langman, L. and Kalekin-Fishman, D. (2006). *The Evolution of Alienation: Trauma, Promise and the Millennium*. Lanham, MD: Rowman and Littlefield.

Leidner, R. (2003). *Fast Food, Fast Talk: Service Work and the Routinization of Everyday Life*. Berkeley, CA: University of California Press.

Marx, K. (1977 [1844]). The economic and philosophical manuscripts of 1844. In: R. Tucker (ed), *The Marx-Engels Reader*, pp. 66–126. New York, NY: WW Norton and Company.

Seeman, M. (1959). On the meaning of alienation. *American Sociological Review*, 24(6), 783–791.

INDEX

Page numbers in italics refer to figures. Page numbers in bold refer to tables.

Abdunnasar 176
Aber, M. S. 48
academic behaviours and student culture 48
academic performance 166
access to education 186
accountability, teacher 149, 150, 151
Action Dyslexia Delhi 178
active citizenship 26
Administering for Excellence (New Zealand) 95
administrators 140, 141, 155
Adult Education Centres 108
adults: literacy programs 49; multiple disadvantages 12; outcomes of educational exclusion 209; *see also* lifelong learning
Advani, L. 81
affective component of human behaviour 187
affirmative action 141
African American parents 48
Ahmad, F. K. 179
Ainscow, M. 13, 83
Aiyyer, Sripath 172
alienation 207–10
Alkire, S. 80
Altbach, P. G. 152
Alternative and Innovative Schools (India) 192; analysis of 205–6; assessment of learners 201–2; classroom environment 199–200; methodology 196–7; parental and community involvement 202–3; research study data collection 195–7; shortcomings 203–4; suggestions and recommendations 204–5; teaching strategies and approaches 197–9
Annual Status of Education Report 148
anomie 208
ANOVA test 164
anti-learning agenda 149
Antrop-Gonzalez, R. 48
apprenticeship education 98–9
Arab Spring 22–3
assistive technology 191
assumptions, unlearning of 45
Atkinson, Richard 66, 68
autistic thinking 68
autonomy, teacher 128, 202
AVRAR (awareness, vision, responsibility, action, and review) 190

Banerji, R. 154
Bangladesh **136**, **137**, **138**, **139**; expansion of education 131–3, **132**; gender parity 133–42
Bawa, Aditya 172
behaviour: academic behaviours and student culture 48; affective component 187; dyslexia 177
Behrman, J. 106
'being-in-the-world' 189
belonging and citizenship 26
Bernier, E. 43

214 Index

Beyond Learning: Democratic Education for a Human Future (Biesta) 40–1
Bhopal, K. 49
bias: mind-sets 16; teachers bias towards students with disabilities 126
Biesta, Gert 40–1
bilingual immigrant students: language development 157–8; research study methodology 159–60; writing skills research study 160–8, *161*, *162*, *163*, **164**, *164*
Billig, S. H. 29
birfurcation of education 38, 39–41
boarding schools 98, 99, 100, 102, 103
Bombay High Court 18
Bouazizi, Mohamed 22
brain *see* neuroscience
Brighouse, Harry 40
Britain *see* United Kingdom
broadstreaming 53, 54–5, **56**
Bronfenbrenner, Urie 187
bullying 102

Cambridge International Examinations 96
capitalism 207–8
caring for learners 199–200
Carter, Julie 49
caste 11, 12, 82, 153, 154, 186; *see also* social class
Centre for Human Rights Research 38
Chakravarthi language 176
Chapman, T. K. 48
Charcot, J. M. 172
charter schools 102
Chi, B. 29
child development 187
child-centered education 84, 153–4
child-to-child learning 81
China 24, 152
Chinese logographic orthography 175–6
choice, school *see* school choice
Chomsky, N. 173
church and state 24
citizenship education: curriculum 27–8, 40–1; elements of citizenship 25–7; enhancing inclusion through 29–32; outcomes 28–9; pedagogy 32–3; selected countries 24–5
Civil, M. 43
civil conflict 29
classroom as a society 31
classroom environment 197
classroom processes and practices 200–1
coding of research data 113
co-education: India 80; New Zealand 101

cognitive component to human behaviour 187
cognitive writing strategies 161–3, *162*, **164**
Commission of the European Communities 106, 107
common core curriculum 54, 95
communication and engagement levels 188
community involvement: Alternative and Innovative Schools (India) 197, 202–3, 204, 206; culturally responsive pedagogies 47; school-home-community partnerships 42–4, 47–50
commutative law 62
compensation for deficiencies in learning 72
compensation strategies, while-writing 162, *162*, **164**
compulsory education: Bangladesh 134; Marxist viewpoint 211; New Zealand 83, 93, 94
conative component of human behaviour 187
concentration 70
Constitution (Bangladesh) 133
Constitution (India) 83
constructive pluralistic engagement 44–5
Convention on the Rights of the Child 133, 191
convergent thinking 69
Corbin, J. 113
core creative competencies 53, 71, 73–4
correspondence schools 94, 96, 101
costs: education in Bangladesh 138; higher education in New Zealand 97; *see also* funding
Crawford, D. L. 106
creative learning 55–6; core creative competencies 71; enhancing learning ability 58–9; managing learning difficulties 72–3; multiple intelligence 57–8; phases of 67; special features of the systems model 71–2; symbolic system of learning 59–66; systems model 66–72
critical sociology 208
Cruickshank, W. 172
cultural capital 98
cultural responsiveness 42, 46–7, 91
cultural self-exclusion 12
culture: New Zealand 90; school-home-community partnerships 47–8
curiosity 71–2
curriculum: broadstreaming 55; common core curriculum 54, 95; culturally responsive pedagogies 46–7; gender parity in Bangladesh 141; hidden curriculum 14, 17, 31–2; 'hidden

curriculum' 14; India 150, 151, 153–4; learner-specific strategy 71; New Zealand 95–6; school-home-community partnerships 43; secondary schools in New Zealand 95; *see also* citizenship education
Curriculum Enrichment Model 43

Dakar Framework for Action 54
Dalits 11
Daniels, H. 85
data collection *see* methodology, research
Davis, Ron 191
decision-making: citizenship education 33, 34; school-home-community partnerships 43, 44
deficit theorizing 45–6
Dejerine, J. 172
Delanty, G. 25
Delhi Declaration on Education for All 85
deliberative democracy 30, 32–3, 34
democracy: citizenship education 26, 32; constructive pluralistic engagement 44–5; curriculum considerations 40–1; humanities and arts, teaching of 39–40; role of education in 13
demographics, research study 109, **110**, **112**
developed countries 82
'Developing Citizenship Competencies from Kindergarten through Grade 12' 27–8
developing countries 81–2
'deviant' students 102
dialogue teaching strategies 188, 189
directed thinking 68
disability: barriers to inclusion 186; economic cost of exclusion 9–10; educational policies in Greece 121–2; India 81, 82, 83–4, 85; models of disability 120–1; New Zealand 96, 101–2
Disability Convention, UN 185
Disabled Student Allowance (UK) 190
disadvantaged groups 82, 107–16, 113–16
discussion, classroom 30
District Primary Education Programme (India) 195
divergent thinking 69
diversity: Europe 11; India 85, 152
Douglas, Roger 90
dressing patterns of teachers 199
drop outs 138
duties and citizenship 25–6, 31, 32, 34
Dweck, C. 16
Dyer, C. 85–6
dyslexia 172–80, 191

early childhood education 31, 93–4
Eck, Diana 4
economically disadvantaged students *see* poverty
economics: education agenda 40; European Union 105; Greece 116; New Zealand 90, 97; workplace exclusion of people with disabilities 9–10
education: primary aim of 38–9; societal development, role in 79–81
Education Act 1877 (New Zealand) 94
Education Act 1914 (New Zealand) 95
Education Amendment Act 2000 (New Zealand) 99
Education Commission (India) 83
Education Commission of the States 27
education expansion in Bangladesh 131–3, **132**
education policies *see* policies
Education Review Office (New Zealand) 92
education volunteers (Alternative and Innovative Schools) *see* teachers
Education Watch 138, 139
educational attainment: bilingual immigrant students in Greece 166; gender parity in Bangladesh 137
EFA Global Monitoring Report 54
elementary education: District Primary Education Programme (India) 195; enrolment in India 148; gender parity in Bangladesh 134, 135, 138, 140, 142; India 150; New Zealand 94
elite private schools 98
elitism and higher education 97
emotional brain 56–7
emotional intelligence 188, 189, 192
employment: apprenticeship education in New Zealand 99; disability 122, 190; economic cost of excluding people with disabilities 9–10; India's quota system 14, 17; teen parents 102
engineering education 152
Engler, R. 97
English grammar school system 95
English orthography 175
enrolment: gender parity in Bangladesh 135–6, **136**, 138, 142; higher education in India 151–2; India 147–8; New Zealand 93, 99
Epstein, Joyce 43
Equal Opportunities, Protection of Rights and Full Participation Act (India) 17
equality of opportunity *vs.* equality of outcomes 16–7

ethnicity: lifelong learning 107; New Zealand 90, 92, 97, 100–1
Euro-centric educational notions 91
Europe, immigrants in 11
European Union 105, 107, 116
evaluation *see* testing and assessment
existential philosophy 189
exploitation and capitalism 207–8
export education 103

facial expressions of teachers 199
faculty, higher education 140
false consciousness 209
families, as resource 46
flourishing as aim of education 39, 40, 41, 45, 47, 49
Frames of Mind (Gardner) 57
Fraser, Peter 90
free access to lifelong learning 114–5
free education: Bangladesh 134; New Zealand 94, 95
Freire, Paulo 43–4
Friends of Dyslexia 178
Full Participation Act 1995 (India) 179
funding: Alternative and Innovative Schools (India) 203; Bangladesh 134–5; early childhood education in New Zealand 94; higher education in New Zealand 97; lifelong learning 108; New Zealand educational research 92; research funding 152; *see also* costs

Galaburda, A. M. 173, 174–5
Galston, W. A. 29
Gandhi, Mohandas 183–4
Gardner, Howard 57, 84
Garner, P. 85
Gay, G. 42
gender: Bangladesh 133–42, **136**, **137**, **138**, **139**; barriers to inclusion 186; India 82, 86; New Zealand 101; peer culture 48; religious prejudice 17–18
genetics and dyslexia 174–5
geography-based issues: Alternative and Innovative Schools (India) 192–3; New Zealand 99–100; quality of education in India 149
German orthography 175
Germany 24
girls' education *See* gender
globalisation, challenges of 11–2
goals 187
Goffman, E. 120
Goleman, Daniel 57
Gordon-Burns, D. 89, 91

government: core values 13–4; deliberative democracy 30, 32
government policies *see* policies
Government services employment (India) 17
graduate institutions 151
Grant, Carl 44, 45, 48
Greece: bilingual immigrant students' writing skills 159–68, *161*, *162*, *163*, **164**, *164*; educational policies and disability 120–1; language development 157–8; lifelong learning outcomes 108–16; teachers' professional development and disability issues 122–8
grounded theory research methodology 113
group thinking 16
grouping of learners 200
Guskey, T. 127
Gutmann, A. 26, 32

Haji Ali Dargah 7
Hallahan, D. 172
happiness 186–7
Harvard University Pluralism Project 44
health issues 186
hidden curriculum 14, 17, 31–2
hierarchical pyramid of needs 189
high intensity short term interventions 187
higher education: enrolment in India 148; gender parity in Bangladesh 135–6, 140, 142; India 151–2; New Zealand 90, 96–7, 99, 102–3
Hobbes, Thomas 25
holistic approaches 15, 18–19
home assignments 202
home schooling 103
Howard, T. C. 48
Hulme, H. 79
Human Development Index 79, 80

identical patterns 65
identity: citizenship 25–6; culturally responsive pedagogies 47; intersectionality 45–6; right to retain 13
ideology 90
IEA Civic Education Study 29
imaging studies, brain 174
immigrants: Europe 10, 11; lifelong learning 107; school-home partnerships 49; *see also* bilingual immigrant students
inclusive education: definition 13; special needs students in the United Kingdom 190–1
inclusive learning 187–9; barriers to 185–7; definition 183; model of change 189–90; UNESCO 184–5

Index   217

India: caste system 11; challenges for education and inclusiveness in 147–55; citizenship education 24; data collection for the Alternative and Innovative Schools (India) research study 195–6; District Primary Education Programme 195; dyslexia 176–80; exclusion from school, categories of 82–3; learning disabilities **177**; mind-sets, formation of 16; people with disabilities, inclusion of 9–10; quota systems 14; quotas 17; religious prejudice against women 17–8; societal development and inclusive education 79–86; students with learning disabilities 171, 172; *see also* Alternative and Innovative Schools (India)
indifference, teacher 11
indigenous peoples 90
information processing theory 66–70
infrastructure 84, 121, 122, 126, 203, 204
inner cities 187, 189
in-service teacher education 150
Inside Primary Schools (Bhattacharjea, Wadhwa and Banerji) 148–9
integration as distinct from inclusion 83
intelligence quotient 188, 189, 192
interaction and citizenship 26–7
interactive learning 188, 192
inter-intelligence 62
intermediate education 94
internal efficiency indicators 137–40
internal self-management tools 191
International Association for the Evaluation of Education 91–2
International Baccalaureate Diploma Programme 96
international comparisons 91–2
International Conference on 'Educational and Social Inclusion' 1
international examinations 96
International Journal of Inclusive Education 19
international students 102–3
interpersonal intelligence 60
intersectionality 41–2, 47
inter-unit pattern rules 65
intra-intelligence 62
Islam 17–18
Islamophobia 16
Israel 23, 24–5

Janoski, T. 25
Japanese logographic orthography 175–6
Jha, M. M. 13
Julka, A. 83
Juma Masjid 17–18

Kahne, J. 28, 29, 34
Kaiadas 121
Kalekin-Fishman, D. 208
Kamin, S. 80
Kannada language 176
Kelly, S. 48
Kids Learning Centre 178
kinaesthetic intelligence 60
kinaesthetic learning 58
Kokiri, Te Puni 100
Kothari Commission 83
kura 94, 96

labeling learning difficulties 74
Labour Party (New Zealand) 90, 98
language: citizenship education 31, 32; dyslexia 175–6, 178; India 154–5; Maori 94, 96, 101; school-home partnerships 49; symbols 59; *see also* bilingual immigrant students
language development 157–8, 165–6
language disorders 172
language orthography 175–6
Lao Tsu 184
Law 3699/2008 (Greece) 122
learner-specific strategies 71
learning: efficiency of 71, 72; engagement levels of interaction 188; performance-based learning 30–1; styles of 57–8
learning at home 43
learning culture 114
learning disabilities: broadstreaming 53; concept of 172–3; creative learning model applications 72–3; identification 73–4; India 176–80, **177**
legislated inclusion 13
legislation: educational policies and disability in Greece 121–2; Equal Opportunities, Protection of Rights and Full Participation (India) 17; as first step to inclusion 18; Persons with Disabilities Act (India) 82
leisure 114
lifelong learning: and democratic citizenship 40; Europe 105, 107; factors inhibiting participation in 111; outcomes study 108–16, **110**, **111**, **112**
linguistic intelligence 58
Link, B. G. 120
literacy: dyslexia 191; gender parity in Bangladesh 137, **138**; lifelong learning outcomes 115–16
literature 42
logical intelligence 58, 59–60
logographic writing systems 175–6

Look & Say approach 192
Lopez, S. V. 28, 29
low intensity long duration interventions 187
Lyubomirsky, Sonja 186

Madras Dyslexia Association 178
madrasas 135–6, 142
Maharashtra Dyslexia Association 178
mainstreaming 54–5, **56**, 83
Major, B. 120
Malayalam language 176
Maori 90, 91, 92, 94, 96, 97, 100–1
MAPPS (Math and Parent Partnerships in the Southwest) Project 43
marginalised students in India 154–5
Marshall, T. H. 25
Marx, K. 207–8, 211
Mastropieri, M. A. 82
mathematical analysis of symbolic learning 61–2
mathematical intelligence 58, 60
meaninglessness 208, 210, 211
media: Israeli summer 23; role of in the education sector 85; stereotypes 16
media, instruction 73, 154–5
medical model of disability 83–4, 120–1
MELLRA *see* Ministry of Education, Lifelong Learning and Religious Affairs (Greece)
memory 67–8
mental intelligence 188, 189, 192
mentoring, teacher 149
meta-cognitive writing strategies *163*, 163–4, **164**
methodology, research: Alternative and Innovative Schools (India) research study 195–7; coding of research data 113, 114–5; lifelong learning outcomes study 108–10, 113; teachers' professional development and disability issues in Greece 123–4
Middaugh, E. 29
Middle East 22–3
middle-class students 48, 98, 100
migrants *see* immigrants
Millennium Development Goals 84, 133
mind-sets, changing 15–18
Ministry of Education (Bangladesh) 140
Minister of Education (Israel) 23
Ministry of Education (New Zealand) 92, 101–2
Ministry of Education, Lifelong Learning and Religious Affairs (Greece) 125
Ministry of Human Resource Development (India) 86

Ministry of Primary and Mass Education (Bangladesh) 140
Ministry of Social Justice and Empowerment (India) 83–4
misconceptions and mind-sets 16
modal model of information processing 68
model of change 189–90
models: child development 187; creative learning models 53, 55–6, 66–8, 70, 71–4; disability models 82, 83, 120–1, 126, 179; partnership models 43–4
molecular studies of dyslexia 175
Moore, K. 79
motivation: barriers to inclusion 186; inclusive learning 187
multicultural education 39, 42–6
Multi-Grade Learning Centres (India) *see* Alternative and Innovative Schools (India)
multimedia presentations 60
multiple disadvantages 12
multiple intelligences: inclusive learning 189, 192; learning styles 57–8; learning through interaction 188; symbolic system of learning 59–66; total learning 58–9
multi-sensory learning 191

Nalanda Institute 178
National Center for Culturally Responsive Educational Systems 42
National Certificate of Educational Achievement (New Zealand) 96
National Curriculum (United Kingdom) 24
National Curriculum Framework (India) 150
national identity 25–6
National Institute of Neurological Disorders and Stroke (United States) 173
National Joint Committee on Learning Disabilities (United States) 172
National Policy of Education (India) 85
national standards 91, 92, 96
natural abilities 185
neo-liberalism 90, 97, 103
neuroscience 173–4
New Zealand: axes of inclusion/exclusion 98–103; enrolment statistics 93; higher education 96–7; policies of inclusiveness 90–1; pre-school 93–4; primary and intermediate education 94; research findings 91–3; secondary schools 95–6
non-governmental organisations 178
nonworking women 115

normlessness 208, 211
Nussbaum, Martha 39

O'Brien, L. T. 120
observation phase of learning 66–7
OECD *see* Organisation of Economic Cooperation and Development
older individuals 115
Oliver, M. 83
Olkin, R. 120
opportunity, equality of 16–17
Organisation of Economic Cooperation and Development 92
orthography 175–6
outcomes: citizenship education 28–9; equality of 16–17; of exclusion 209; inclusive learning 189–90; lifelong learning study 107–16, **111**, **112**
Overcoming Dyslexia (Shaywitz) 173

Pakeha 94, 97, 100, 103
Pakistan 24
Pandey, R. S. 81
Pareek, U. 80
parents and parental involvement: Alternative and Innovative Schools (India) 202–3; bilingual immigrant students 165–7; of disabled students 127; language development 158; parenting skills 43; parenting styles 48; school-home-community partnerships 42–4, 48–50
Parikh, Samir 180
participation and citizenship 30
participation and citizenship education 26, 31, 32–3, 34
Pasifika 92, 94
pattern making rules 63–5
pedagogy: approaches 41–2; broadstreaming 55; citizenship education 29, 32–3; culturally responsive teaching 42, 46–7; Gandhi, Mahatma 80; India 85; intersectionality 45–6; multicultural education 42–5; school-home-community partnerships 47–50; teachers' professional development and disability issues in Greece 122–7
peer culture 48
peer evaluation by learners 202
performance-based learning 30–1
personality development 38–41, 45, 48, 49–50, 84
Persons with Disabilities Act (India) 82
Phelan, J. C. 120
physical intelligence 188, 189, 192

Picot Report 95
Planning Commission (Bangladesh) 134
Pledger, C. 120
Pluralism Project, Harvard University 44
pluralistic engagement 44–5
policies: Alternative and Innovative Schools (India) 205; Bangladesh 133–5; gender parity in Bangladesh 142; New Zealand 90–1
political philosophy 26
politics: legislation as first step to inclusion 18; transmission of core values through education 13–14
pop culture 46
positive psychology 186–7
postgraduate education 127–8
Potter, Aubree 44
poverty: barriers to inclusion 186; disabled population 84; India 82, 84; New Zealand 98
powerlessness 208, 210, 211
Prakash, Vijoy 55, 61
Pratham 148, 154
presentation: students' skills 69–70; teaching strategies 188–9
pre-writing processes and strategies 161, *161*
primary education *see* elementary education
Prime Minister of India 9–10
Pritchett, L. 149
private schools: higher education in India 151–2; India 81; New Zealand 94, 98, 103
private tutors 139, 140
processive phase of learning 67, 67–9
production phase of learning 69–70
professional development, teachers' 119–20, 122–8
protests 22–3
psycholinguistic models of dyslexia 175–6
psychological alienation 208–10
Public Private Partnership (India) 151

qualitative analysis: bilingual immigrant students' writing skills 160; lifelong learning outcomes study 109, 113–14
quality of education 149
quality of life 39, 40
quantitative data 108–10
questioning learners 201
quotas 14, 17

race 48
rapid curriculum 154

Rashtriya Madhayamik Shiksha Abhiyan 151
rational brain 56–7
receptive phase of learning 66–7
reform in New Zealand 95–6
regular pattern rules 65
religion: private schools and home schooling 103; women, prejudice against 17–18
replicated patterns 65
research, university 97
research methodology see methodology, research
retention 202
Reynolds, R. 48
Right of Children for Free and Compulsory Education Act (India) 148, 149, 154
Right to Education Act (India) 206
rights: citizenship education 25, 33; pedagogy 32
Ritzer, G. 45
'Rogernomics' 90, 95, 97
role-play 29
Roma 10, 38
rural students 99, 101, 148

Salamanca Statement 9, 179
Salamanca World Conference 153
SAMDEVA Research and Training Centre Kolkata 178
Santos, M. E. 80
Sargent Report 83
Sarva Shiksha Abhiyan 86, 148, 149, 150, 195
Sayeed, Y. 83
scholarships 99
School Certificate exams 95, 96
school choice 100
school culture 47–8
school managing committees (Bangladesh) 140, 141, 142
school-home-community partnerships 42–4, 47–50
science and technology education 39–40, 134
Scruggs, T. E. 82
seating patterns 200
Sebba, J. 13
secondary education: Bangladesh 134–5; enrolment in India 148; gender parity in Bangladesh 135, 138–9, **139**, 141, 142; India 150–1; New Zealand 90, 95–6, 102, 103; teachers' professional development and disability issues in Greece 124–7
Seeman, M. 208, 209

self-containment 114
self-development 84
self-esteem 115, 186–7
self-estrangement 208, 210, 211
self-evaluation 163
self-exclusion 12
self-learning 71–2, 191, 192
semi-skilled labour 99
sensory memory 68
service-learning 29
sexual orientation 102
shallow orthographics 175
Shani Shingnapur temple 18
Shantiniketan, West Bengal 80
Shaywitz, S. E. 173
Shepherd, A. 79
Shiffrin, Richard 66, 68
short-term memory 68
single-sex education 101
skills development and lifelong learning 107
Sleeter, C. E. 48
social capital 45, 98, 108, 113, 114
social class: barriers to inclusion 186; New Zealand 92, 97, 98–9, 100; peer culture 48; school-home partnerships 49; see also caste
social isolation 208, 210, 211
social issues and gender parity 141
social justice 44–5
social model of disability 120, 126
social promotion 102
social psychological alienation 208–10
social self-exclusion 12
socialisation 11, 16, 122
socially disadvantaged children 82, 84
societal development 79–86
society, classroom as a 31
socioeconomic status see social class
sociology of education 89
socio-political knowledge 46
South Africa 29
Soysal, Y. 25
spatial arrangement of symbols 63–5
spatial intelligence and learning 58, 60, 61
spatial periodicity patterns 65
special education: Greece 122; India 81, 85; New Zealand 101–2; teacher training 126, 127–8
Special Educational Needs Coordinators 172
special needs students: India 86; New Zealand 94, 96; UNESCO declarations 9–10; United Kingdom 190–1; see also learning disabilities
spiritual component of human behaviour 187

spiritual intelligence 188, 189, 192
Stacey, N. 106
standardisation of symbols and patterns 65–6
state schools 94, 95–6, 99
stereotypes: changing mind-sets 15–18; intersectionality and the unlearning of 45; of parents 48; teacher education 15
stigma: disability 84, 120, 190; Roma 10
Strathdee, R. 97
Strauss, A. 113
streaming/tracking 95, 99
structural alienation 208–9
student cultures 47–8
subjectivity of students 41
substantive citizenship 26
suburban schools 48–9
symbols: citizenship education 31, 32; symbolic patterns 61, 63; symbolic system of learning 59–66; thinking 68
synthetic teaching strategies 188, 189
systems model of creative learning 55–6, 71–2

Taare Zameen Par (film) 178
Tagore, Rabindranath 80–1
Tata Interactive Learning Disability Forum 178
teacher education: addressing stereotypes 15; Bangladesh 135; changing mind-sets 16; dyslexia 179; failure to include multicultural curriculum 39; gender parity in Bangladesh 141; India 150; in-service teacher education 150
teachers: Alternative and Innovative Schools (India) 197–201, 198–9; attitudes towards disadvantaged students 155; Bangladesh 135; delivery of curriculum 14–15; dyslexia 179–80; dyslexia in the Indian context 176–7; gender parity in Bangladesh 135, 136–7, **137**, 140; India 149, 151, 153–4; indifference to minority needs 11; language development 157–8; as listeners 33; professional development and disability issues 119–20, 122–8; responsibility of 41; teacher gap 86
teaching to the test 92
technical education 95, 98–9
technological intelligence 60
technology: culturally responsible pedagogies 46; potential of 15
teen parents 102
temporal pattern arrangements 61, 65
terminology: creative learning 55; educational inclusion 13

tertiary education *see* higher education
testing and assessment: Alternative and Innovative Schools (India) 197, 201–2; dyslexia 178; gender parity in Bangladesh 139; India 155; New Zealand 95, 96; teaching to the test 92
thinking and creative learning 68–9
third way government (New Zealand) 90–1
Thomas report (New Zealand) 95
Thompson, D. 26, 32
three-dimensional pattern rules 65
Thrupp, M. 100
Tomorrow's Schools Program (New Zealand) 95
topic introduction 200
Torney-Purta, J. 28, 29
total learning 58–9
tracking *see* streaming/tracking
training teachers *see* teacher education
Transformative Education Context 43–4
trauma: barriers to inclusion 186; inclusive learning 187
Traveller people 10, 38, 48, 49
Treaty of Waitangi 91
tuition 97
Tunisia 22
Turnock, K. 102
two-dimensional pattern rules 64

unemployment: European Union 105; lifelong learning 107
UNESCO: declarations on inclusion 9–10; inclusive learning 184–5; interactive learning 188; Salamanca statement 179; statement on education for all 81, 82; teacher gap 86
uni-dimensional pattern rules 64
unit patterns 63
United Kingdom: citizenship education 24; exclusion from school 82; mind-sets, formation of 16; special needs teaching 190–1; Traveller parents, adult literacy programmes for 49
United Nations: Convention on the Rights of the Child 191; declarations of inclusion 9; Millennium Development Goals 184
United Nations Development Programme 80
United States: citizenship education 25; school-home-community partnerships 43–4
universal education: elementary education in India 195; goals of 185; India 148, 150

universities *see* higher education
Universal Declaration of Human Rights 38–9, 41
university entrance exams 95
Uno, Akira 172
unskilled labour 99
Untouchables 11
upper class 98
upward social mobility 99

validation 42
value education 153
verbal intelligence 58, 59, 61
Verma, G. K. 86
visualisation teaching strategy 188, 189
volunteers 43

Watkins, N. D. 48
welfare programs 14
Western Europe 10
Westheimer, J. 28, 34
while-writing processes and strategies 161–4, *162*, *163*
whole school approach 14, 18–19, 82, 98, 157, 184

women, religious prejudice against 17–8
workers 207–8
World Assembly of the Disabled People's International 9
World Bank 80
World Conference on Education, UNESCO 9
World Conference on Special Needs Education 54
World Declaration on Education for All 53
World Economic Forum 185
World Federation of Neurology 172–3
World Health Organization 84
writing skills: bilingual immigrant students 160–8; issues and strategies 158–9; pre-writing processes *161*; research study methodology 159–60; while-writing strategies *162*, *163*, **164**; writing difficulties *164*

youth culture 46
youth labour market 99

zoning 99–100
Zwier, E. 45